MATA HARI

BERGER BOOKS
TM AN IMPRINT OF
DARK HORSE COMICS

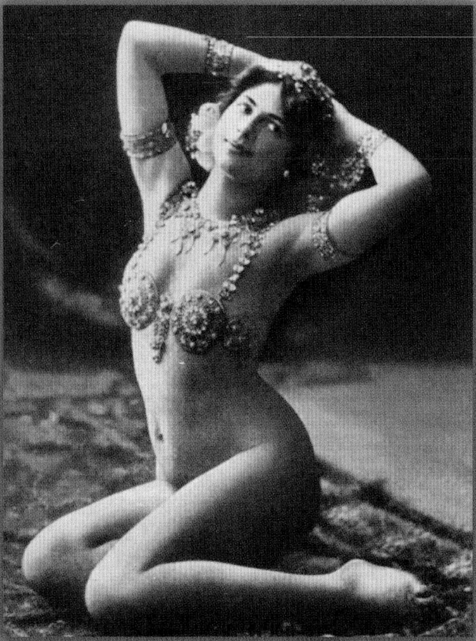

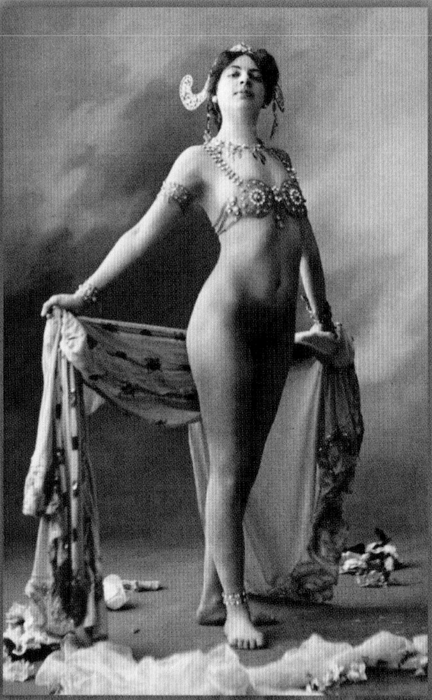

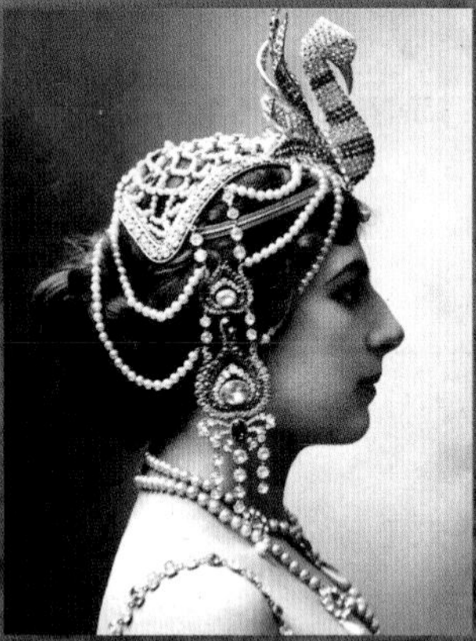

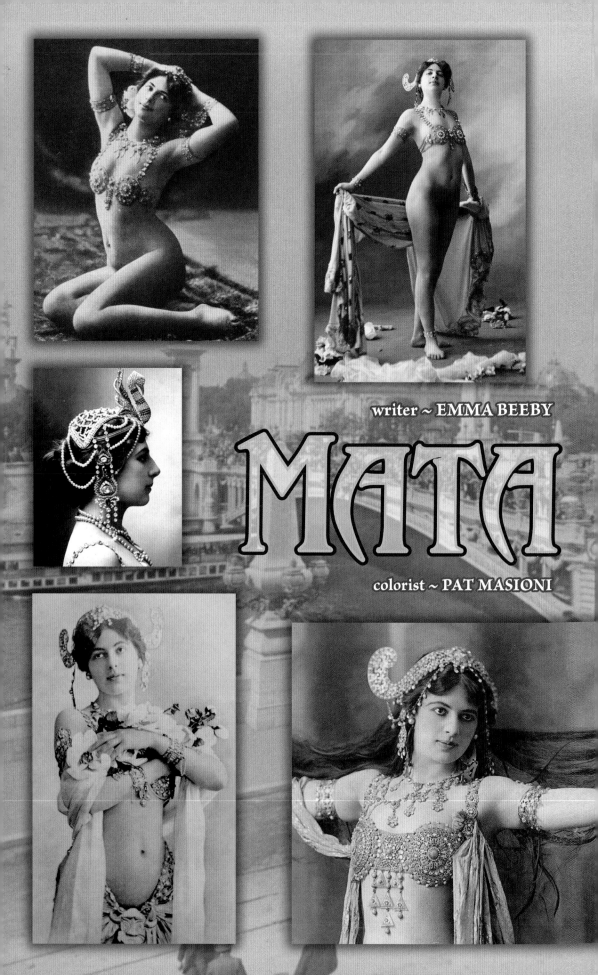

writer ~ EMMA BEEBY

MATA

colorist ~ PAT MASIONI

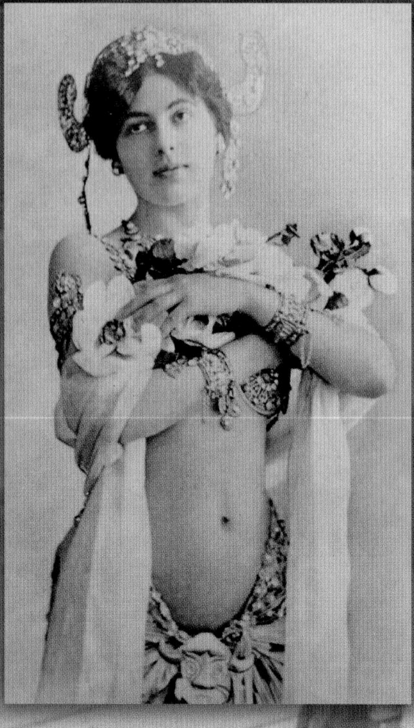

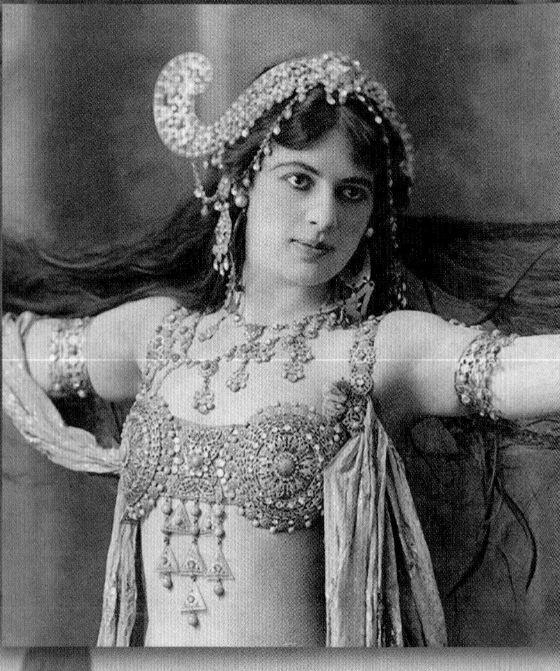

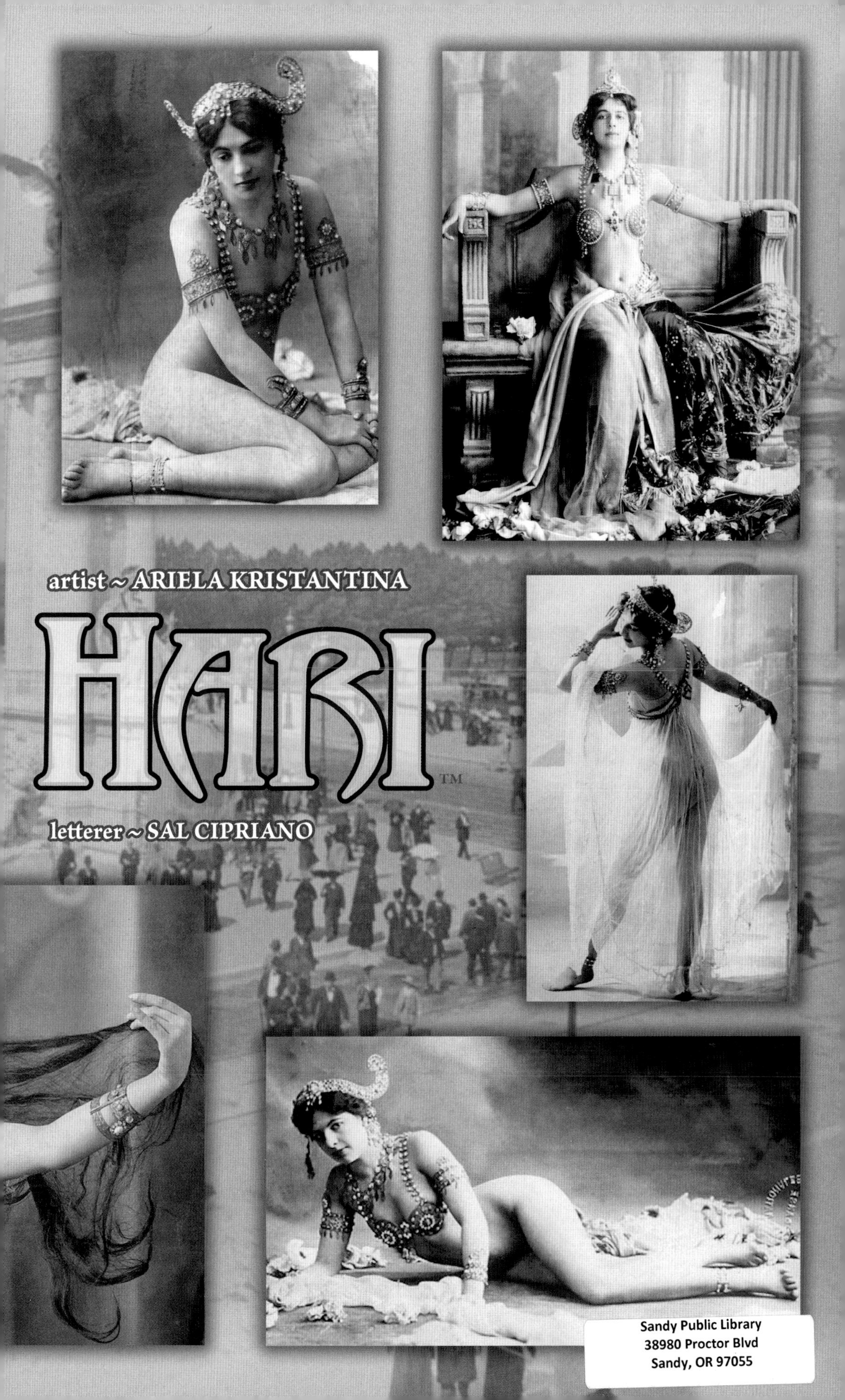
artist ~ ARIELA KRISTANTINA
HARI™
letterer ~ SAL CIPRIANO

KAREN BERGER
Editor

✦

RICHARD BRUNING
Logo/Book Designer

✦

ADAM PRUETT
Digital Art Technician

✦

MIKE RICHARDSON
Publisher

✦

This volume collects
issues #1–#5 of
MATA HARI
from Berger Books

SALOMÉ *quotes translated*
from the French by Lord Alfred Douglas

Published by Dark Horse Books

A division of
Dark Horse Comics LLC
10956 SE Main Street
Milwaukie, OR 97222

DarkHorse.com
ComicShopLocator.com

First Edition: April 2019
ISBN: 978-1-50670-561-3
Digital ISBN: 978-1-50670-590-3

Printed in Hong Kong
10 9 8 7 6 5 4 3 2 1

❧

CHAPTER ONE
BARE·FACED

"You are always looking at her.
You look at her too much.
It is dangerous to look
at people in such fashion.
Something terrible may happen."

SALOMÉ:
A TRAGEDY IN ONE ACT
~ OSCAR WILDE ~

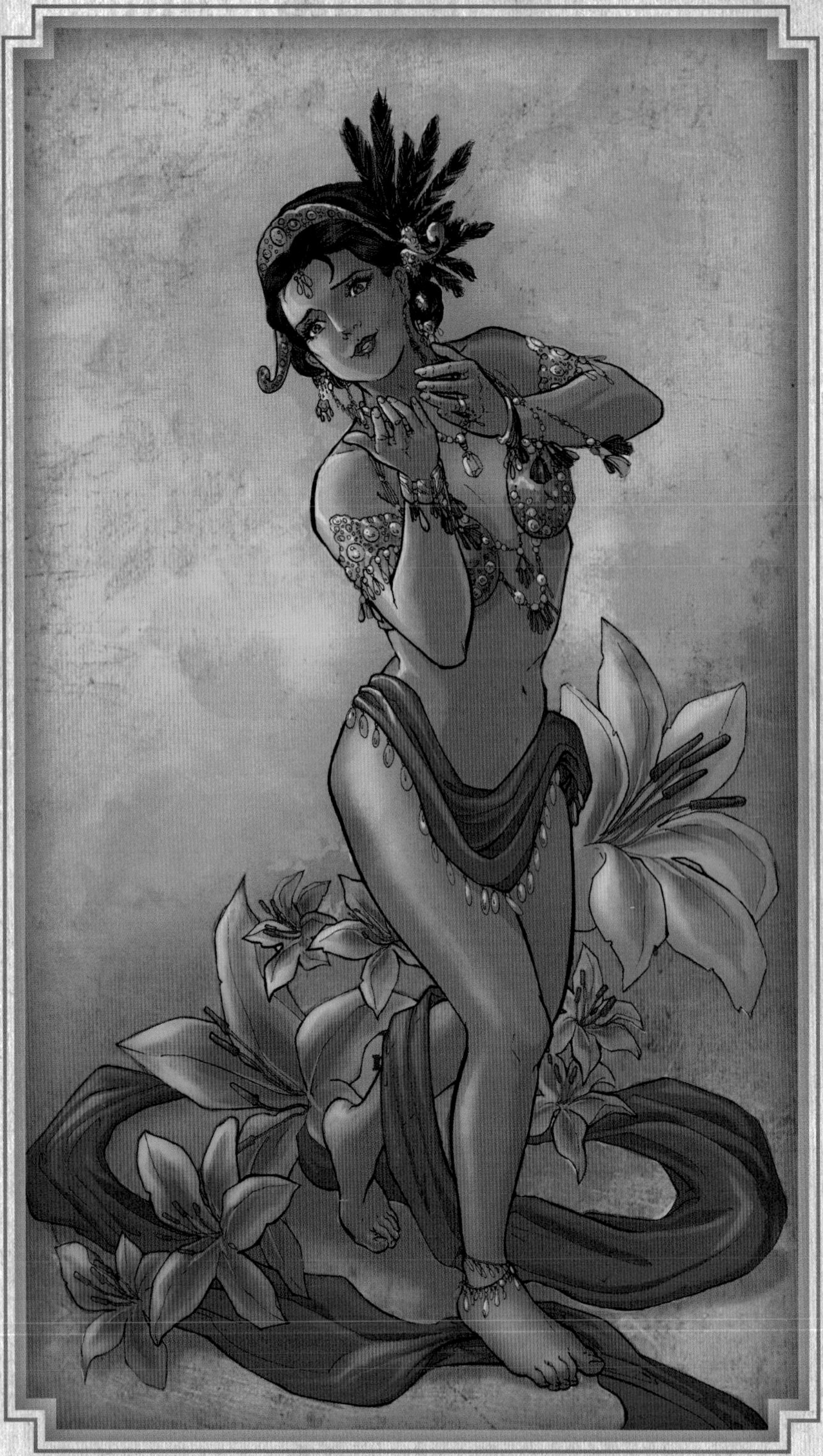

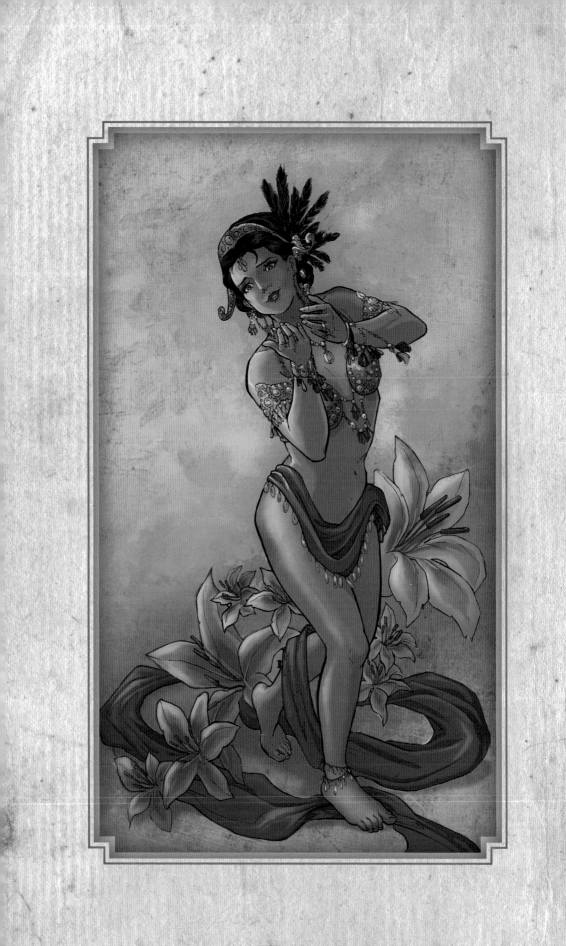

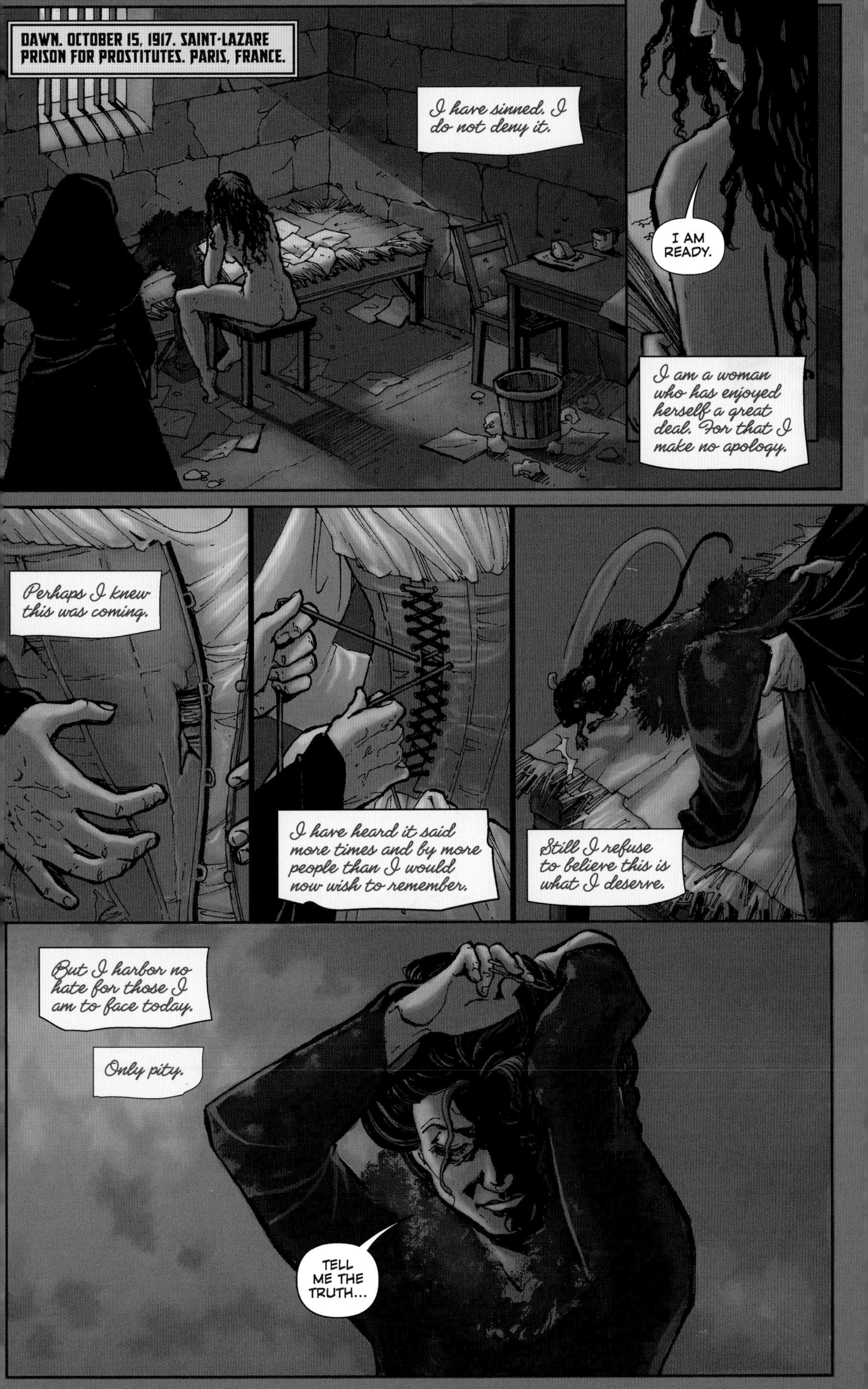
DAWN. OCTOBER 15, 1917. SAINT-LAZARE PRISON FOR PROSTITUTES. PARIS, FRANCE.
I have sinned. I do not deny it.
I AM READY.
I am a woman who has enjoyed herself a great deal. For that I make no apology.
Perhaps I knew this was coming.
I have heard it said more times and by more people than I would now wish to remember.
Still I refuse to believe this is what I deserve.
But I harbor no hate for those I am to face today.
Only pity.
TELL ME THE TRUTH...

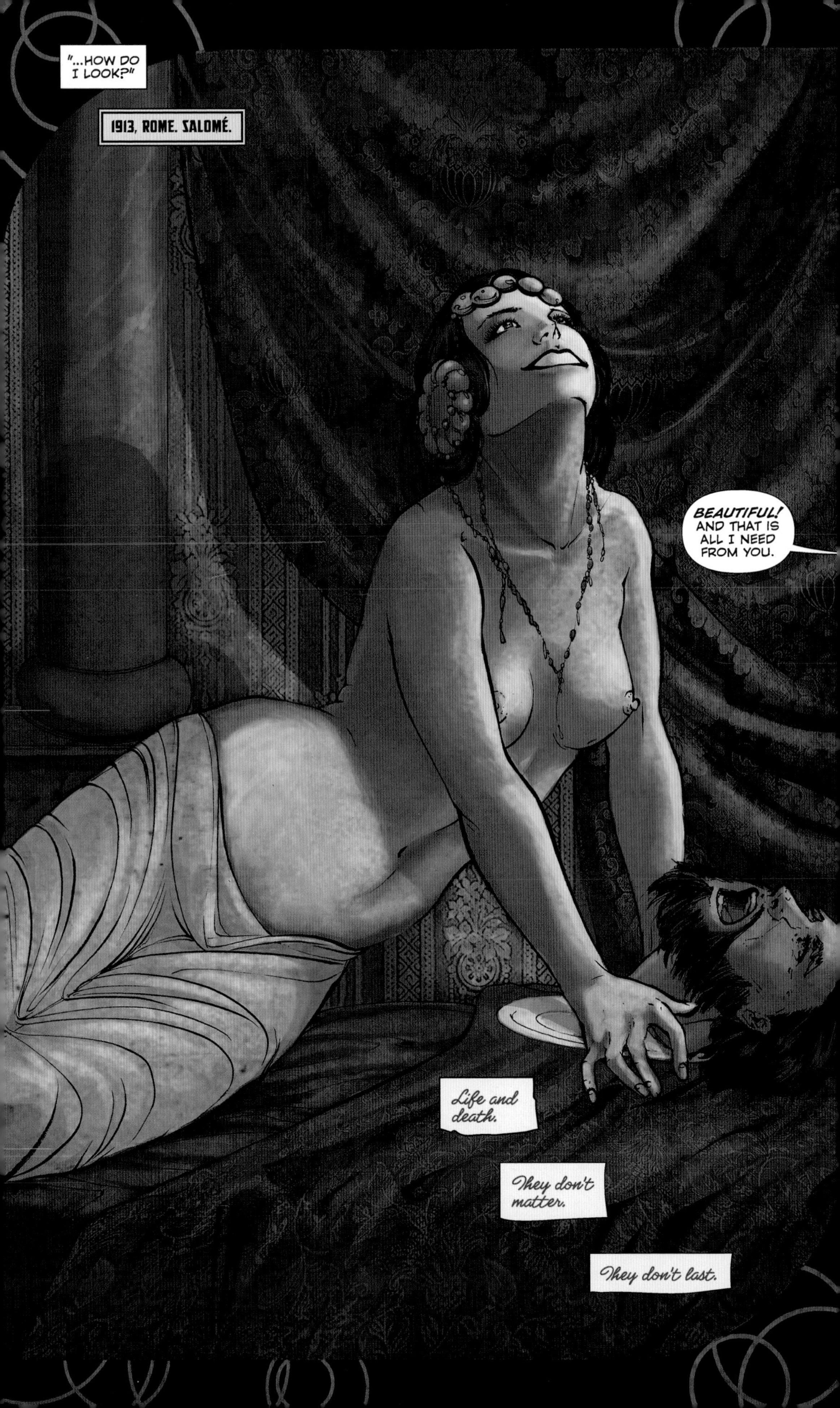
"...HOW DO I LOOK?"
1913, ROME. SALOMÉ.
BEAUTIFUL! AND THAT IS ALL I NEED FROM YOU.
Life and death.
They don't matter.
They don't last.

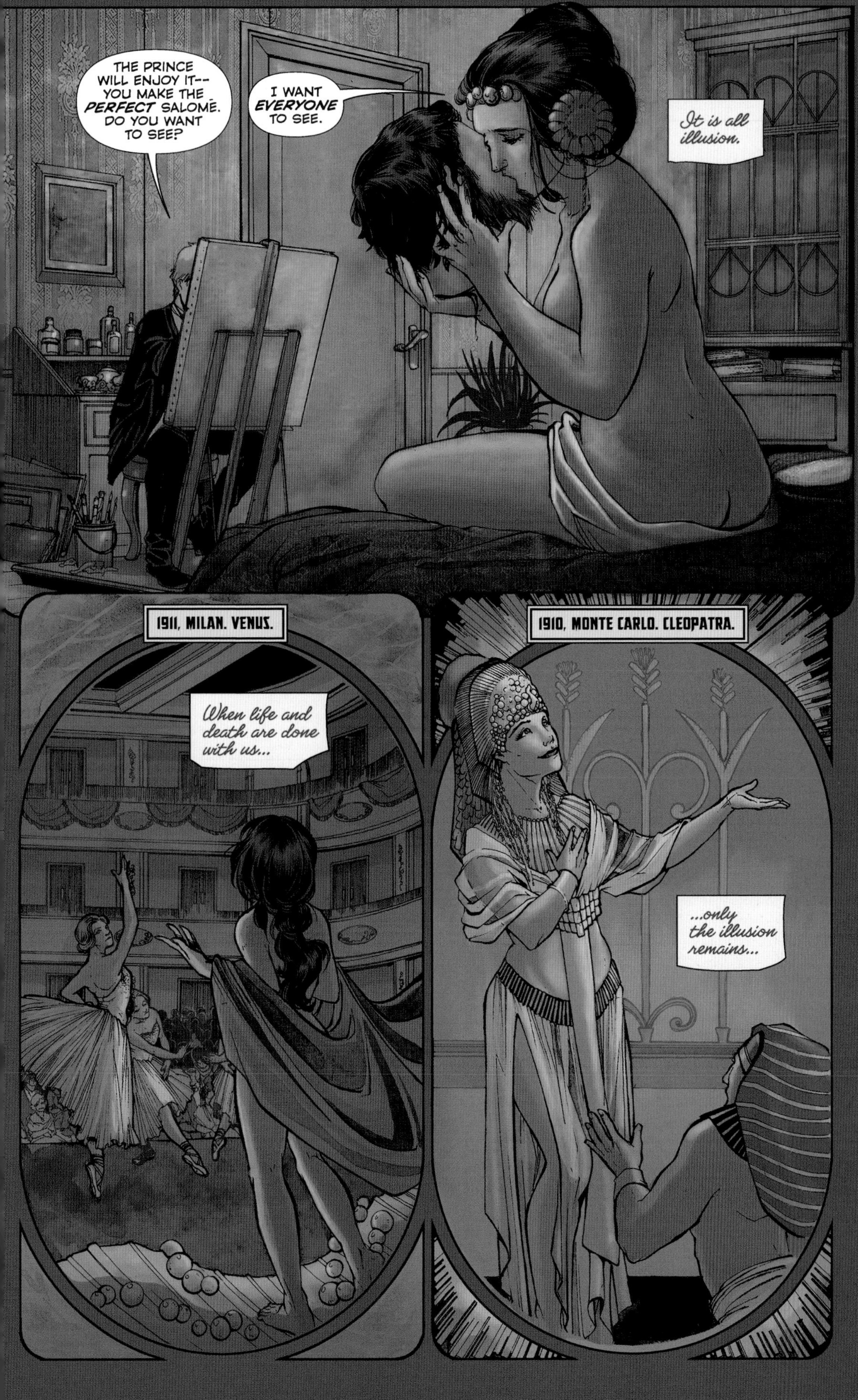
THE PRINCE WILL ENJOY IT-- YOU MAKE THE *PERFECT* SALOMÉ. DO YOU WANT TO SEE?
I WANT *EVERYONE* TO SEE.
It is all illusion.
1911, MILAN. VENUS.
When life and death are done with us...
1910, MONTE CARLO. CLEOPATRA.
...only the illusion remains...

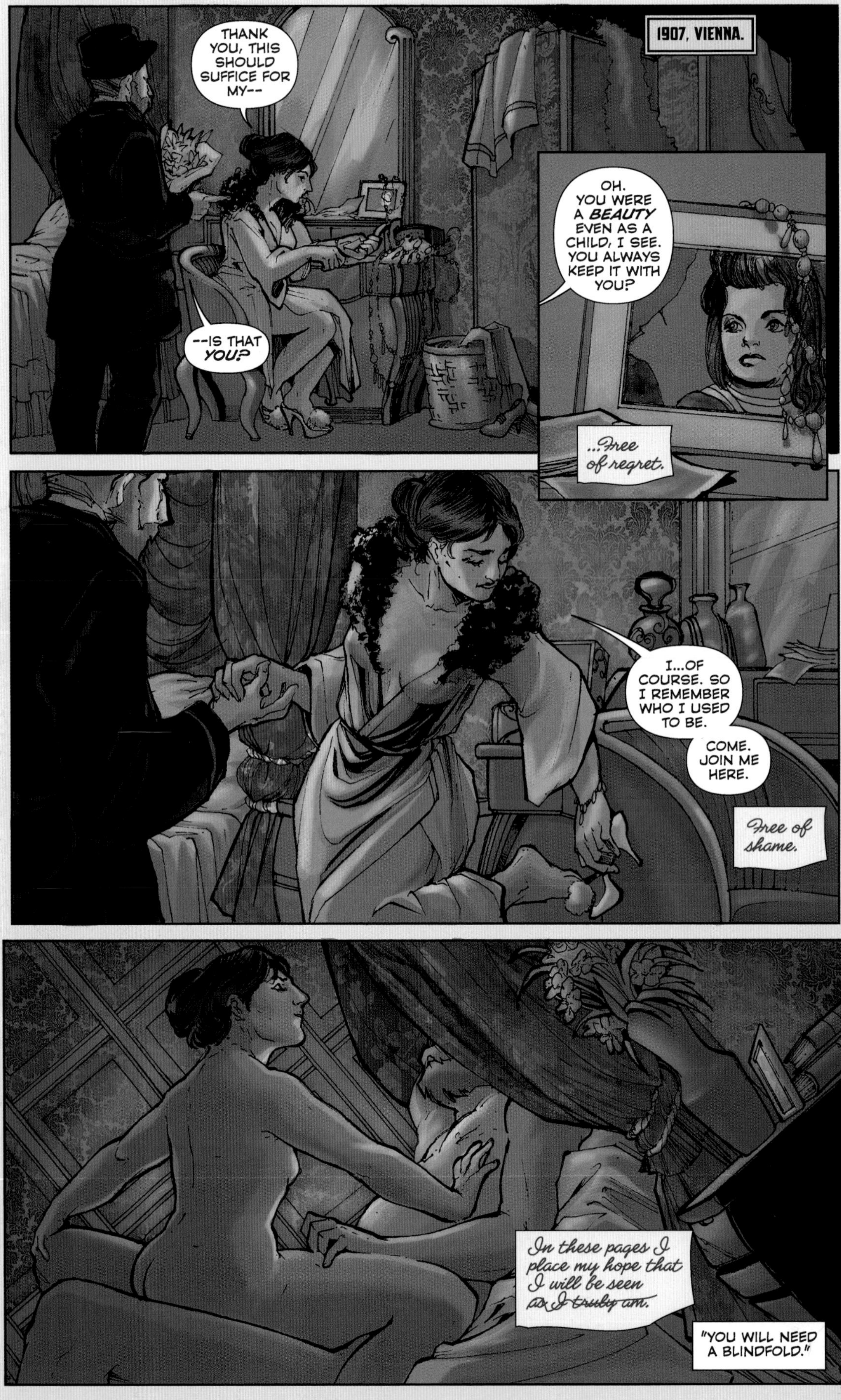
1907, VIENNA.
THANK YOU, THIS SHOULD SUFFICE FOR MY--
--IS THAT *YOU?*
OH. YOU WERE A *BEAUTY* EVEN AS A CHILD, I SEE. YOU ALWAYS KEEP IT WITH YOU?
...Free of regret.
I...OF COURSE. SO I REMEMBER WHO I USED TO BE.
COME. JOIN ME HERE.
Free of shame.
In these pages I place my hope that I will be seen ~~as I truly am.~~
"YOU WILL NEED A BLINDFOLD."

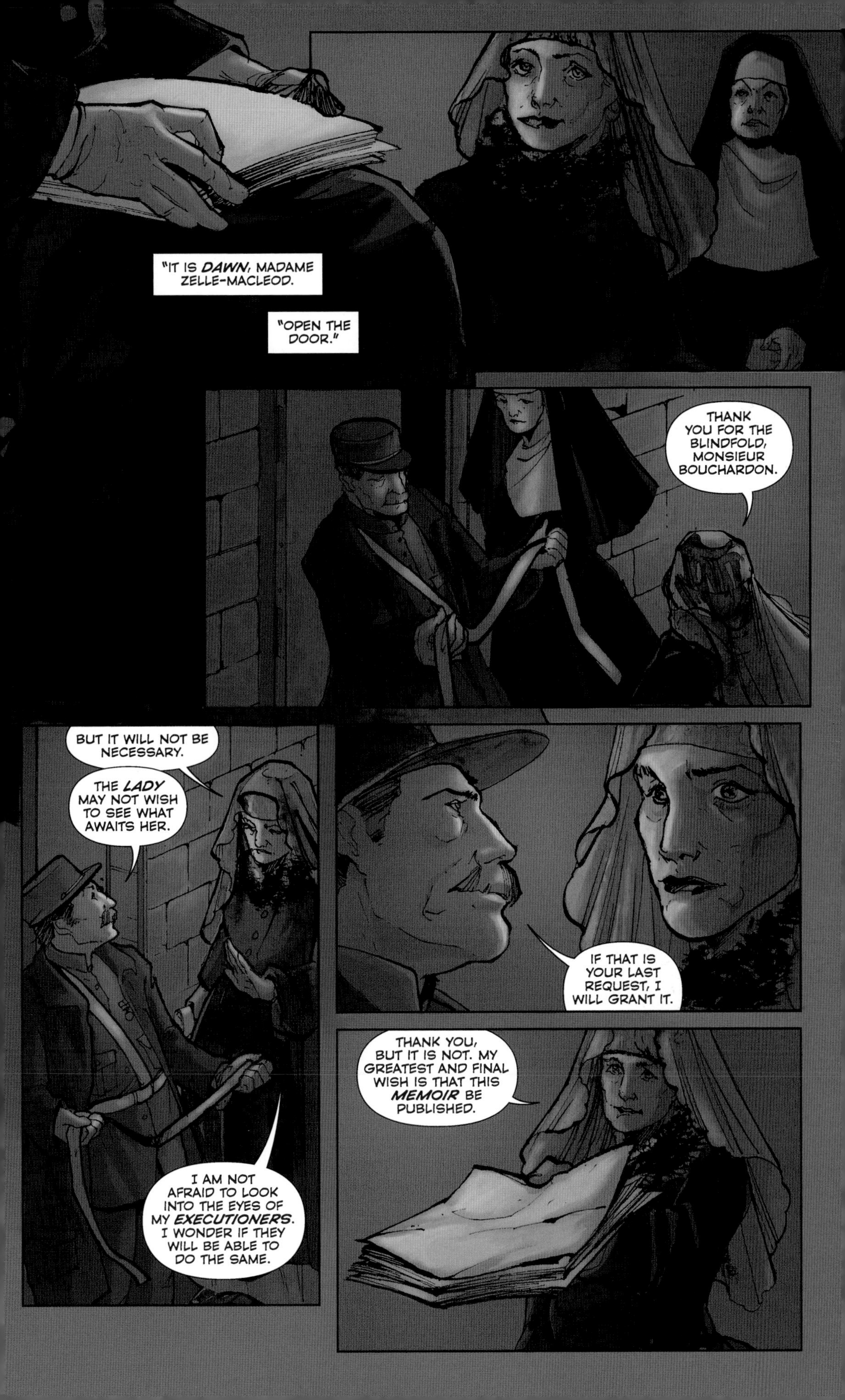
"IT IS DAWN, MADAME ZELLE-MACLEOD.
"OPEN THE DOOR."
THANK YOU FOR THE BLINDFOLD, MONSIEUR BOUCHARDON.
BUT IT WILL NOT BE NECESSARY.
THE LADY MAY NOT WISH TO SEE WHAT AWAITS HER.
IF THAT IS YOUR LAST REQUEST, I WILL GRANT IT.
I AM NOT AFRAID TO LOOK INTO THE EYES OF MY EXECUTIONERS. I WONDER IF THEY WILL BE ABLE TO DO THE SAME.
THANK YOU, BUT IT IS NOT. MY GREATEST AND FINAL WISH IS THAT THIS MEMOIR BE PUBLISHED.

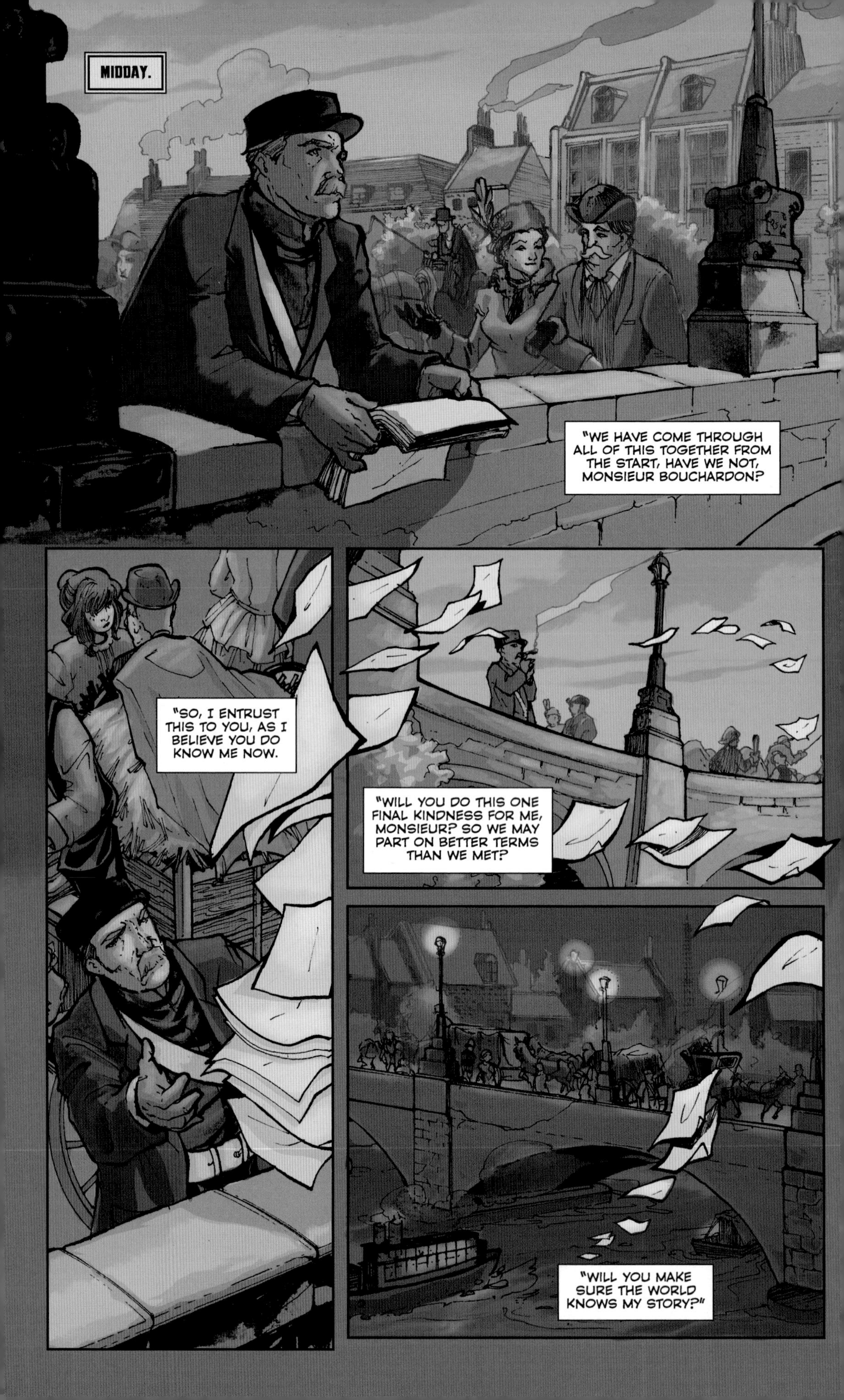
MIDDAY.
"WE HAVE COME THROUGH ALL OF THIS TOGETHER FROM THE START, HAVE WE NOT, MONSIEUR BOUCHARDON?
"SO, I ENTRUST THIS TO YOU, AS I BELIEVE YOU DO KNOW ME NOW.
"WILL YOU DO THIS ONE FINAL KINDNESS FOR ME, MONSIEUR? SO WE MAY PART ON BETTER TERMS THAN WE MET?
"WILL YOU MAKE SURE THE WORLD KNOWS MY STORY?"

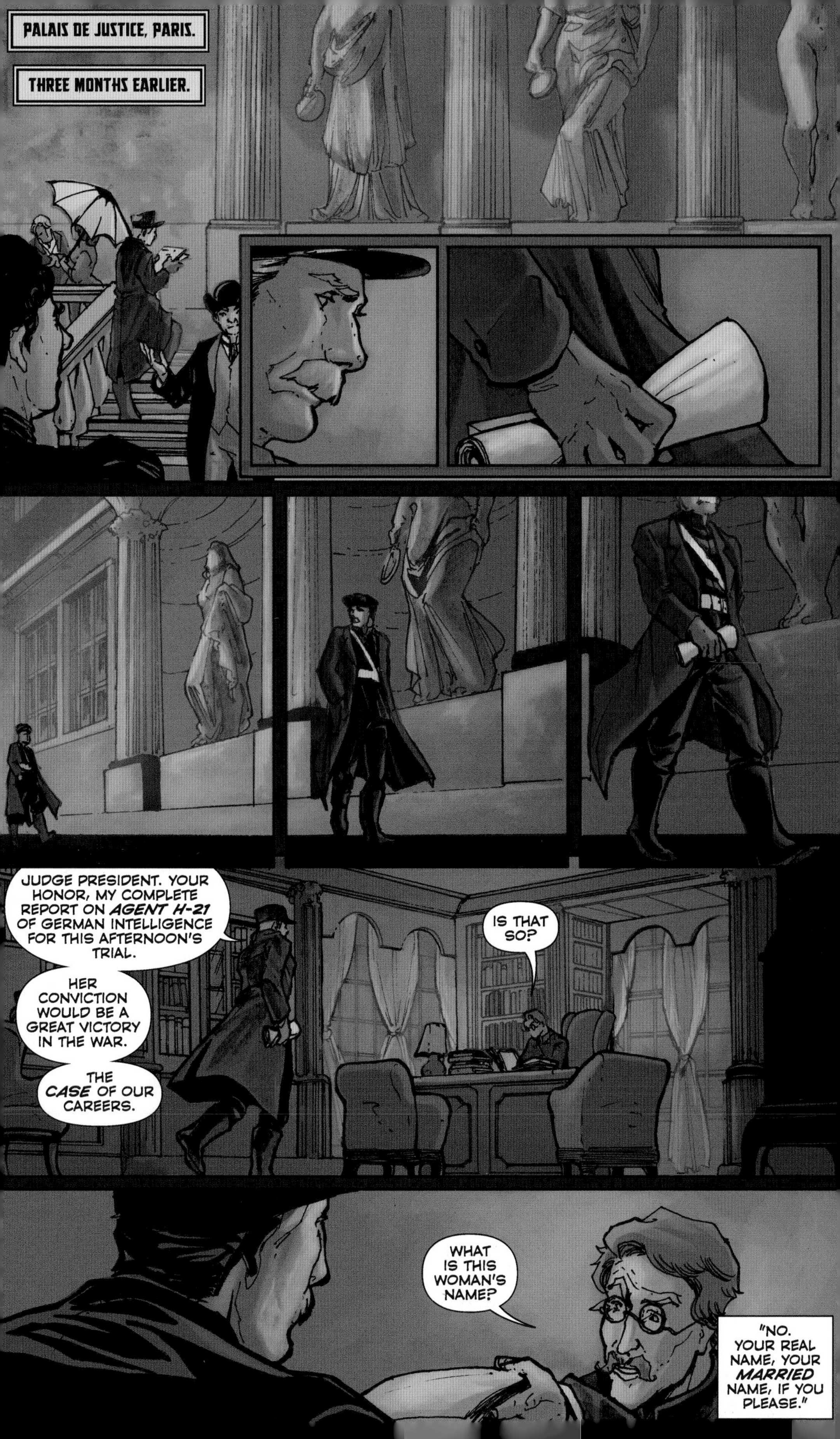
PALAIS DE JUSTICE, PARIS.
THREE MONTHS EARLIER.
JUDGE PRESIDENT. YOUR HONOR, MY COMPLETE REPORT ON *AGENT H-21* OF GERMAN INTELLIGENCE FOR THIS AFTERNOON'S TRIAL.
IS THAT SO?
HER CONVICTION WOULD BE A GREAT VICTORY IN THE WAR.
THE *CASE* OF OUR CAREERS.
WHAT IS THIS WOMAN'S NAME?
"NO. YOUR REAL NAME, YOUR *MARRIED* NAME, IF YOU PLEASE."

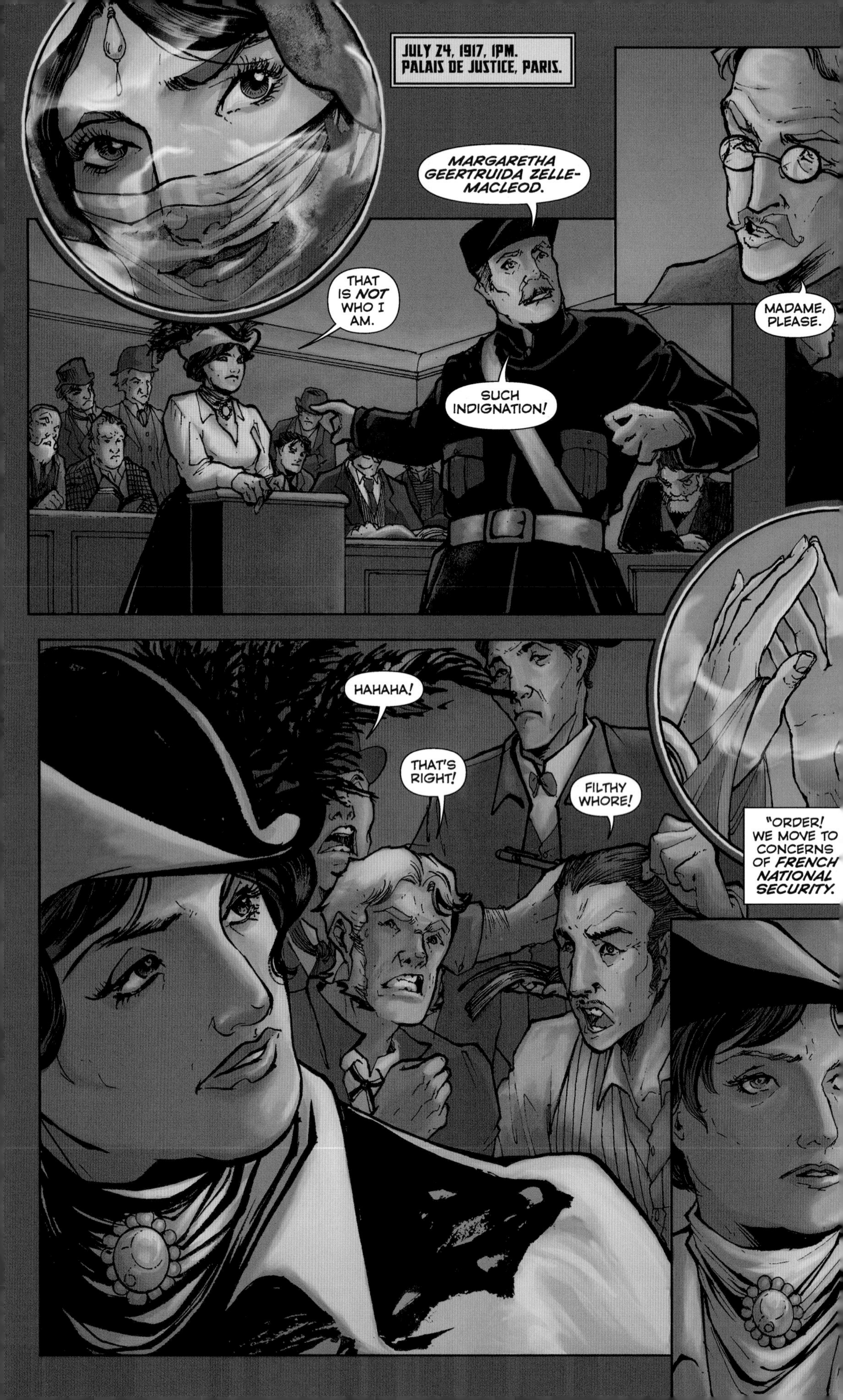
JULY 24, 1917, 1PM.
PALAIS DE JUSTICE, PARIS.
MARGARETHA GEERTRUIDA ZELLE-MACLEOD.
THAT IS NOT WHO I AM.
SUCH INDIGNATION!
MADAME, PLEASE.
HAHAHA!
THAT'S RIGHT!
FILTHY WHORE!
"ORDER! WE MOVE TO CONCERNS OF FRENCH NATIONAL SECURITY.

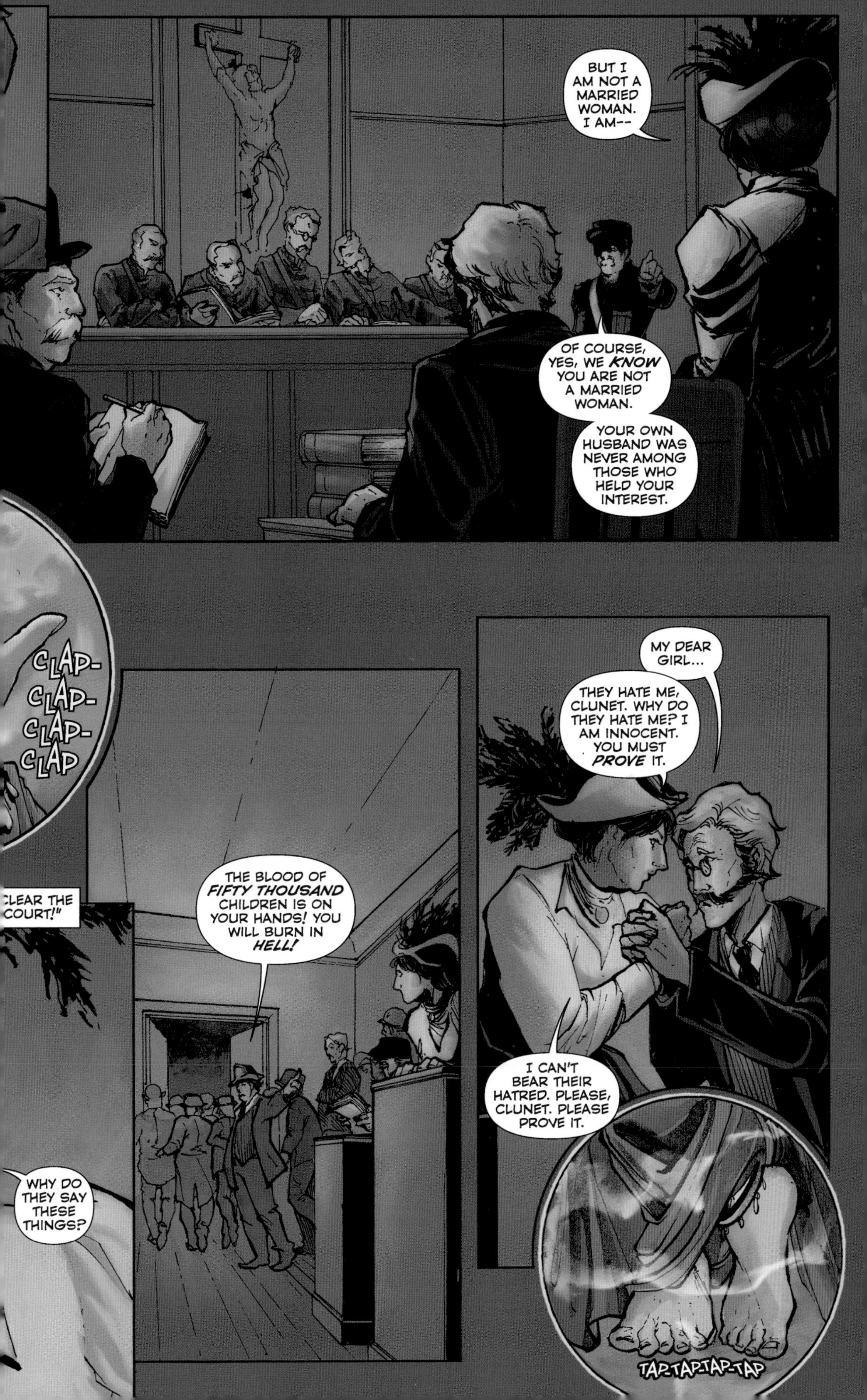
BUT I AM NOT A MARRIED WOMAN. I AM--
OF COURSE, YES, WE *KNOW* YOU ARE NOT A MARRIED WOMAN.
YOUR OWN HUSBAND WAS NEVER AMONG THOSE WHO HELD YOUR INTEREST.
CLAP-CLAP-CLAP-CLAP
"CLEAR THE COURT!"
THE BLOOD OF *FIFTY THOUSAND* CHILDREN IS ON YOUR HANDS! YOU WILL BURN IN *HELL!*
WHY DO THEY SAY THESE THINGS?
MY DEAR GIRL...
THEY HATE ME, CLUNET. WHY DO THEY HATE ME? I AM INNOCENT. YOU MUST *PROVE* IT.
I CAN'T BEAR THEIR HATRED. PLEASE, CLUNET. PLEASE PROVE IT.
TAP-TAP-TAP-TAP

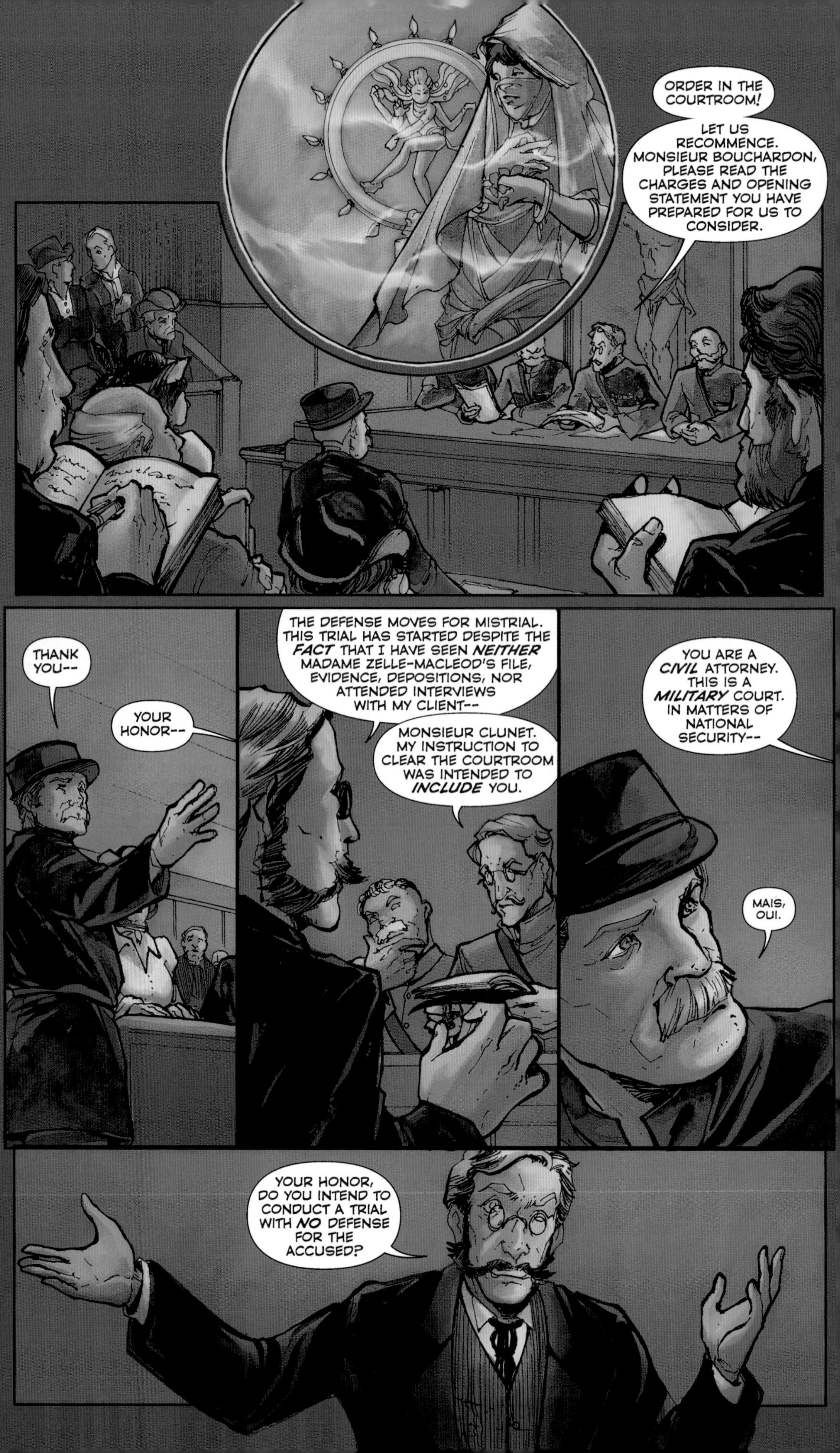
ORDER IN THE COURTROOM!
LET US RECOMMENCE. MONSIEUR BOUCHARDON, PLEASE READ THE CHARGES AND OPENING STATEMENT YOU HAVE PREPARED FOR US TO CONSIDER.
THANK YOU--
YOUR HONOR--
THE DEFENSE MOVES FOR MISTRIAL. THIS TRIAL HAS STARTED DESPITE THE FACT THAT I HAVE SEEN NEITHER MADAME ZELLE-MACLEOD'S FILE, EVIDENCE, DEPOSITIONS, NOR ATTENDED INTERVIEWS WITH MY CLIENT--
MONSIEUR CLUNET. MY INSTRUCTION TO CLEAR THE COURTROOM WAS INTENDED TO INCLUDE YOU.
YOU ARE A CIVIL ATTORNEY. THIS IS A MILITARY COURT. IN MATTERS OF NATIONAL SECURITY--
MAIS, OUI.
YOUR HONOR, DO YOU INTEND TO CONDUCT A TRIAL WITH NO DEFENSE FOR THE ACCUSED?

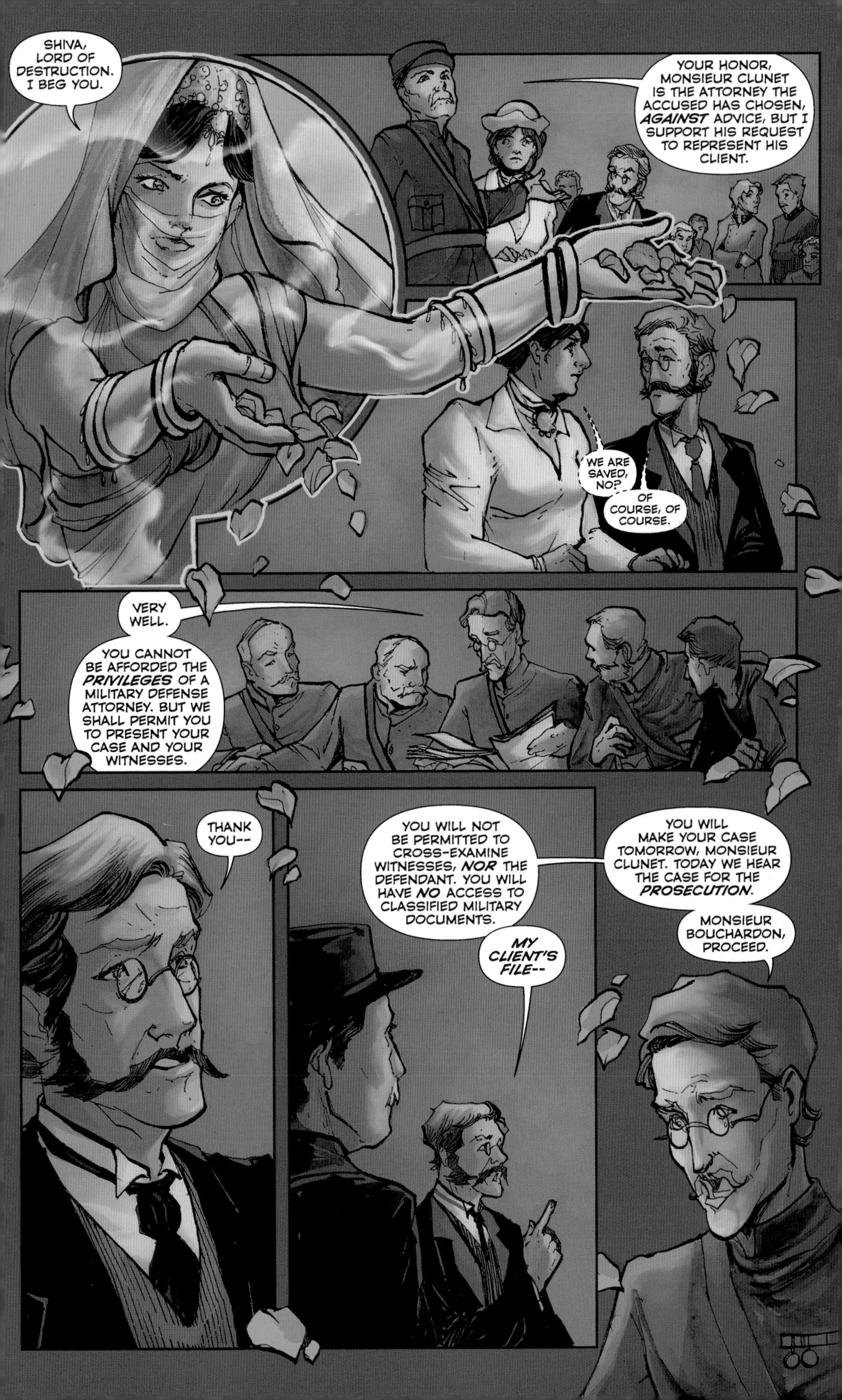
SHIVA, LORD OF DESTRUCTION. I BEG YOU.
YOUR HONOR, MONSIEUR CLUNET IS THE ATTORNEY THE ACCUSED HAS CHOSEN, AGAINST ADVICE, BUT I SUPPORT HIS REQUEST TO REPRESENT HIS CLIENT.
WE ARE SAVED, NO?
OF COURSE, OF COURSE.
VERY WELL.
YOU CANNOT BE AFFORDED THE PRIVILEGES OF A MILITARY DEFENSE ATTORNEY. BUT WE SHALL PERMIT YOU TO PRESENT YOUR CASE AND YOUR WITNESSES.
THANK YOU--
YOU WILL NOT BE PERMITTED TO CROSS-EXAMINE WITNESSES, NOR THE DEFENDANT. YOU WILL HAVE NO ACCESS TO CLASSIFIED MILITARY DOCUMENTS.
MY CLIENT'S FILE--
YOU WILL MAKE YOUR CASE TOMORROW, MONSIEUR CLUNET. TODAY WE HEAR THE CASE FOR THE PROSECUTION.
MONSIEUR BOUCHARDON, PROCEED.

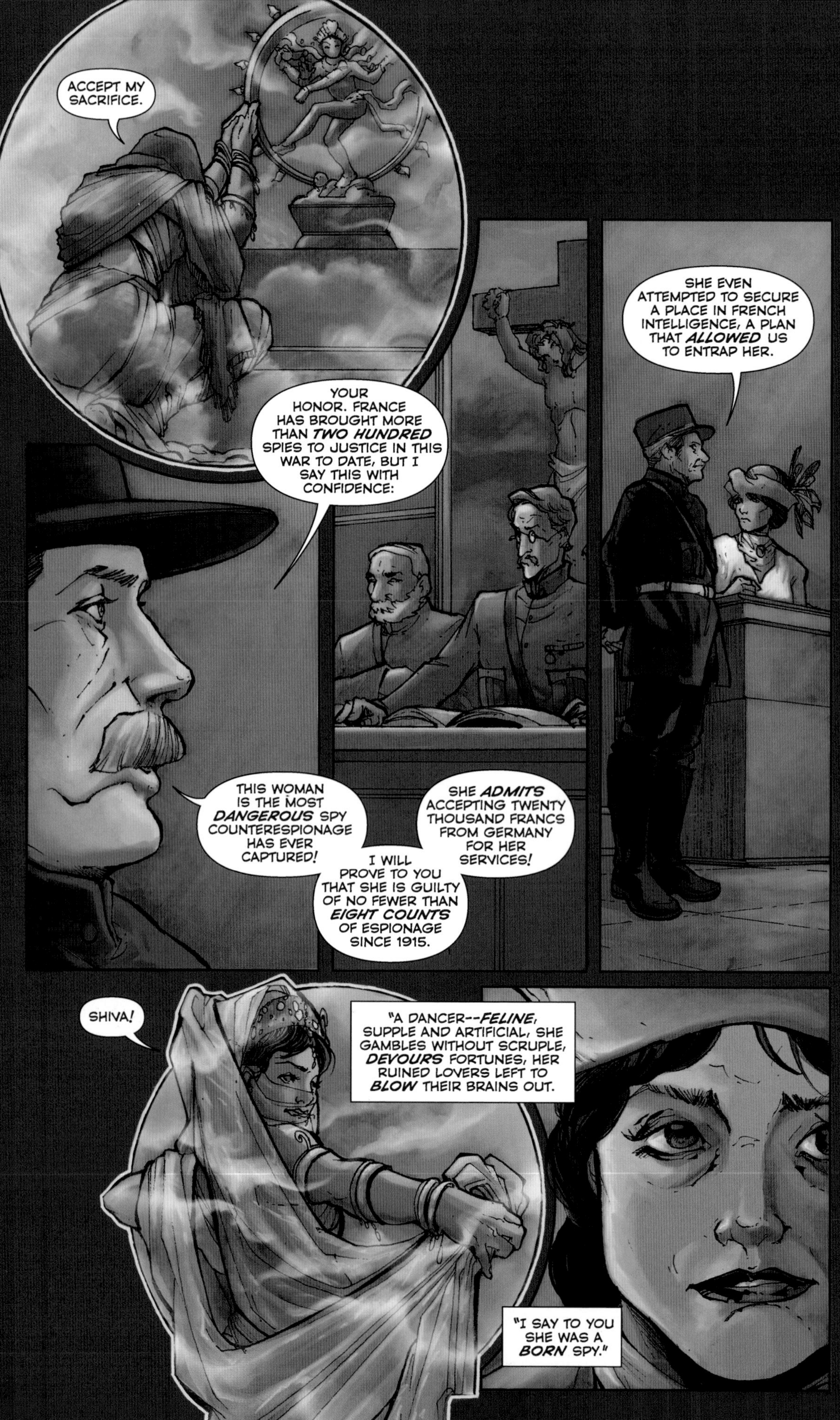
ACCEPT MY SACRIFICE.
YOUR HONOR. FRANCE HAS BROUGHT MORE THAN TWO HUNDRED SPIES TO JUSTICE IN THIS WAR TO DATE, BUT I SAY THIS WITH CONFIDENCE:
SHE EVEN ATTEMPTED TO SECURE A PLACE IN FRENCH INTELLIGENCE, A PLAN THAT ALLOWED US TO ENTRAP HER.
THIS WOMAN IS THE MOST DANGEROUS SPY COUNTERESPIONAGE HAS EVER CAPTURED!
I WILL PROVE TO YOU THAT SHE IS GUILTY OF NO FEWER THAN EIGHT COUNTS OF ESPIONAGE SINCE 1915.
SHE ADMITS ACCEPTING TWENTY THOUSAND FRANCS FROM GERMANY FOR HER SERVICES!
SHIVA!
"A DANCER--FELINE, SUPPLE AND ARTIFICIAL, SHE GAMBLES WITHOUT SCRUPLE, DEVOURS FORTUNES, HER RUINED LOVERS LEFT TO BLOW THEIR BRAINS OUT.
"I SAY TO YOU SHE WAS A BORN SPY."

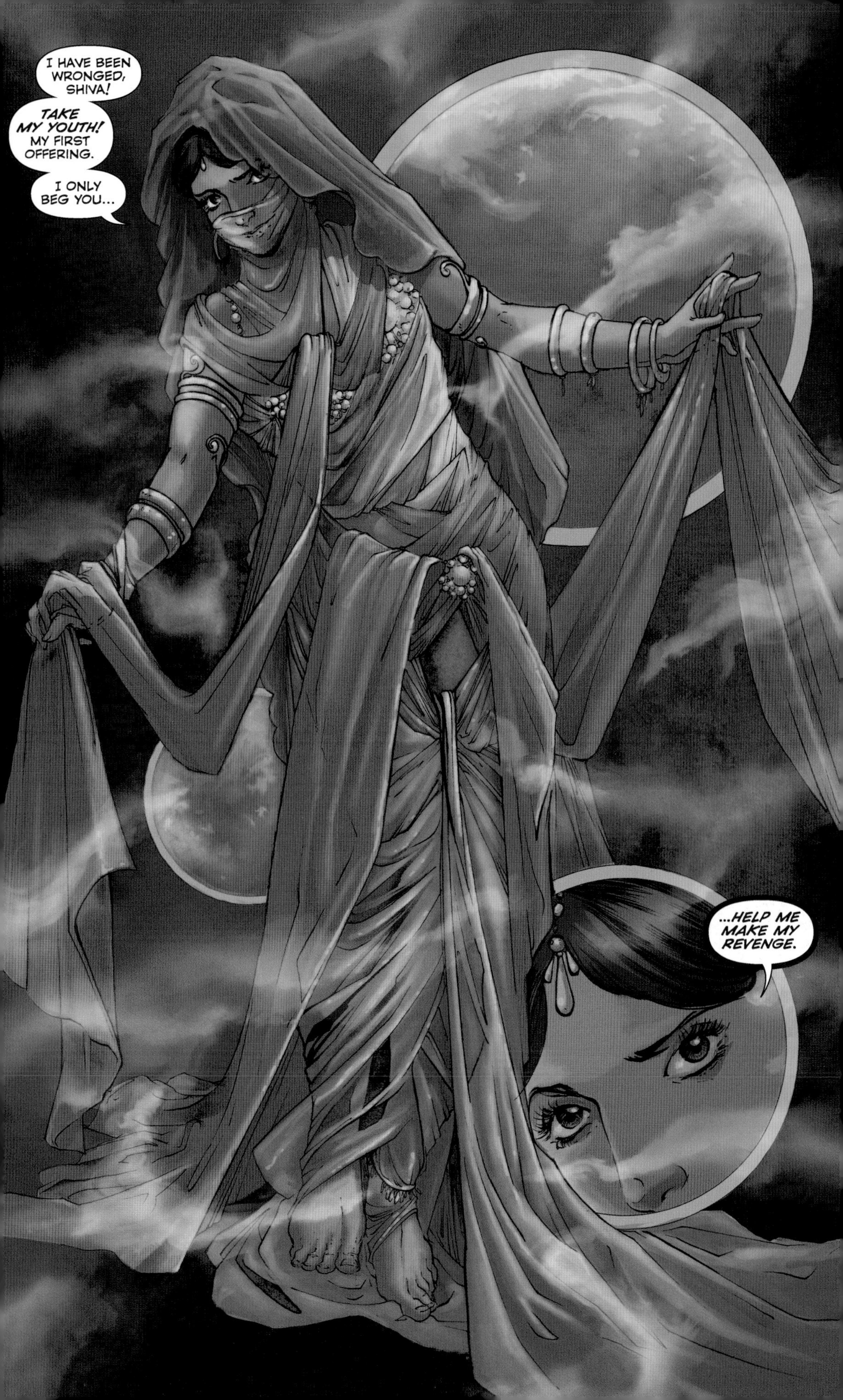

I HAVE BEEN WRONGED, SHIVA!
TAKE MY YOUTH! MY FIRST OFFERING.
I ONLY BEG YOU...
...HELP ME MAKE MY REVENGE.

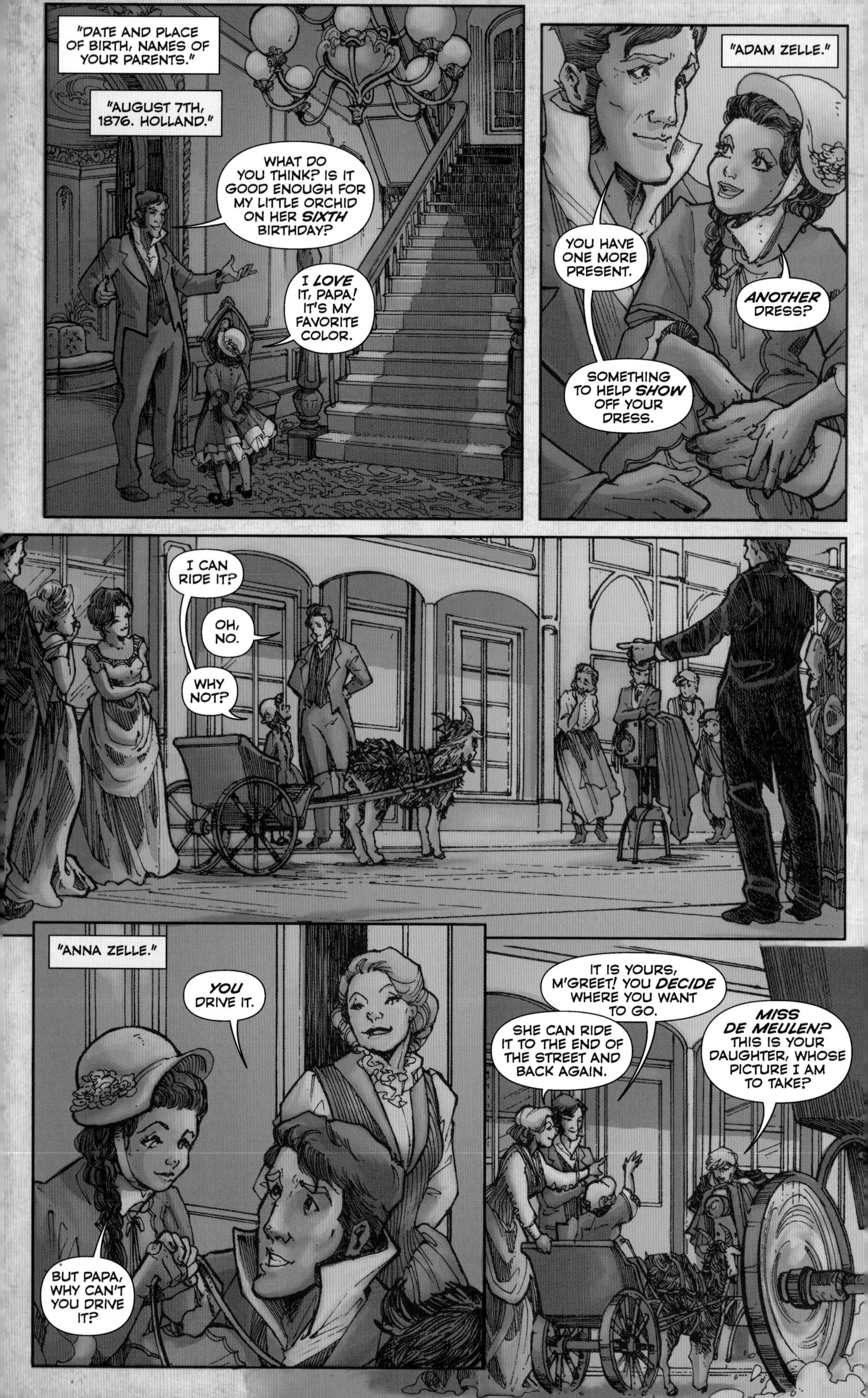
"DATE AND PLACE OF BIRTH, NAMES OF YOUR PARENTS."
"AUGUST 7TH, 1876. HOLLAND."
WHAT DO YOU THINK? IS IT GOOD ENOUGH FOR MY LITTLE ORCHID ON HER SIXTH BIRTHDAY?
I LOVE IT, PAPA! IT'S MY FAVORITE COLOR.
"ADAM ZELLE."
YOU HAVE ONE MORE PRESENT.
ANOTHER DRESS?
SOMETHING TO HELP SHOW OFF YOUR DRESS.
I CAN RIDE IT?
OH, NO.
WHY NOT?
"ANNA ZELLE."
YOU DRIVE IT.
BUT PAPA, WHY CAN'T YOU DRIVE IT?
IT IS YOURS, M'GREET! YOU DECIDE WHERE YOU WANT TO GO.
SHE CAN RIDE IT TO THE END OF THE STREET AND BACK AGAIN.
MISS DE MEULEN? THIS IS YOUR DAUGHTER, WHOSE PICTURE I AM TO TAKE?

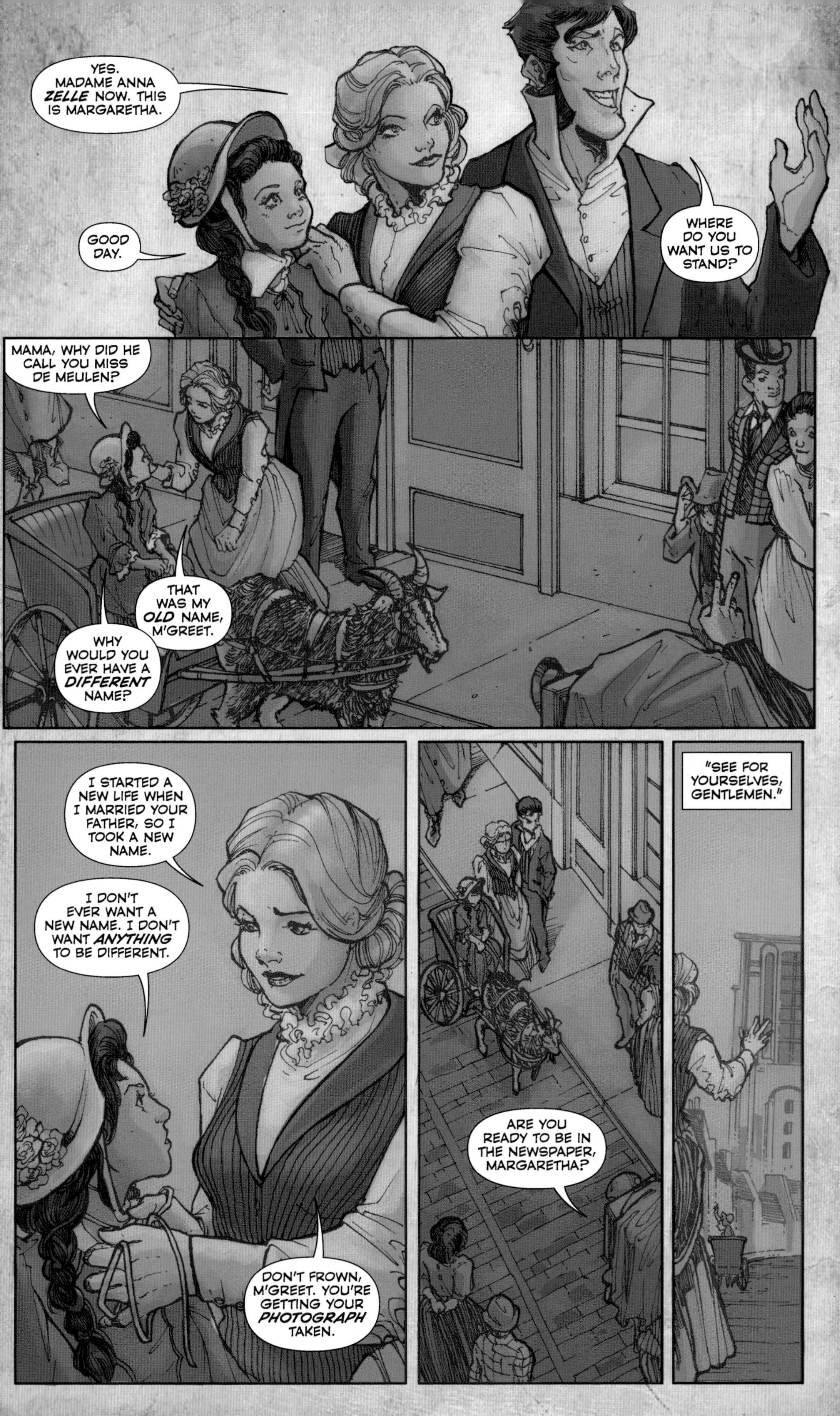
YES. MADAME ANNA ZELLE NOW. THIS IS MARGARETHA.
GOOD DAY.
WHERE DO YOU WANT US TO STAND?
MAMA, WHY DID HE CALL YOU MISS DE MEULEN?
THAT WAS MY OLD NAME, M'GREET.
WHY WOULD YOU EVER HAVE A DIFFERENT NAME?
I STARTED A NEW LIFE WHEN I MARRIED YOUR FATHER, SO I TOOK A NEW NAME.
I DON'T EVER WANT A NEW NAME. I DON'T WANT ANYTHING TO BE DIFFERENT.
DON'T FROWN, M'GREET. YOU'RE GETTING YOUR PHOTOGRAPH TAKEN.
ARE YOU READY TO BE IN THE NEWSPAPER, MARGARETHA?
"SEE FOR YOURSELVES, GENTLEMEN."

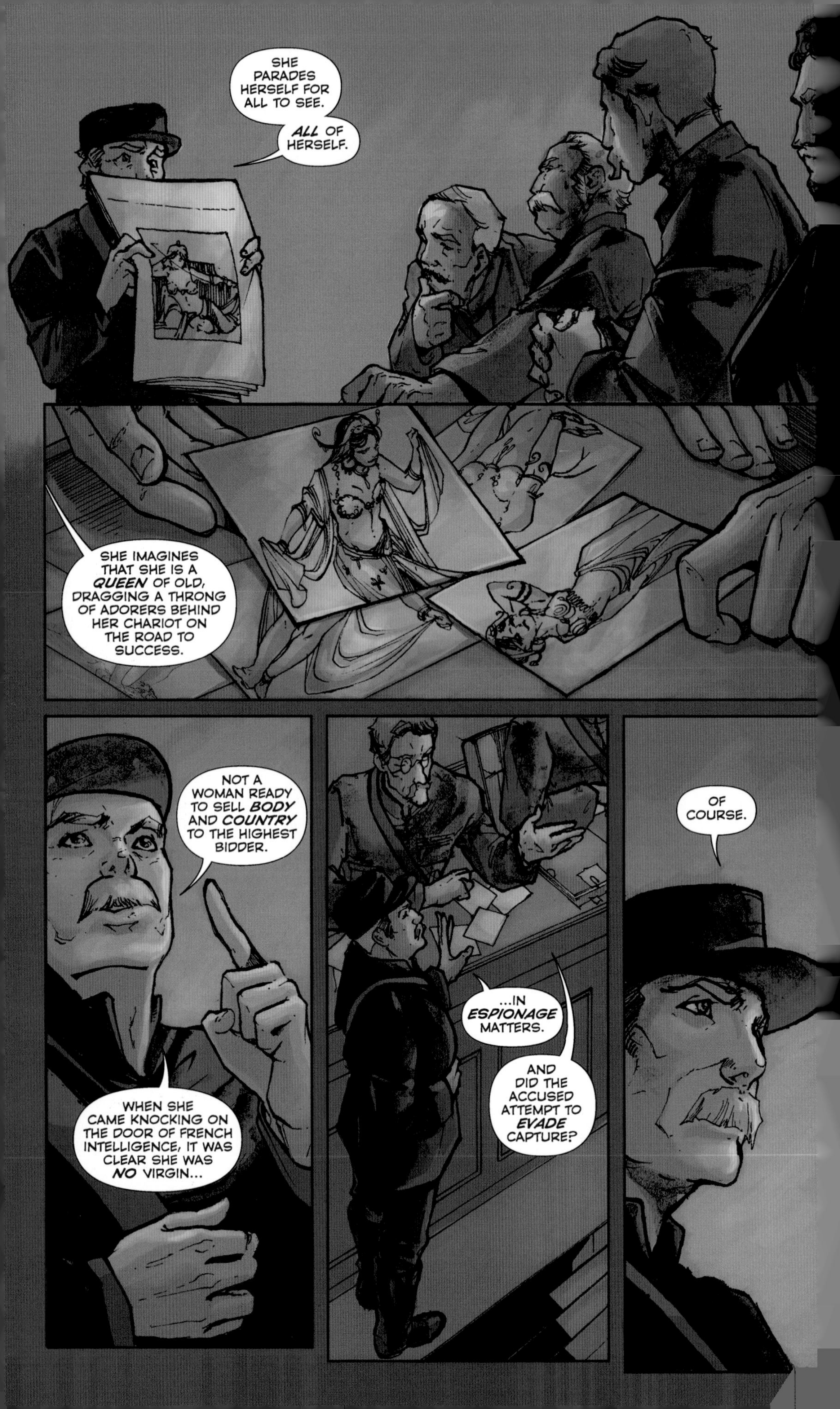
SHE PARADES HERSELF FOR ALL TO SEE.
ALL OF HERSELF.
SHE IMAGINES THAT SHE IS A *QUEEN* OF OLD, DRAGGING A THRONG OF ADORERS BEHIND HER CHARIOT ON THE ROAD TO SUCCESS.
NOT A WOMAN READY TO SELL *BODY* AND *COUNTRY* TO THE HIGHEST BIDDER.
WHEN SHE CAME KNOCKING ON THE DOOR OF FRENCH INTELLIGENCE, IT WAS CLEAR SHE WAS *NO* VIRGIN...
...IN *ESPIONAGE* MATTERS.
AND DID THE ACCUSED ATTEMPT TO *EVADE* CAPTURE?
OF COURSE.

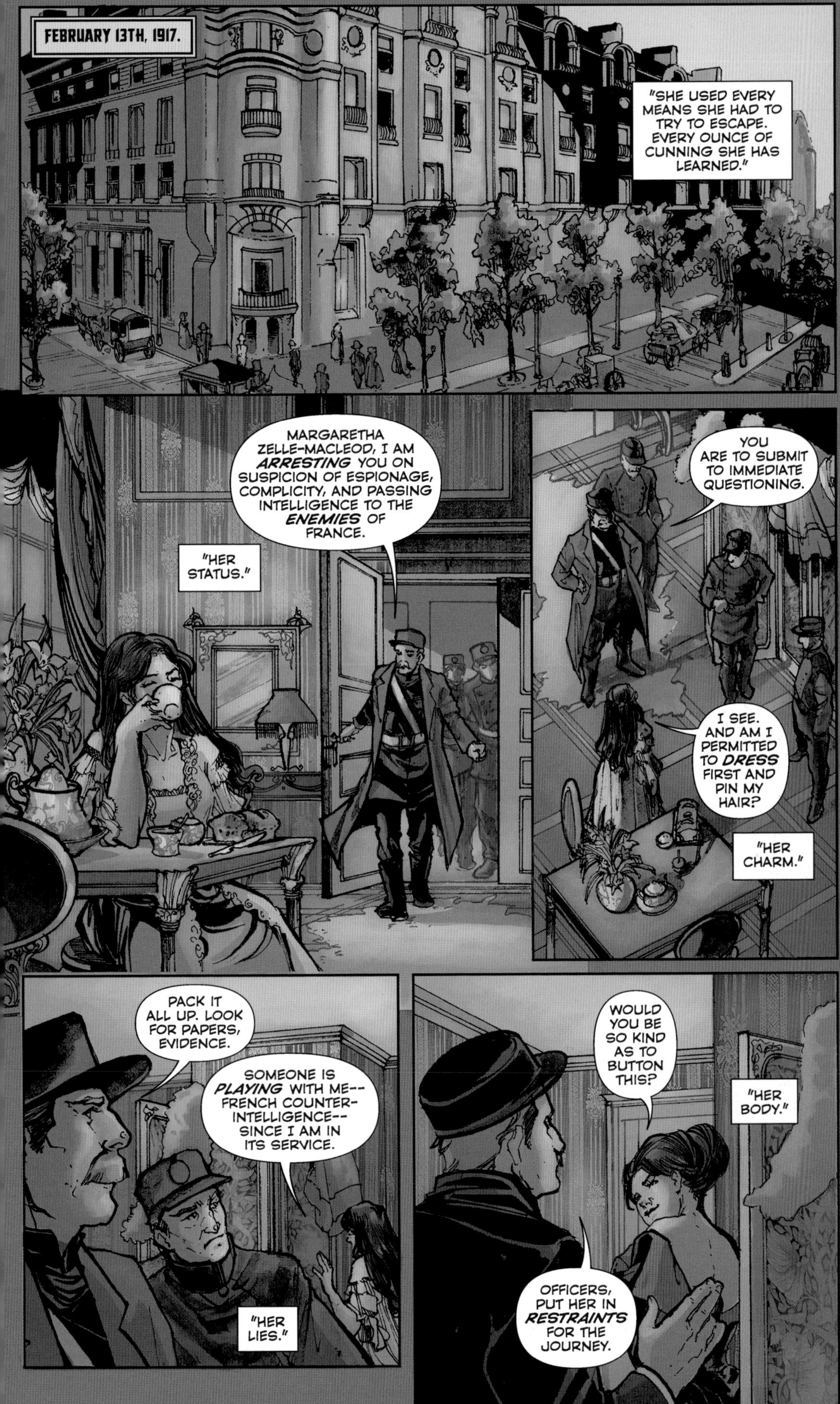
FEBRUARY 13TH, 1917.
"SHE USED EVERY MEANS SHE HAD TO TRY TO ESCAPE. EVERY OUNCE OF CUNNING SHE HAS LEARNED."
MARGARETHA ZELLE-MACLEOD, I AM ARRESTING YOU ON SUSPICION OF ESPIONAGE, COMPLICITY, AND PASSING INTELLIGENCE TO THE ENEMIES OF FRANCE.
"HER STATUS."
YOU ARE TO SUBMIT TO IMMEDIATE QUESTIONING.
I SEE. AND AM I PERMITTED TO DRESS FIRST AND PIN MY HAIR?
"HER CHARM."
PACK IT ALL UP. LOOK FOR PAPERS, EVIDENCE.
SOMEONE IS PLAYING WITH ME-- FRENCH COUNTER-INTELLIGENCE-- SINCE I AM IN ITS SERVICE.
"HER LIES."
WOULD YOU BE SO KIND AS TO BUTTON THIS?
"HER BODY."
OFFICERS, PUT HER IN RESTRAINTS FOR THE JOURNEY.

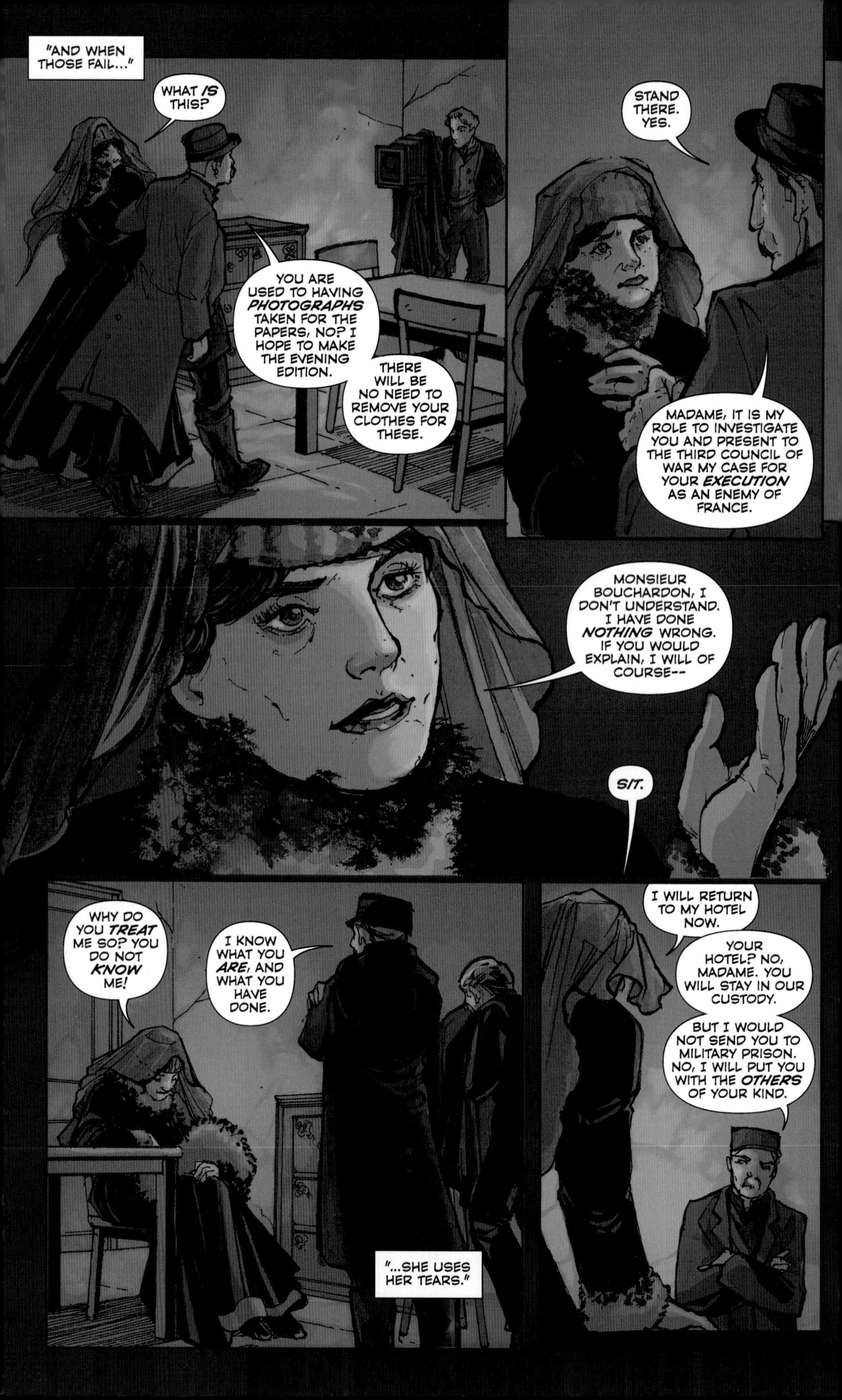
"AND WHEN THOSE FAIL..."
WHAT IS THIS?
YOU ARE USED TO HAVING PHOTOGRAPHS TAKEN FOR THE PAPERS, NO? I HOPE TO MAKE THE EVENING EDITION.
THERE WILL BE NO NEED TO REMOVE YOUR CLOTHES FOR THESE.
STAND THERE. YES.
MADAME, IT IS MY ROLE TO INVESTIGATE YOU AND PRESENT TO THE THIRD COUNCIL OF WAR MY CASE FOR YOUR EXECUTION AS AN ENEMY OF FRANCE.
MONSIEUR BOUCHARDON, I DON'T UNDERSTAND. I HAVE DONE NOTHING WRONG. IF YOU WOULD EXPLAIN, I WILL OF COURSE--
SIT.
WHY DO YOU TREAT ME SO? YOU DO NOT KNOW ME!
I KNOW WHAT YOU ARE, AND WHAT YOU HAVE DONE.
I WILL RETURN TO MY HOTEL NOW.
YOUR HOTEL? NO, MADAME. YOU WILL STAY IN OUR CUSTODY.
BUT I WOULD NOT SEND YOU TO MILITARY PRISON. NO, I WILL PUT YOU WITH THE OTHERS OF YOUR KIND.
"...SHE USES HER TEARS."

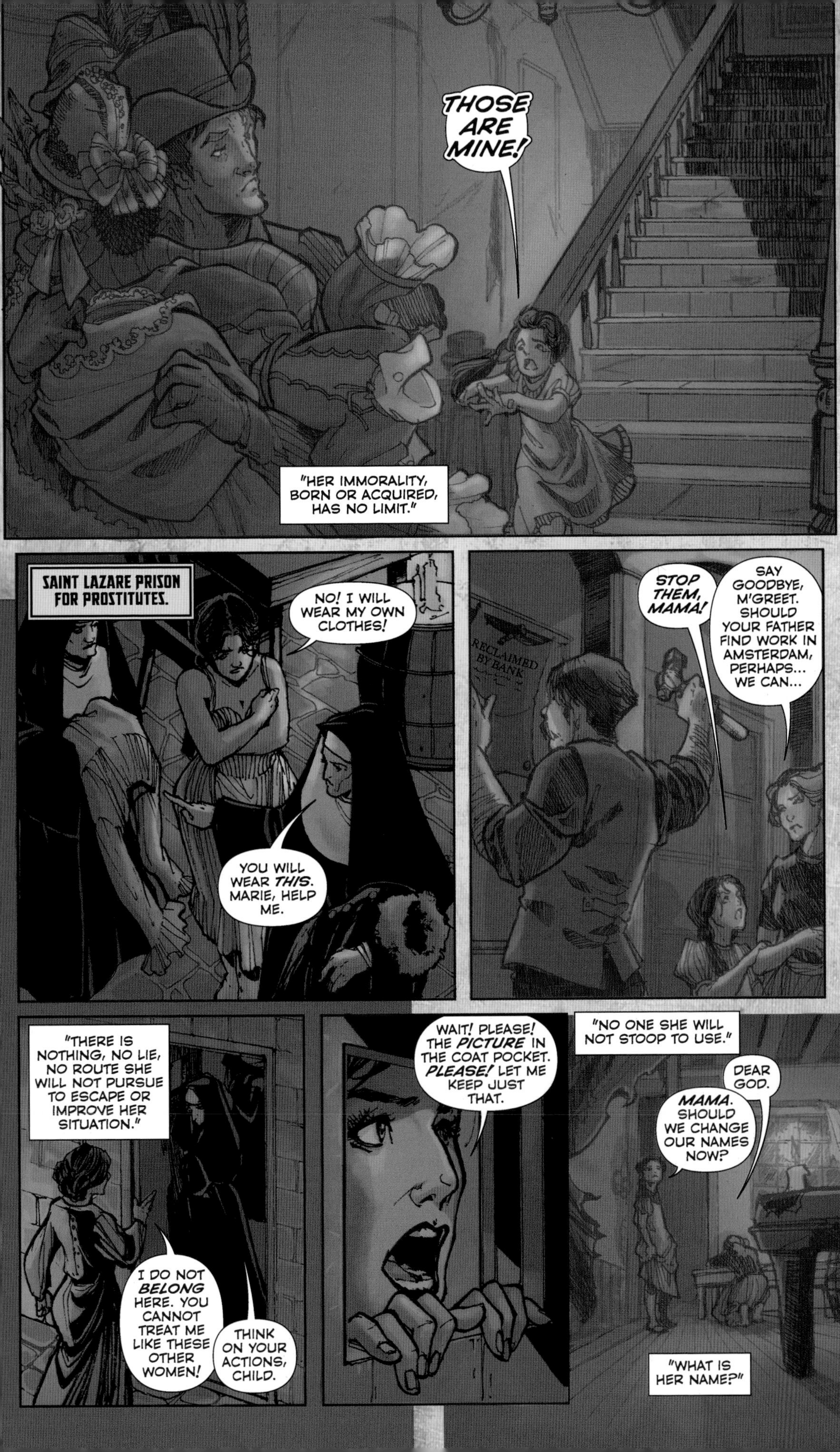
THOSE ARE MINE!
"HER IMMORALITY, BORN OR ACQUIRED, HAS NO LIMIT."
SAINT LAZARE PRISON FOR PROSTITUTES.
NO! I WILL WEAR MY OWN CLOTHES!
YOU WILL WEAR THIS. MARIE, HELP ME.
RECLAIMED BY BANK
STOP THEM, MAMA!
SAY GOODBYE, M'GREET. SHOULD YOUR FATHER FIND WORK IN AMSTERDAM, PERHAPS... WE CAN...
"THERE IS NOTHING, NO LIE, NO ROUTE SHE WILL NOT PURSUE TO ESCAPE OR IMPROVE HER SITUATION."
I DO NOT BELONG HERE. YOU CANNOT TREAT ME LIKE THESE OTHER WOMEN!
THINK ON YOUR ACTIONS, CHILD.
WAIT! PLEASE! THE PICTURE IN THE COAT POCKET. PLEASE! LET ME KEEP JUST THAT.
"NO ONE SHE WILL NOT STOOP TO USE."
DEAR GOD.
MAMA. SHOULD WE CHANGE OUR NAMES NOW?
"WHAT IS HER NAME?"

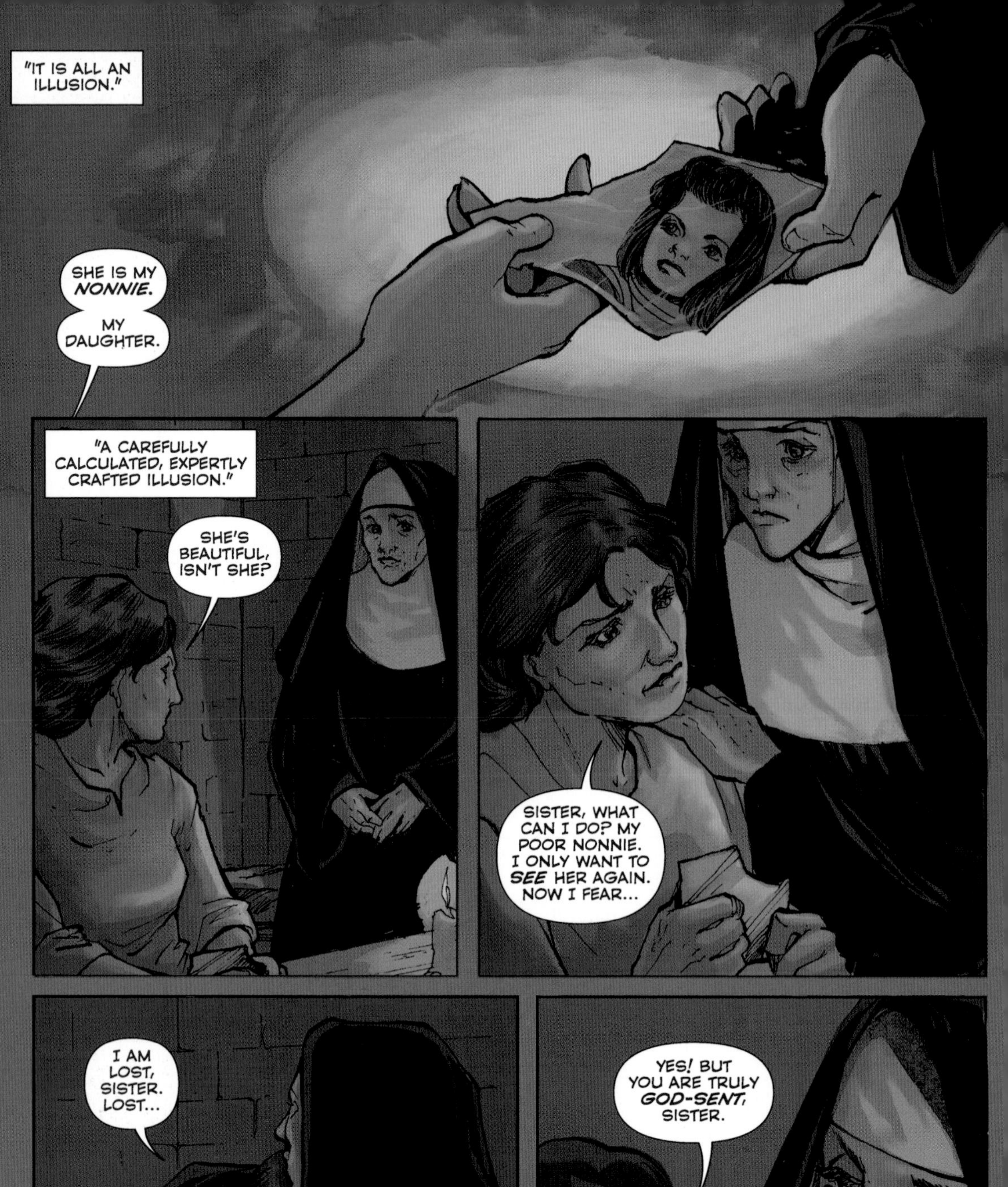
"IT IS ALL AN ILLUSION."
SHE IS MY NONNIE.
MY DAUGHTER.
"A CAREFULLY CALCULATED, EXPERTLY CRAFTED ILLUSION."
SHE'S BEAUTIFUL, ISN'T SHE?
SISTER, WHAT CAN I DO? MY POOR NONNIE. I ONLY WANT TO SEE HER AGAIN. NOW I FEAR...
I AM LOST, SISTER. LOST...
NOW, NOW, THERE IS NO NEED FOR TEARS. YOU LOOK TO ME LIKE A WOMAN WHO WILL FIGHT. YOU WILL TELL THEM YOUR STORY, WILL YOU NOT?
YES! BUT YOU ARE TRULY GOD-SENT, SISTER.
IF YOU WOULD PERMIT ME PEN AND PAPER, I WILL TELL THEM MY STORY, AND THEY WILL NEVER FORGET IT.

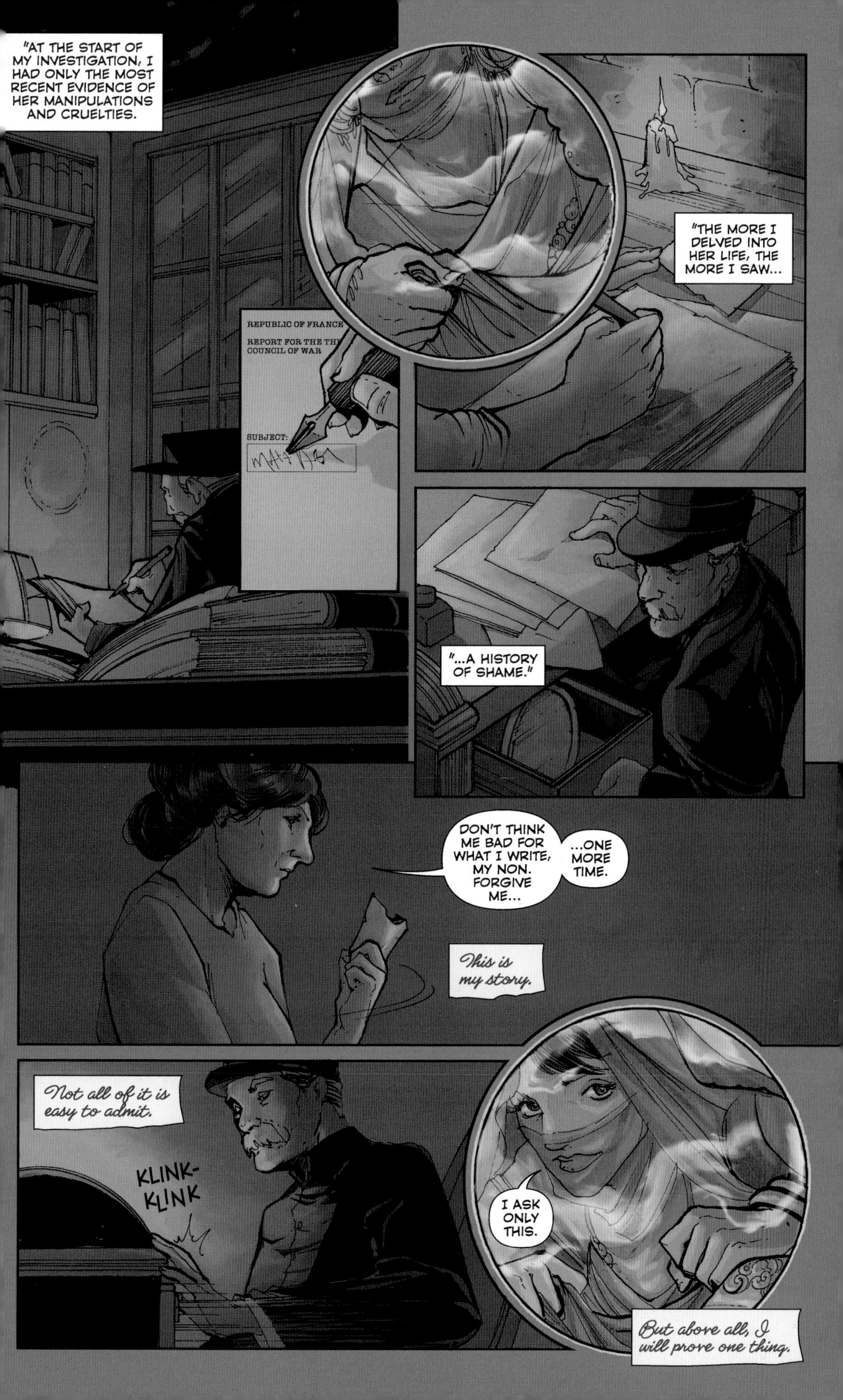
"AT THE START OF MY INVESTIGATION, I HAD ONLY THE MOST RECENT EVIDENCE OF HER MANIPULATIONS AND CRUELTIES.
REPUBLIC OF FRANCE
REPORT FOR THE TH
COUNCIL OF WAR
SUBJECT:
"THE MORE I DELVED INTO HER LIFE, THE MORE I SAW...
"...A HISTORY OF SHAME."
DON'T THINK ME BAD FOR WHAT I WRITE, MY NON. FORGIVE ME...
...ONE MORE TIME.
This is my story.
Not all of it is easy to admit.
KLINK-KLINK
I ASK ONLY THIS.
But above all, I will prove one thing.

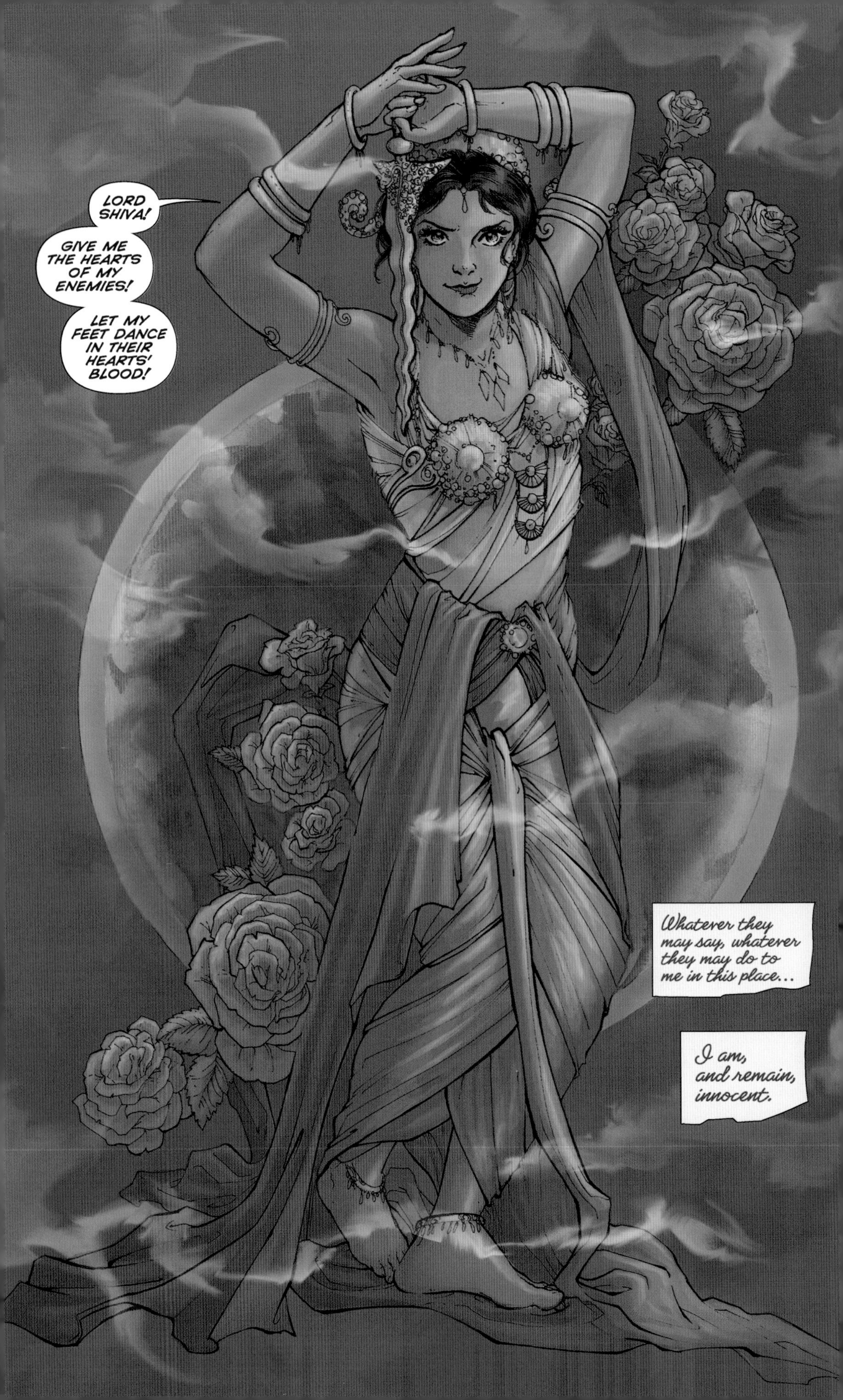
LORD SHIVA!
GIVE ME THE HEARTS OF MY ENEMIES!
LET MY FEET DANCE IN THEIR HEARTS' BLOOD!
Whatever they may say, whatever they may do to me in this place...
I am, and remain, innocent.

CHAPTER TWO

BARE·BREAST

"I have kissed thy mouth.
There was a bitter taste on thy lips.
Was it the taste of blood?
But perchance it is the taste of love...
They say that love hath a bitter taste...
But what of that? What of that?"

SALOMÉ:
A TRAGEDY IN ONE ACT
~ OSCAR WILDE ~

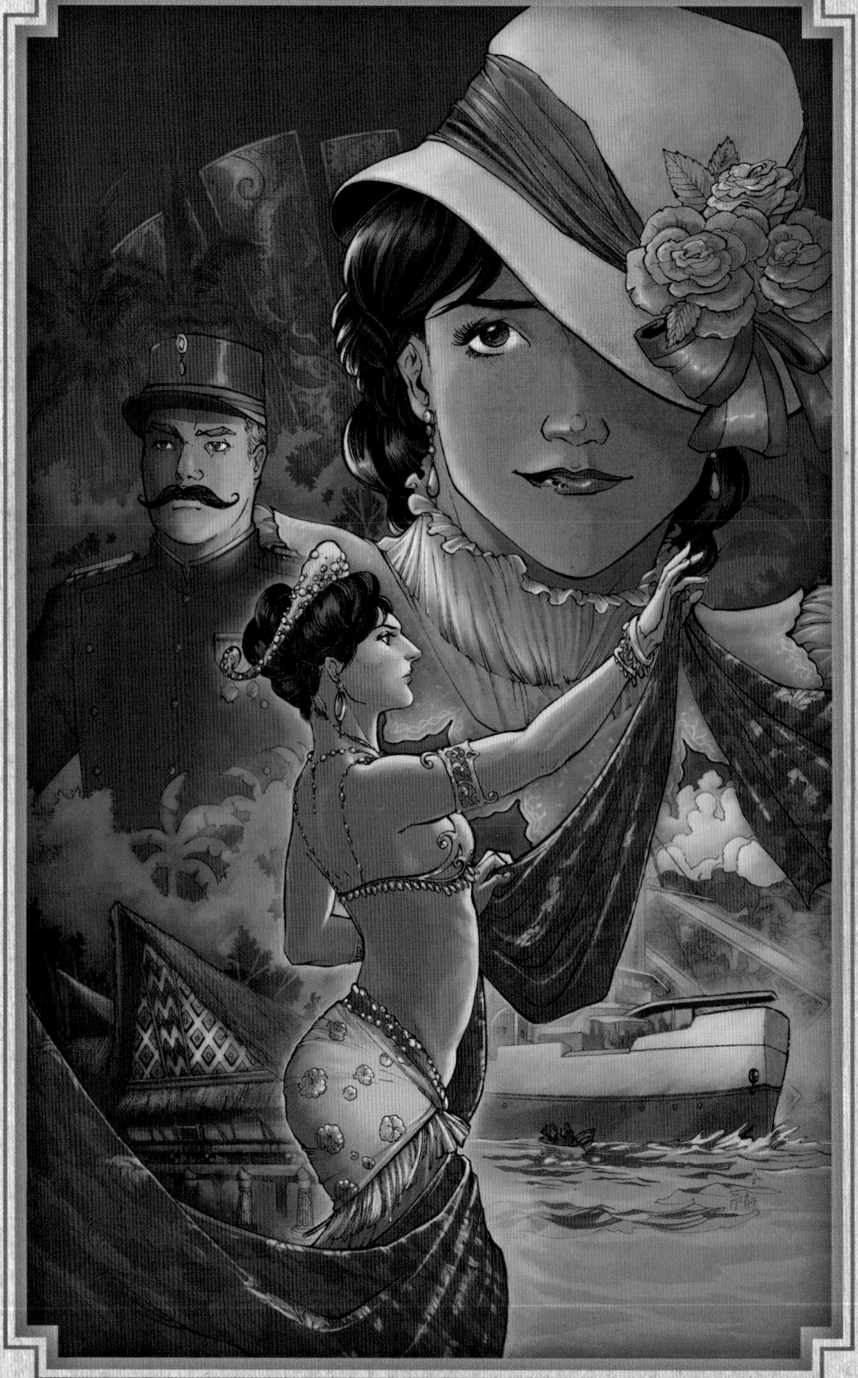

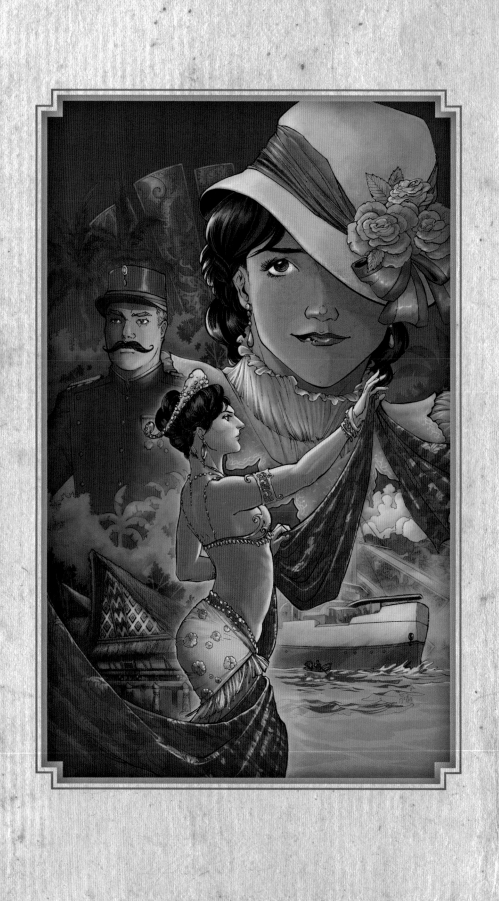

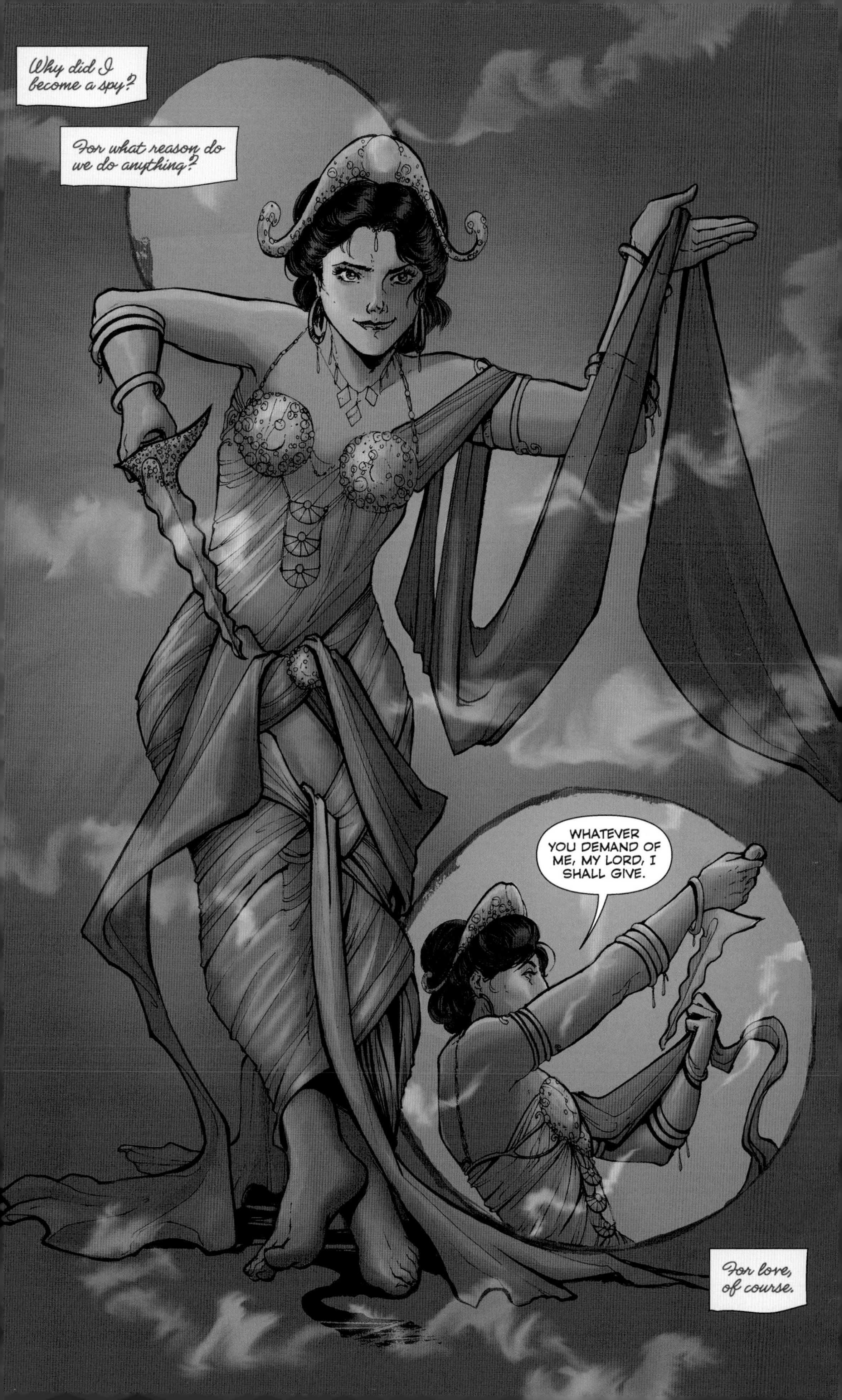
Why did I become a spy?
For what reason do we do anything?
WHATEVER YOU DEMAND OF ME, MY LORD, I SHALL GIVE.
For love, of course.

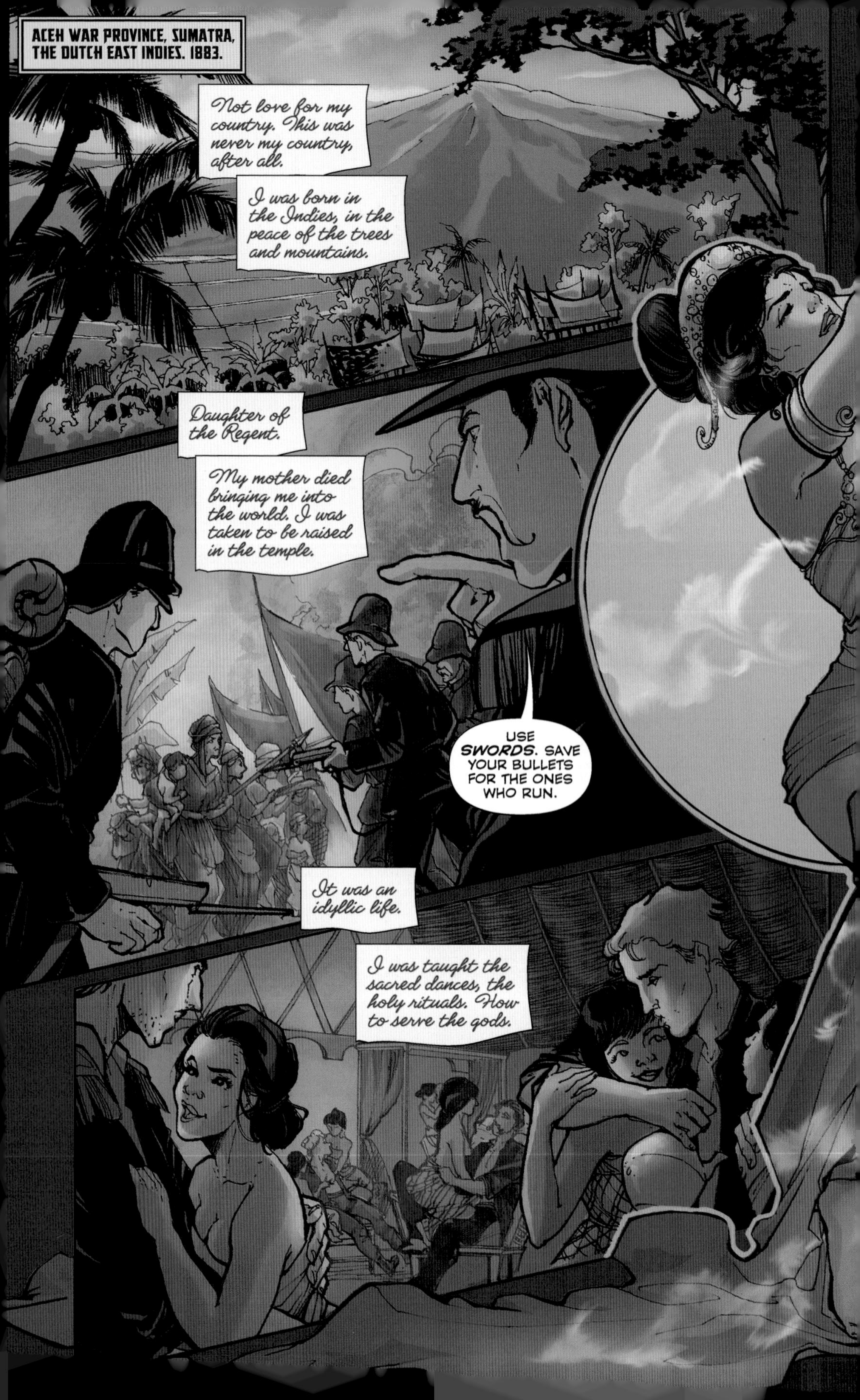
ACEH WAR PROVINCE, SUMATRA, THE DUTCH EAST INDIES. 1883.
Not love for my country. This was never my country, after all.
I was born in the Indies, in the peace of the trees and mountains.
Daughter of the Regent.
My mother died bringing me into the world. I was taken to be raised in the temple.
USE SWORDS. SAVE YOUR BULLETS FOR THE ONES WHO RUN.
It was an idyllic life.
I was taught the sacred dances, the holy rituals. How to serve the gods.

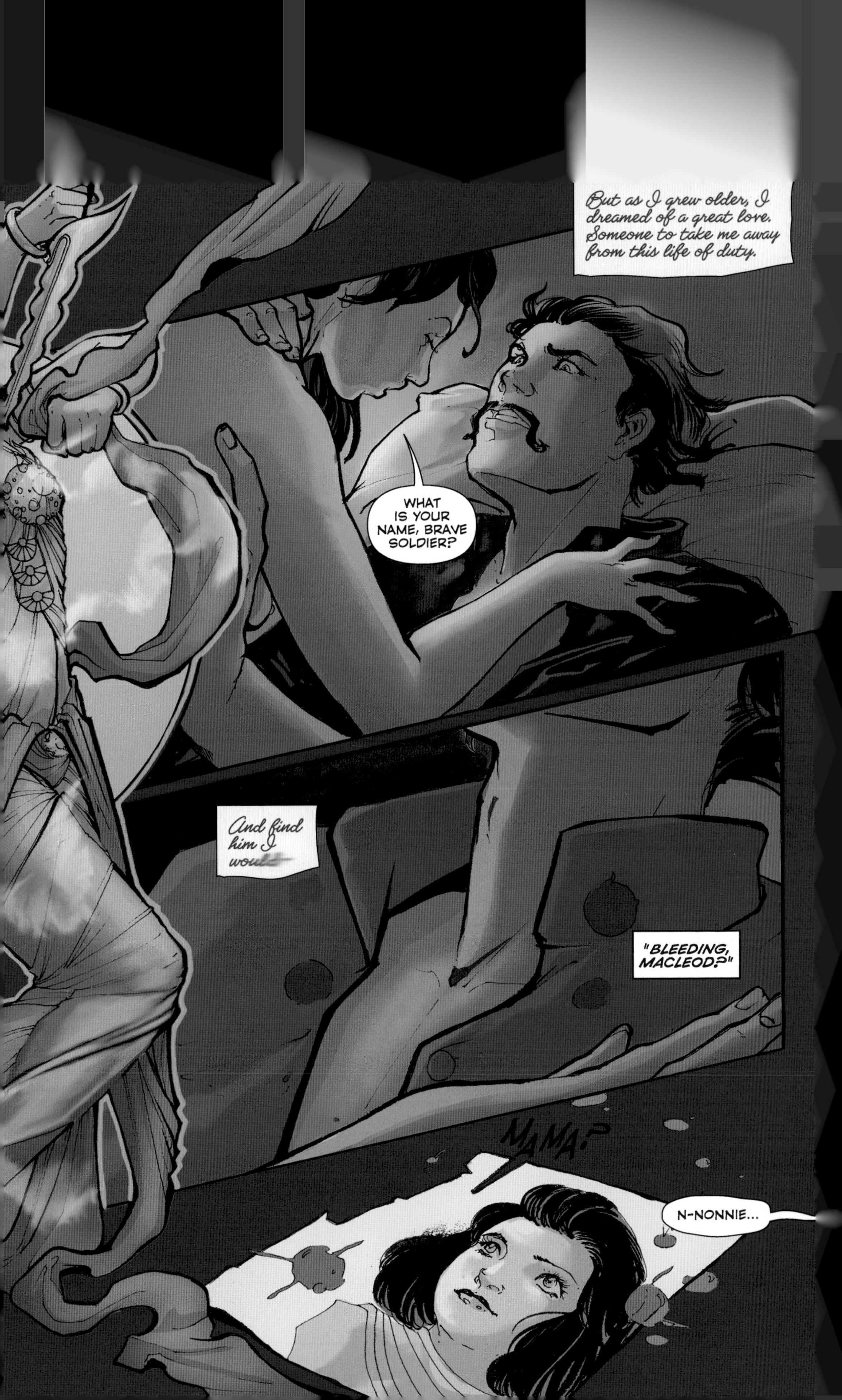

But as I grew older, I dreamed of a great love. Someone to take me away from this life of duty.
WHAT IS YOUR NAME, BRAVE SOLDIER?
And find him I would
"BLEEDING, MACLEOD?"
MAMA?
N-NONNIE...

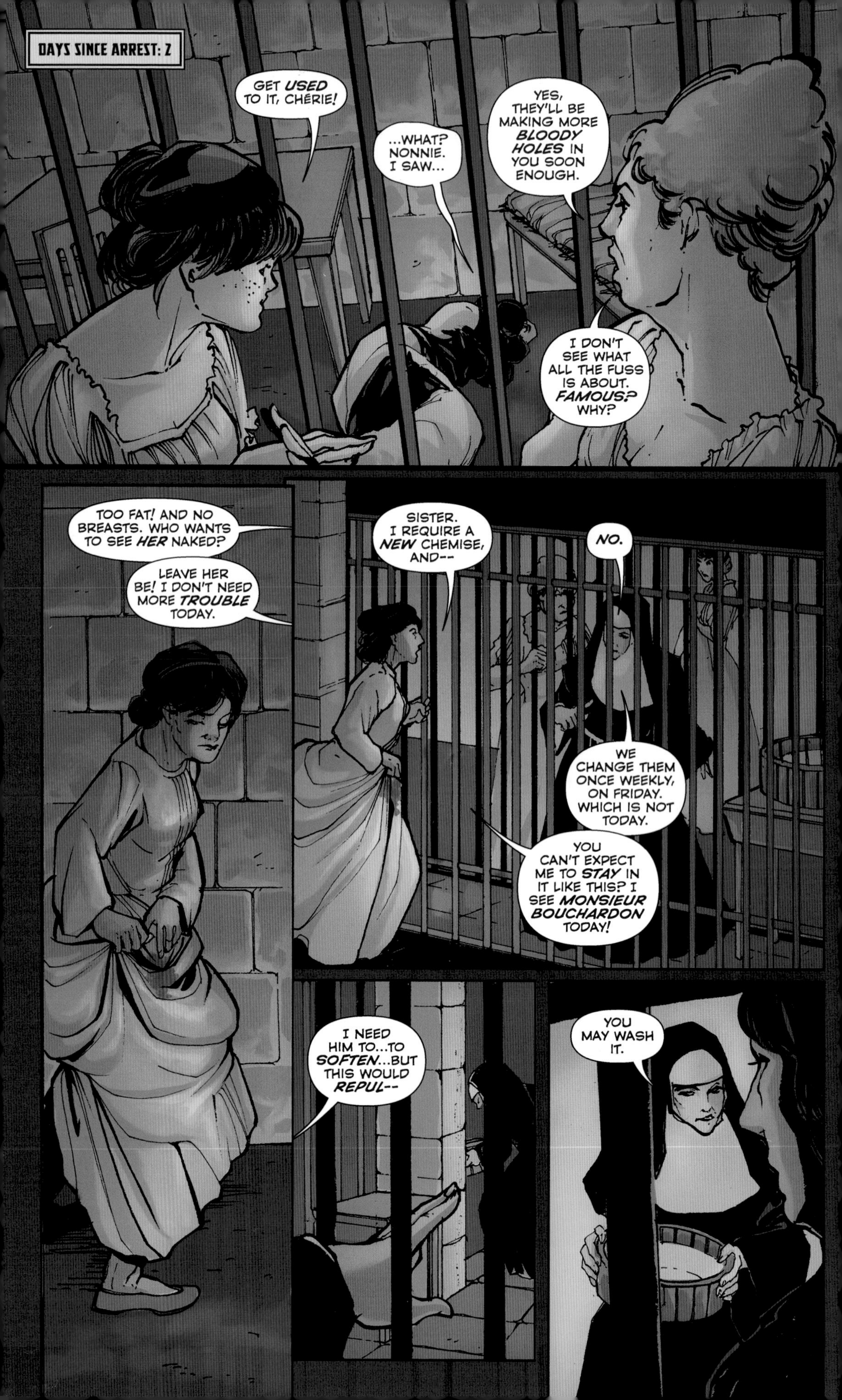
DAYS SINCE ARREST: 2
GET USED TO IT, CHÉRIE!
...WHAT? NONNIE. I SAW...
YES, THEY'LL BE MAKING MORE BLOODY HOLES IN YOU SOON ENOUGH.
I DON'T SEE WHAT ALL THE FUSS IS ABOUT. FAMOUS? WHY?
TOO FAT! AND NO BREASTS. WHO WANTS TO SEE HER NAKED?
LEAVE HER BE! I DON'T NEED MORE TROUBLE TODAY.
SISTER. I REQUIRE A NEW CHEMISE, AND--
NO.
WE CHANGE THEM ONCE WEEKLY, ON FRIDAY. WHICH IS NOT TODAY.
YOU CAN'T EXPECT ME TO STAY IN IT LIKE THIS? I SEE MONSIEUR BOUCHARDON TODAY!
I NEED HIM TO...TO SOFTEN...BUT THIS WOULD REPUL--
YOU MAY WASH IT.

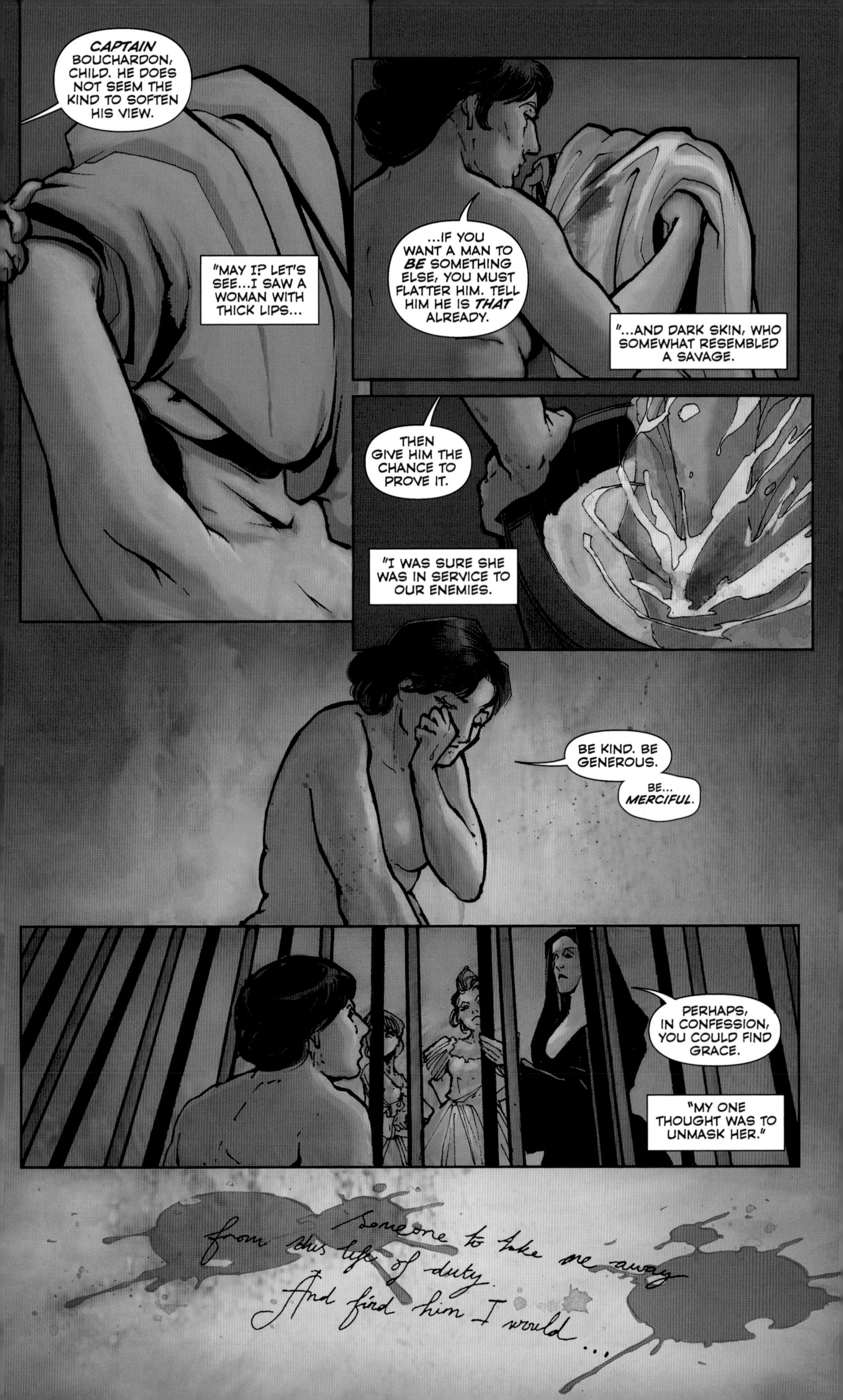
CAPTAIN BOUCHARDON, CHILD. HE DOES NOT SEEM THE KIND TO SOFTEN HIS VIEW.
"MAY I? LET'S SEE...I SAW A WOMAN WITH THICK LIPS...
...IF YOU WANT A MAN TO BE SOMETHING ELSE, YOU MUST FLATTER HIM. TELL HIM HE IS THAT ALREADY.
"...AND DARK SKIN, WHO SOMEWHAT RESEMBLED A SAVAGE.
THEN GIVE HIM THE CHANCE TO PROVE IT.
"I WAS SURE SHE WAS IN SERVICE TO OUR ENEMIES.
BE KIND. BE GENEROUS.
BE... MERCIFUL.
PERHAPS, IN CONFESSION, YOU COULD FIND GRACE.
"MY ONE THOUGHT WAS TO UNMASK HER."
Someone to take me away
from this life of duty.
And find him I would...

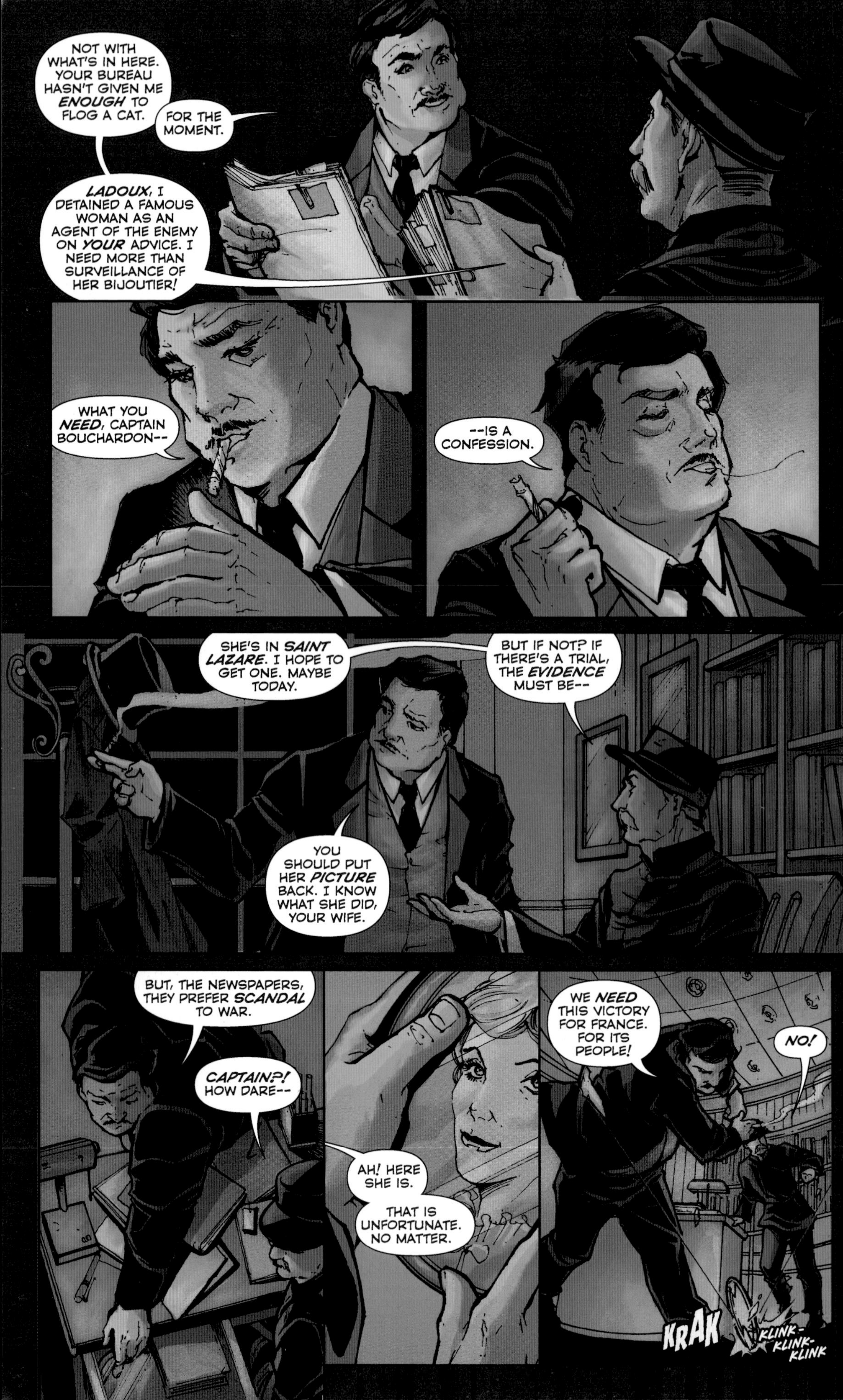
NOT WITH WHAT'S IN HERE. YOUR BUREAU HASN'T GIVEN ME ENOUGH TO FLOG A CAT.
FOR THE MOMENT.
LADOUX, I DETAINED A FAMOUS WOMAN AS AN AGENT OF THE ENEMY ON YOUR ADVICE. I NEED MORE THAN SURVEILLANCE OF HER BIJOUTIER!
WHAT YOU NEED, CAPTAIN BOUCHARDON--
--IS A CONFESSION.
SHE'S IN SAINT LAZARE. I HOPE TO GET ONE. MAYBE TODAY.
BUT IF NOT? IF THERE'S A TRIAL, THE EVIDENCE MUST BE--
YOU SHOULD PUT HER PICTURE BACK. I KNOW WHAT SHE DID, YOUR WIFE.
BUT, THE NEWSPAPERS, THEY PREFER SCANDAL TO WAR.
CAPTAIN?! HOW DARE--
AH! HERE SHE IS.
THAT IS UNFORTUNATE. NO MATTER.
WE NEED THIS VICTORY FOR FRANCE. FOR ITS PEOPLE!
NO!
KRAK
KLINK-KLINK-KLINK

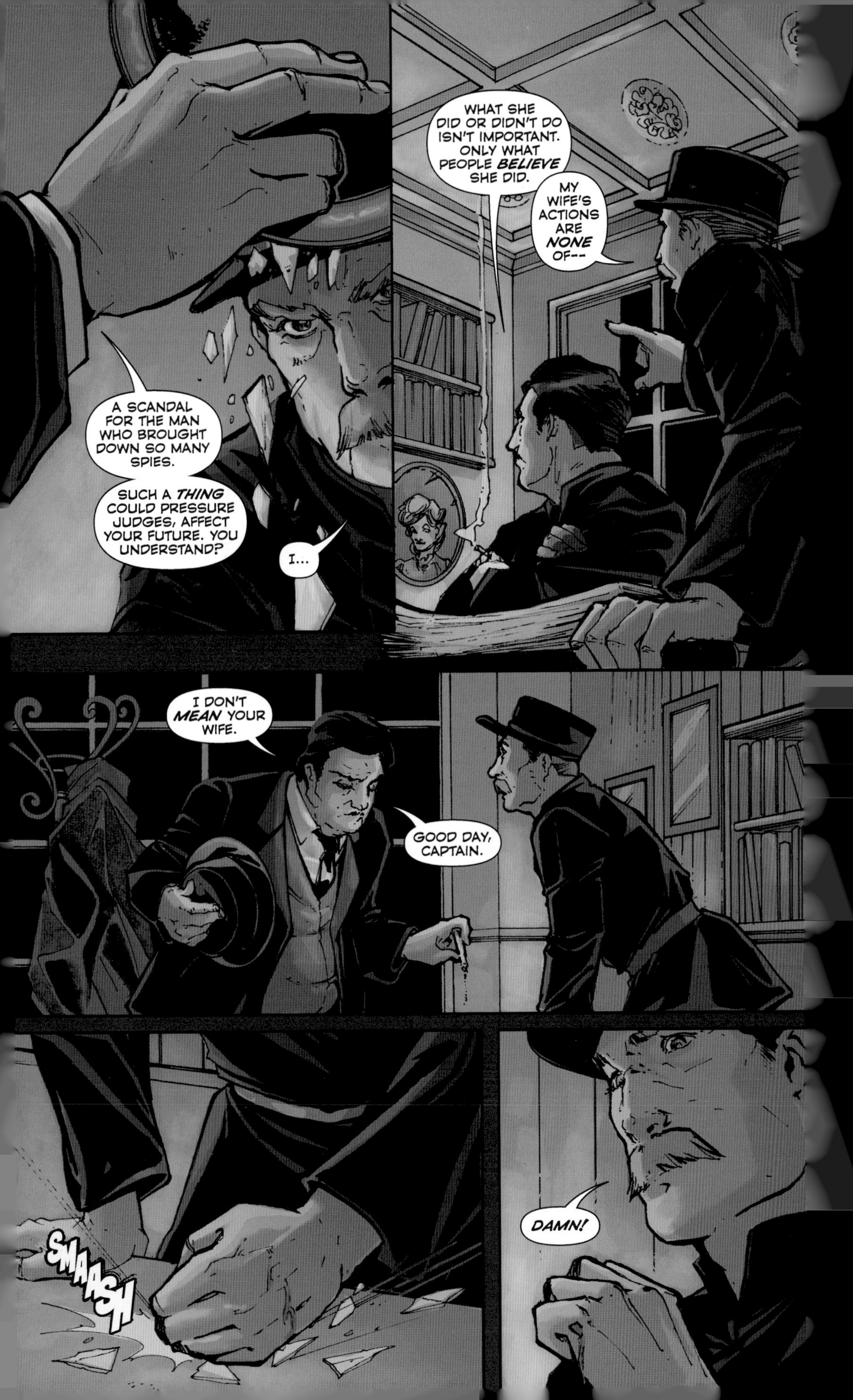
A SCANDAL FOR THE MAN WHO BROUGHT DOWN SO MANY SPIES.
SUCH A THING COULD PRESSURE JUDGES, AFFECT YOUR FUTURE. YOU UNDERSTAND?
I...
WHAT SHE DID OR DIDN'T DO ISN'T IMPORTANT. ONLY WHAT PEOPLE BELIEVE SHE DID.
MY WIFE'S ACTIONS ARE NONE OF--
I DON'T MEAN YOUR WIFE.
GOOD DAY, CAPTAIN.
SMAASH
DAMN!

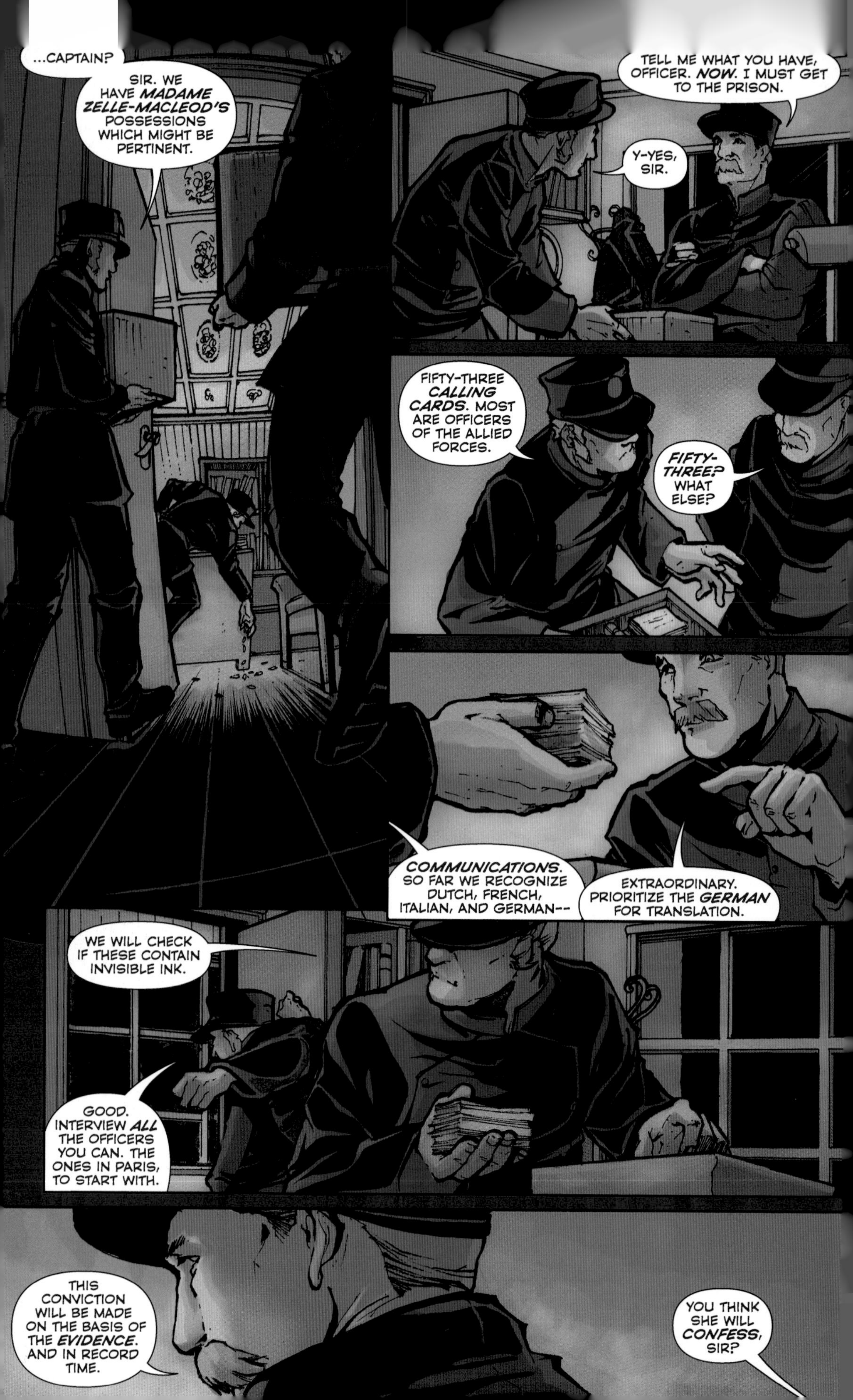
...CAPTAIN?
SIR. WE HAVE MADAME ZELLE-MACLEOD'S POSSESSIONS WHICH MIGHT BE PERTINENT.
TELL ME WHAT YOU HAVE, OFFICER. NOW. I MUST GET TO THE PRISON.
Y-YES, SIR.
FIFTY-THREE CALLING CARDS. MOST ARE OFFICERS OF THE ALLIED FORCES.
FIFTY-THREE? WHAT ELSE?
COMMUNICATIONS. SO FAR WE RECOGNIZE DUTCH, FRENCH, ITALIAN, AND GERMAN--
EXTRAORDINARY. PRIORITIZE THE GERMAN FOR TRANSLATION.
WE WILL CHECK IF THESE CONTAIN INVISIBLE INK.
GOOD. INTERVIEW ALL THE OFFICERS YOU CAN. THE ONES IN PARIS, TO START WITH.
THIS CONVICTION WILL BE MADE ON THE BASIS OF THE EVIDENCE. AND IN RECORD TIME.
YOU THINK SHE WILL CONFESS, SIR?

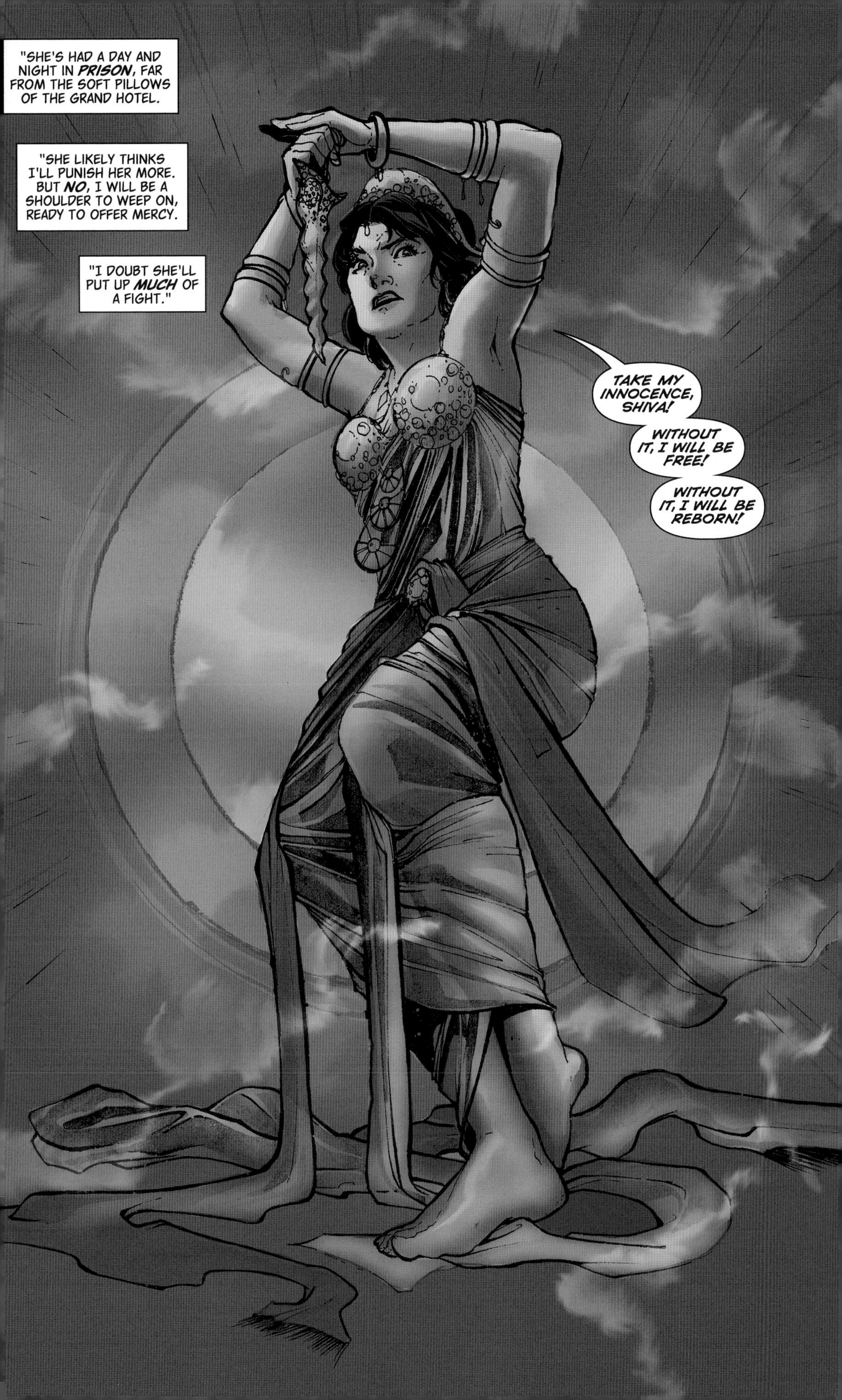
"SHE'S HAD A DAY AND NIGHT IN PRISON, FAR FROM THE SOFT PILLOWS OF THE GRAND HOTEL.
"SHE LIKELY THINKS I'LL PUNISH HER MORE. BUT NO, I WILL BE A SHOULDER TO WEEP ON, READY TO OFFER MERCY.
"I DOUBT SHE'LL PUT UP MUCH OF A FIGHT."
TAKE MY INNOCENCE, SHIVA!
WITHOUT IT, I WILL BE FREE!
WITHOUT IT, I WILL BE REBORN!

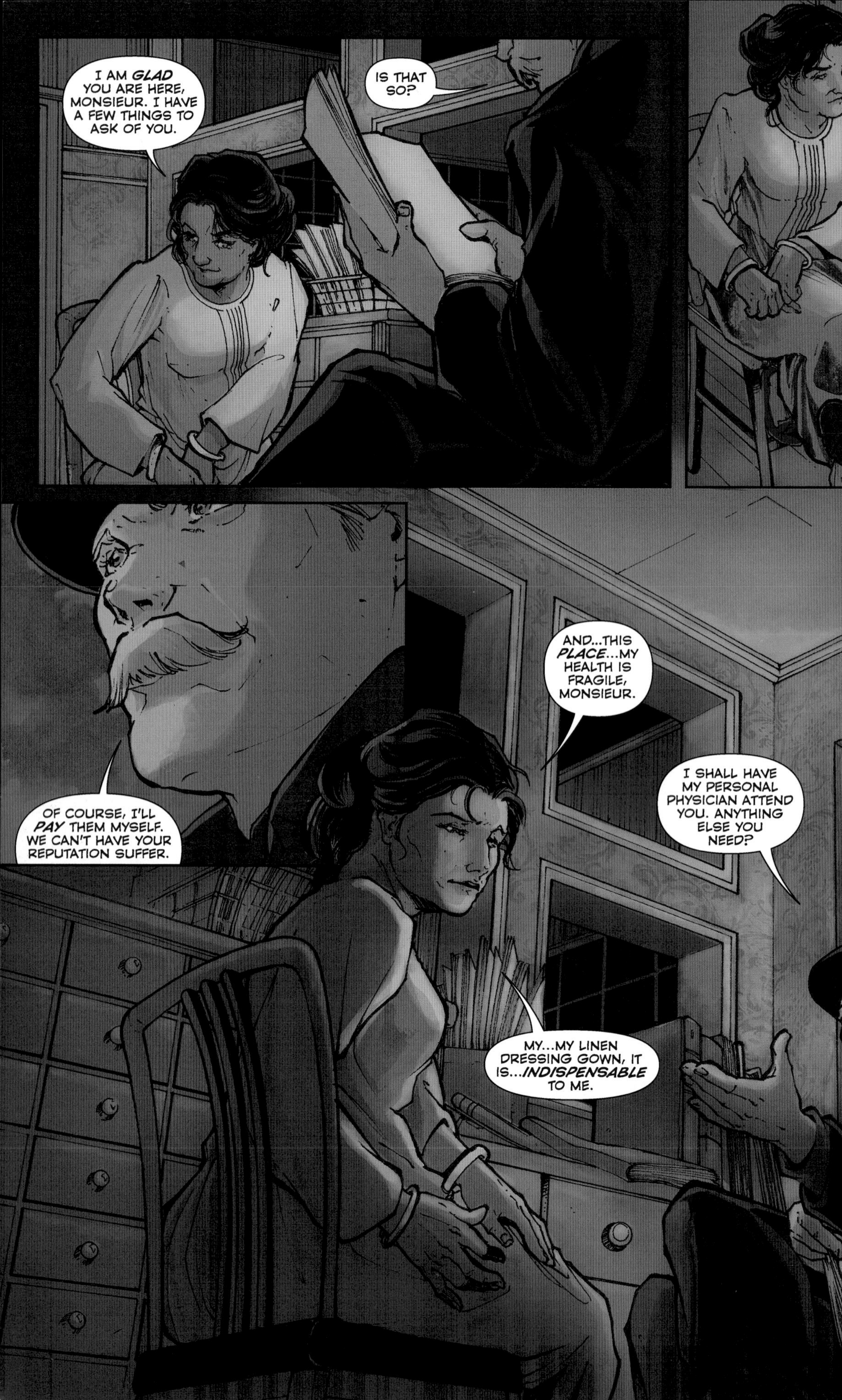
I AM GLAD YOU ARE HERE, MONSIEUR. I HAVE A FEW THINGS TO ASK OF YOU.
IS THAT SO?
OF COURSE, I'LL PAY THEM MYSELF. WE CAN'T HAVE YOUR REPUTATION SUFFER.
AND...THIS PLACE...MY HEALTH IS FRAGILE, MONSIEUR.
I SHALL HAVE MY PERSONAL PHYSICIAN ATTEND YOU. ANYTHING ELSE YOU NEED?
MY...MY LINEN DRESSING GOWN, IT IS...INDISPENSABLE TO ME.

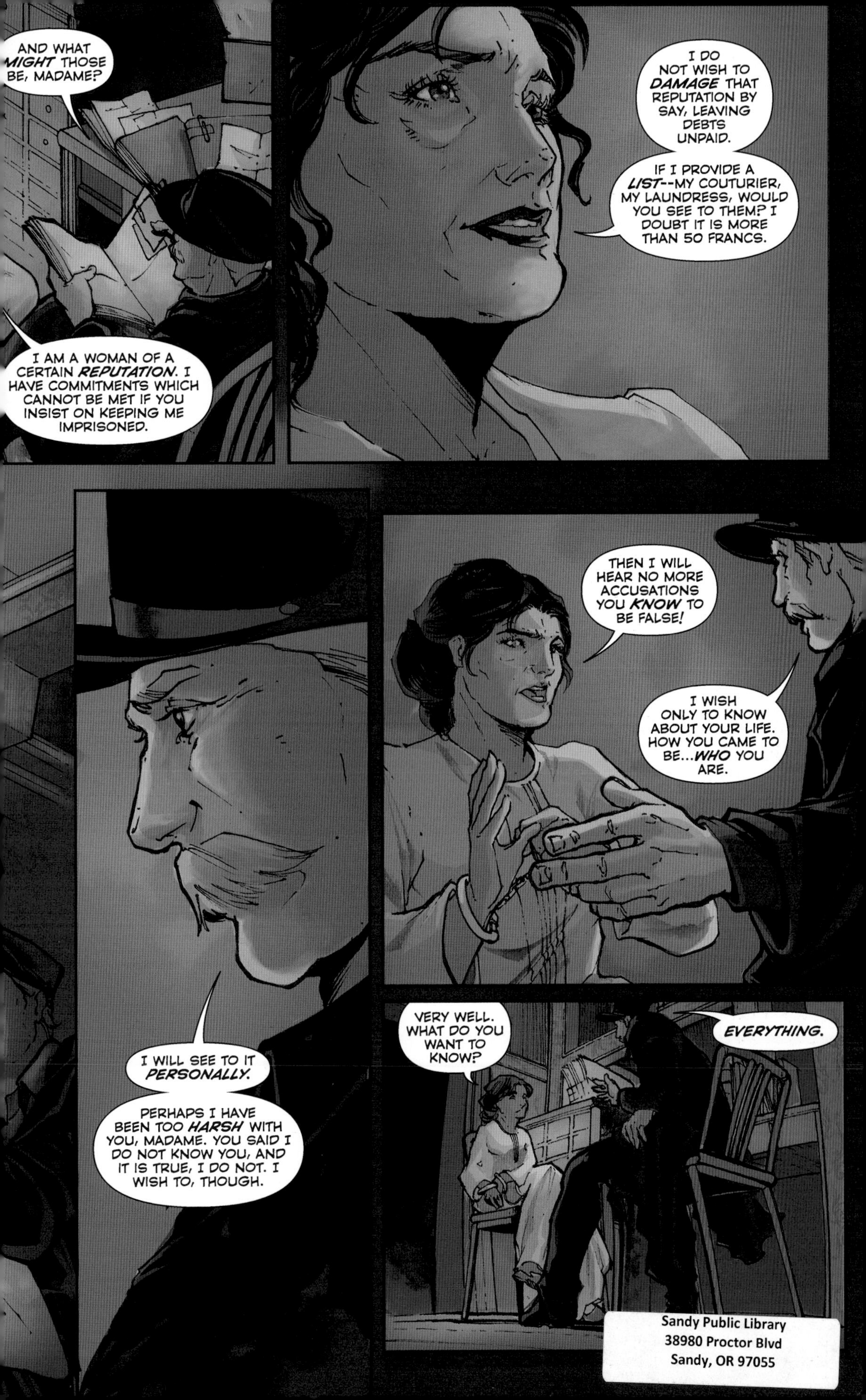
AND WHAT *MIGHT* THOSE BE, MADAME?
I AM A WOMAN OF A CERTAIN *REPUTATION*. I HAVE COMMITMENTS WHICH CANNOT BE MET IF YOU INSIST ON KEEPING ME IMPRISONED.
I DO NOT WISH TO *DAMAGE* THAT REPUTATION BY SAY, LEAVING DEBTS UNPAID.
IF I PROVIDE A *LIST*--MY COUTURIER, MY LAUNDRESS, WOULD YOU SEE TO THEM? I DOUBT IT IS MORE THAN 50 FRANCS.
I WILL SEE TO IT *PERSONALLY*.
PERHAPS I HAVE BEEN TOO *HARSH* WITH YOU, MADAME. YOU SAID I DO NOT KNOW YOU, AND IT IS TRUE, I DO NOT. I WISH TO, THOUGH.
THEN I WILL HEAR NO MORE ACCUSATIONS YOU *KNOW* TO BE FALSE!
I WISH ONLY TO KNOW ABOUT YOUR LIFE. HOW YOU CAME TO BE...*WHO* YOU ARE.
VERY WELL. WHAT DO YOU WANT TO KNOW?
EVERYTHING.

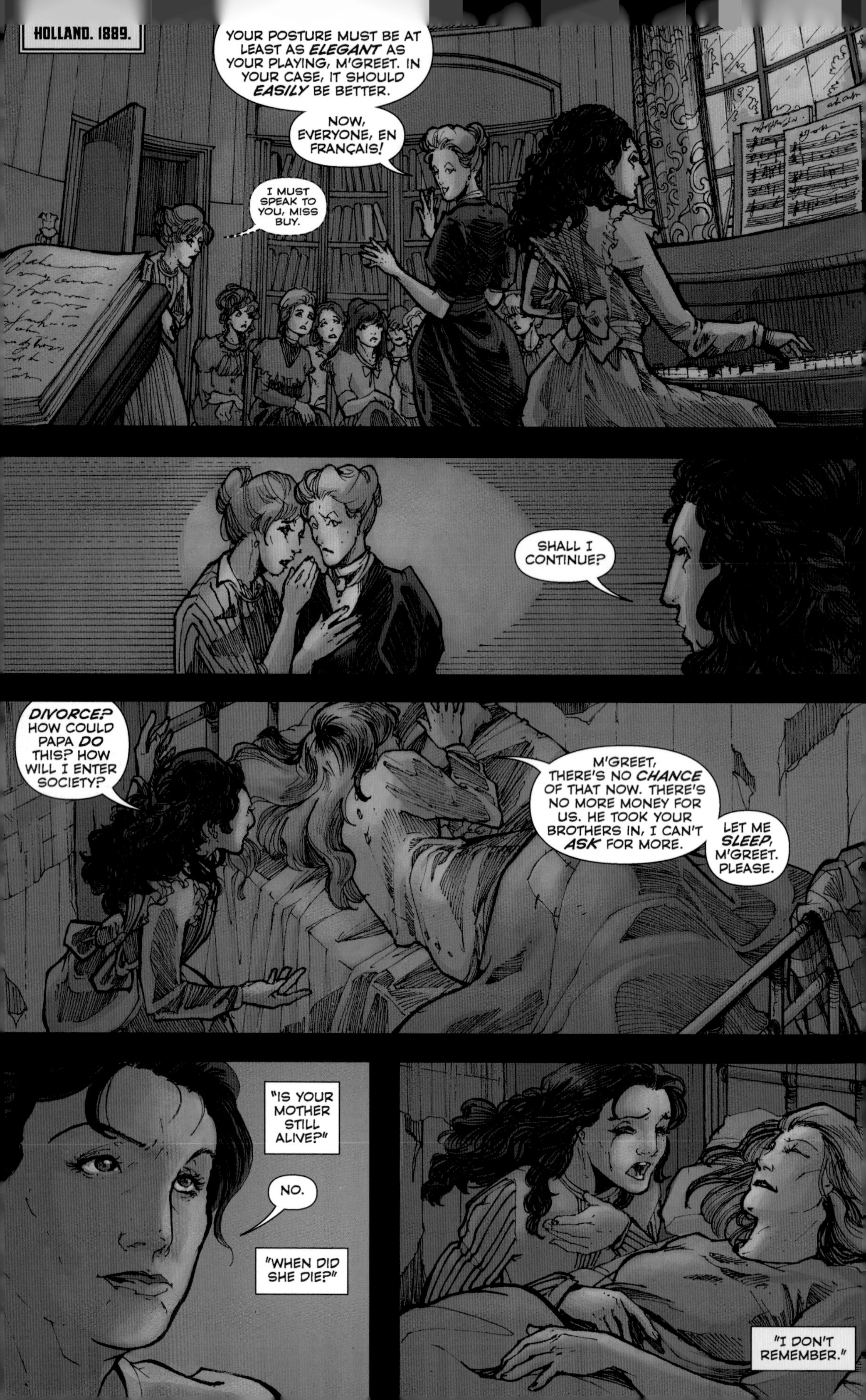
HOLLAND. 1889.
YOUR POSTURE MUST BE AT LEAST AS ELEGANT AS YOUR PLAYING, M'GREET. IN YOUR CASE, IT SHOULD EASILY BE BETTER.
NOW, EVERYONE, EN FRANÇAIS!
I MUST SPEAK TO YOU, MISS BUY.
SHALL I CONTINUE?
DIVORCE? HOW COULD PAPA DO THIS? HOW WILL I ENTER SOCIETY?
M'GREET, THERE'S NO CHANCE OF THAT NOW. THERE'S NO MORE MONEY FOR US. HE TOOK YOUR BROTHERS IN, I CAN'T ASK FOR MORE.
LET ME SLEEP, M'GREET. PLEASE.
"IS YOUR MOTHER STILL ALIVE?"
NO.
"WHEN DID SHE DIE?"
"I DON'T REMEMBER."

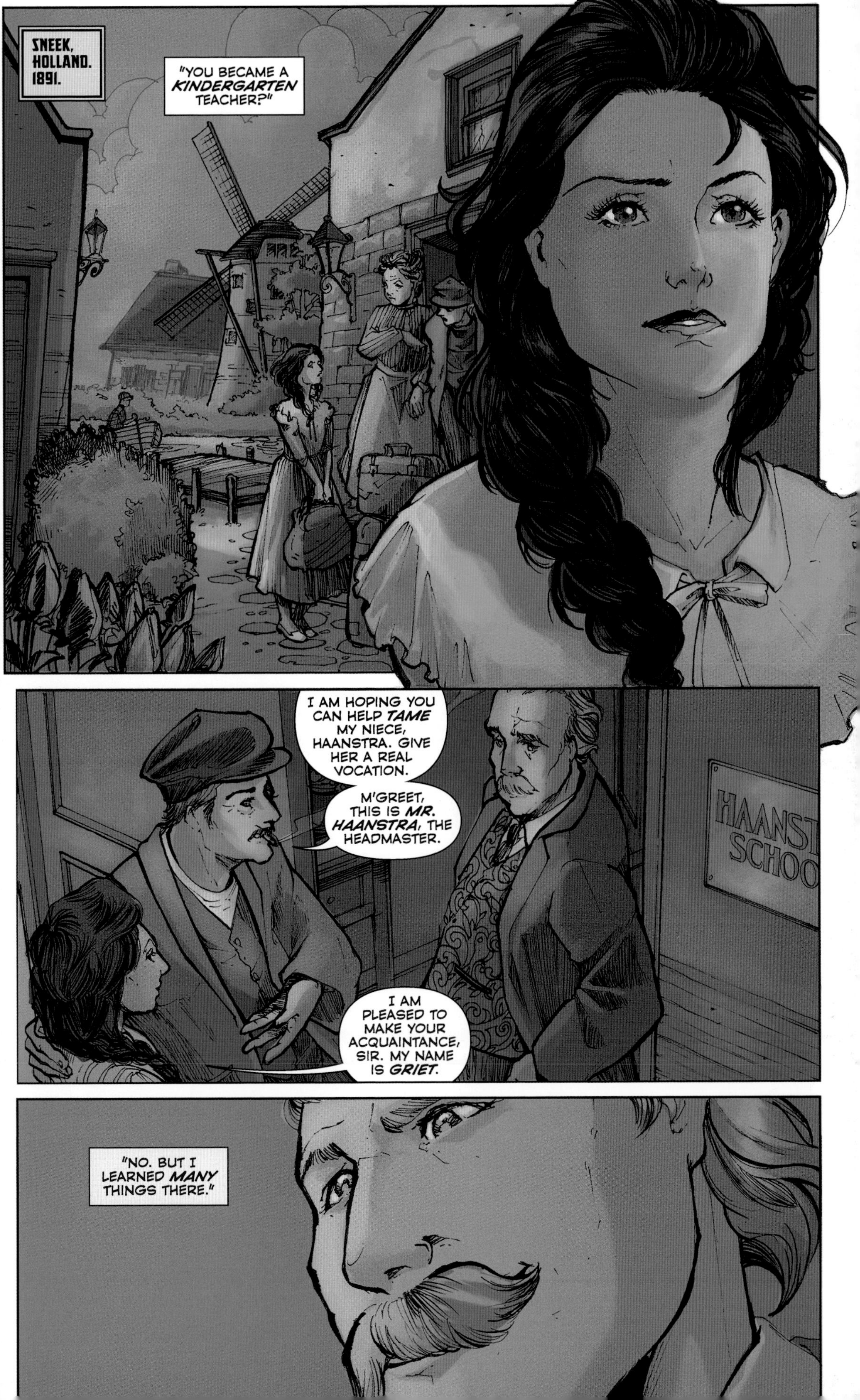

SNEEK, HOLLAND. 1891.
"YOU BECAME A KINDERGARTEN TEACHER?"
I AM HOPING YOU CAN HELP TAME MY NIECE, HAANSTRA. GIVE HER A REAL VOCATION.
M'GREET, THIS IS MR. HAANSTRA, THE HEADMASTER.
HAANST SCHOO
I AM PLEASED TO MAKE YOUR ACQUAINTANCE, SIR. MY NAME IS GRIET.
"NO. BUT I LEARNED MANY THINGS THERE."

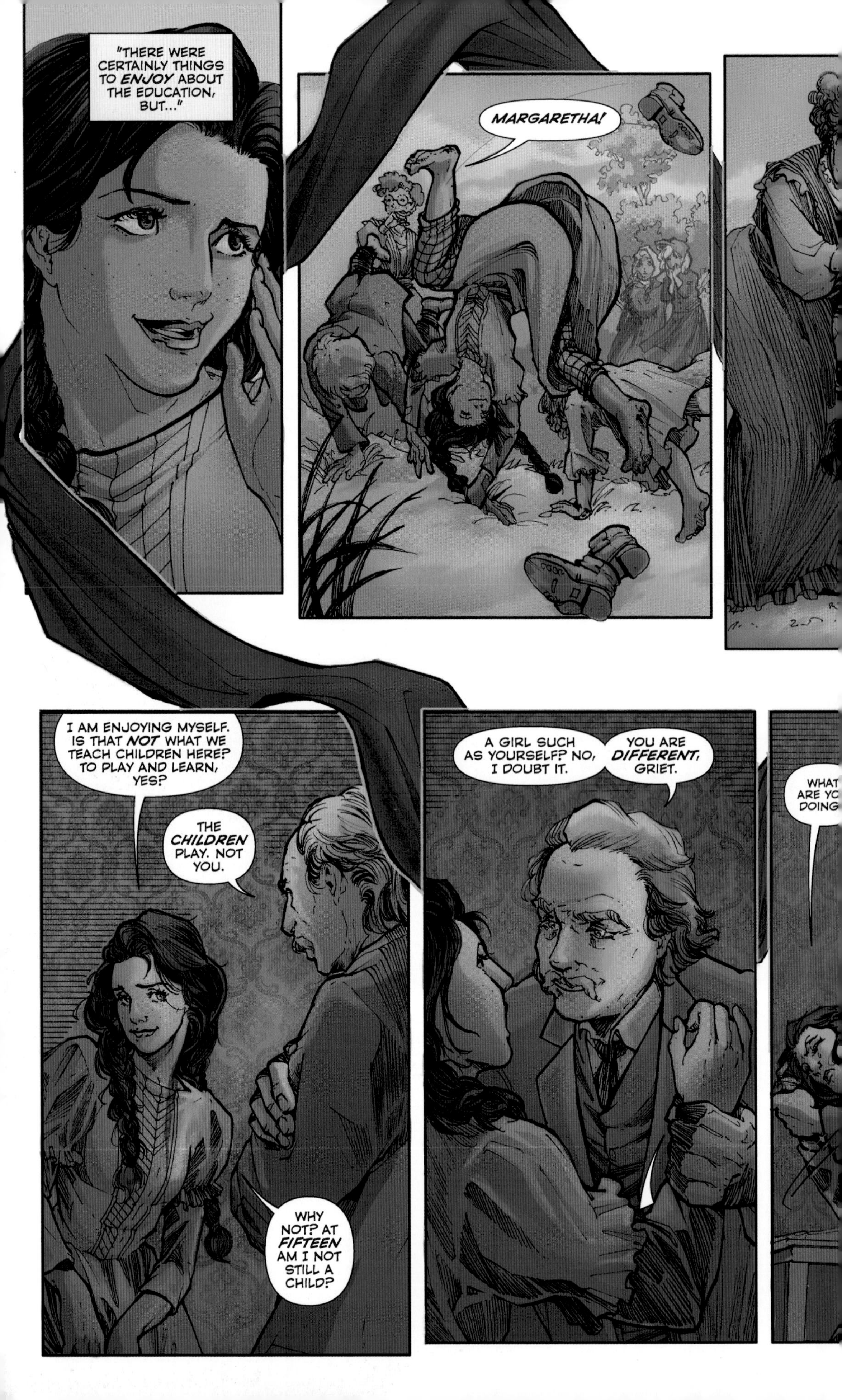
"THERE WERE CERTAINLY THINGS TO ENJOY ABOUT THE EDUCATION, BUT..."
MARGARETHA!
I AM ENJOYING MYSELF. IS THAT NOT WHAT WE TEACH CHILDREN HERE? TO PLAY AND LEARN, YES?
THE CHILDREN PLAY. NOT YOU.
WHY NOT? AT FIFTEEN AM I NOT STILL A CHILD?
A GIRL SUCH AS YOURSELF? NO, I DOUBT IT.
YOU ARE DIFFERENT, GRIET.

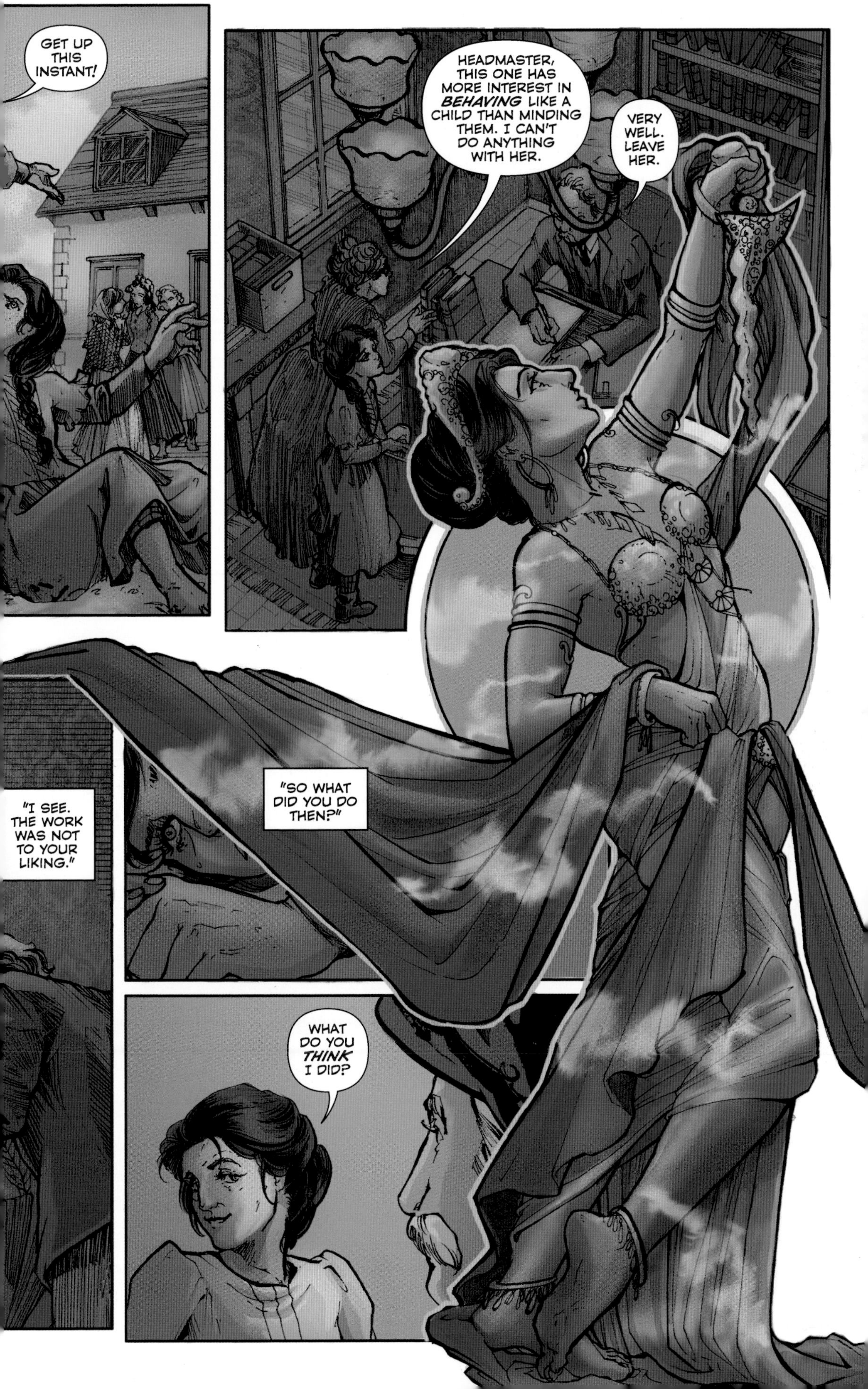
GET UP THIS INSTANT!
HEADMASTER, THIS ONE HAS MORE INTEREST IN BEHAVING LIKE A CHILD THAN MINDING THEM. I CAN'T DO ANYTHING WITH HER.
VERY WELL. LEAVE HER.
"I SEE. THE WORK WAS NOT TO YOUR LIKING."
"SO WHAT DID YOU DO THEN?"
WHAT DO YOU THINK I DID?

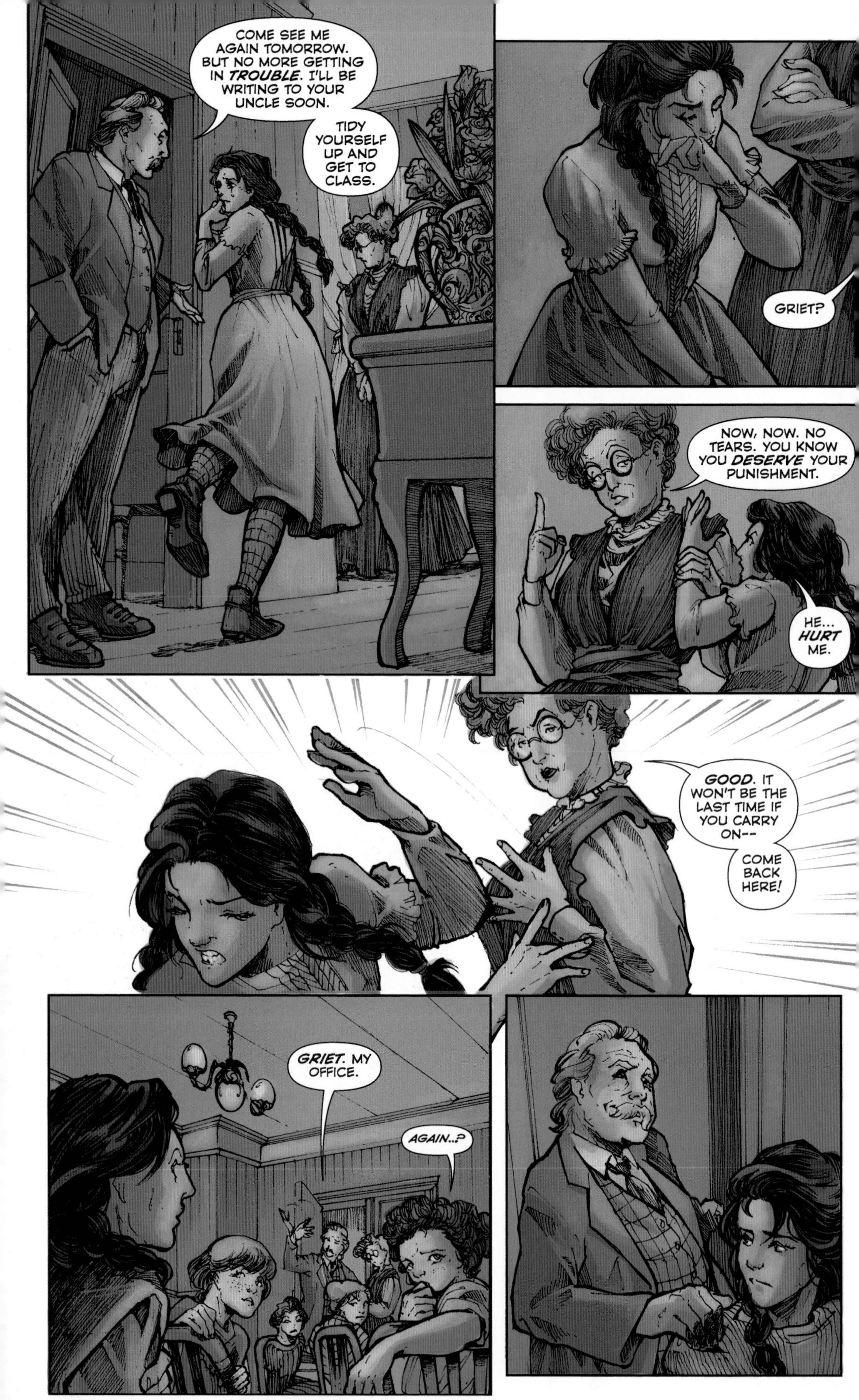
COME SEE ME AGAIN TOMORROW. BUT NO MORE GETTING IN TROUBLE. I'LL BE WRITING TO YOUR UNCLE SOON.
TIDY YOURSELF UP AND GET TO CLASS.
GRIET?
NOW, NOW. NO TEARS. YOU KNOW YOU DESERVE YOUR PUNISHMENT.
HE... HURT ME.
GOOD. IT WON'T BE THE LAST TIME IF YOU CARRY ON--
COME BACK HERE!
GRIET. MY OFFICE.
AGAIN...?

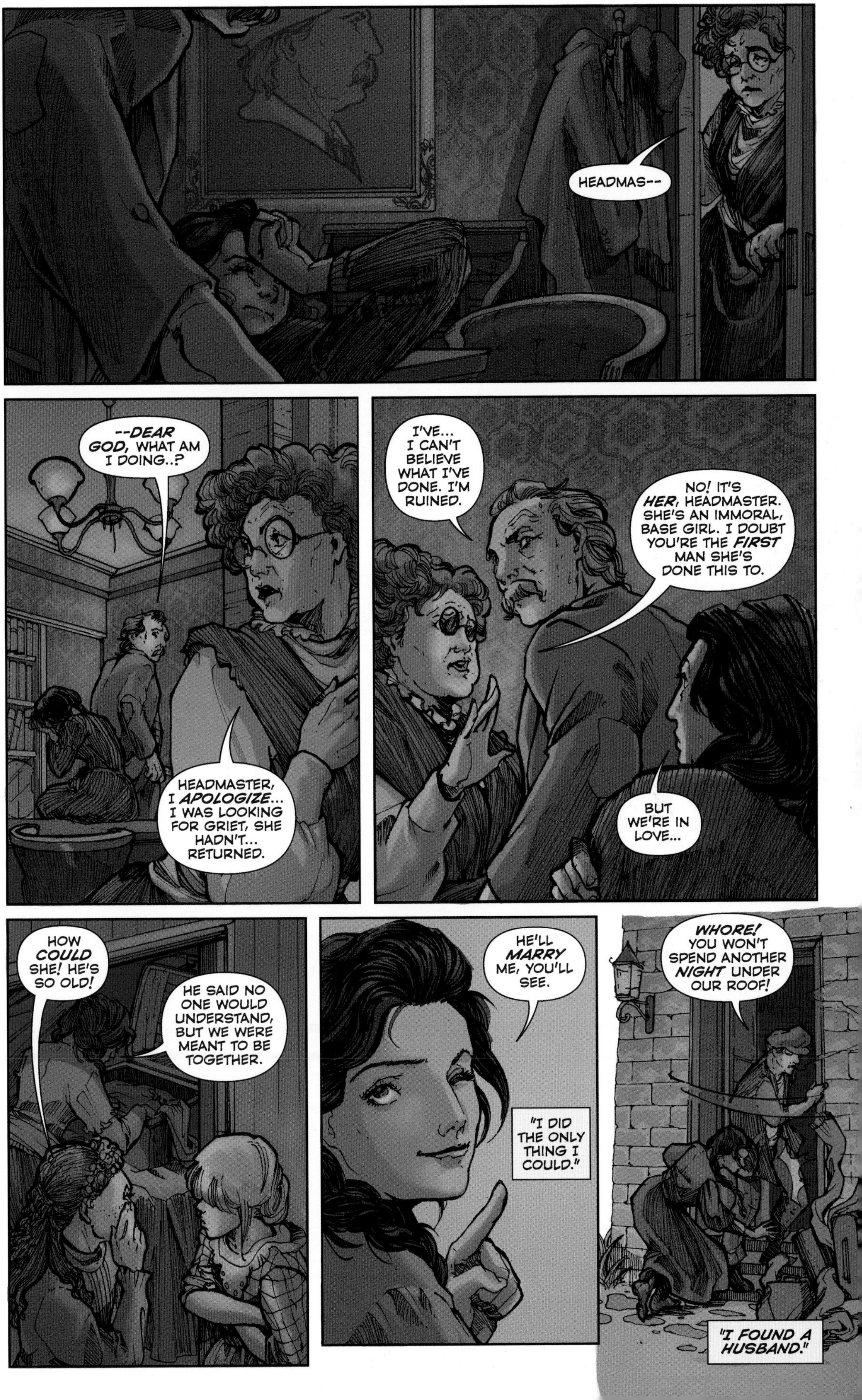
HEADMAS--
--DEAR GOD, WHAT AM I DOING..?
HEADMASTER, I APOLOGIZE... I WAS LOOKING FOR GRIET, SHE HADN'T... RETURNED.
I'VE... I CAN'T BELIEVE WHAT I'VE DONE. I'M RUINED.
NO! IT'S HER, HEADMASTER. SHE'S AN IMMORAL, BASE GIRL. I DOUBT YOU'RE THE FIRST MAN SHE'S DONE THIS TO.
BUT WE'RE IN LOVE...
HOW COULD SHE! HE'S SO OLD!
HE SAID NO ONE WOULD UNDERSTAND, BUT WE WERE MEANT TO BE TOGETHER.
HE'LL MARRY ME, YOU'LL SEE.
"I DID THE ONLY THING I COULD."
WHORE! YOU WON'T SPEND ANOTHER NIGHT UNDER OUR ROOF!
"I FOUND A HUSBAND."

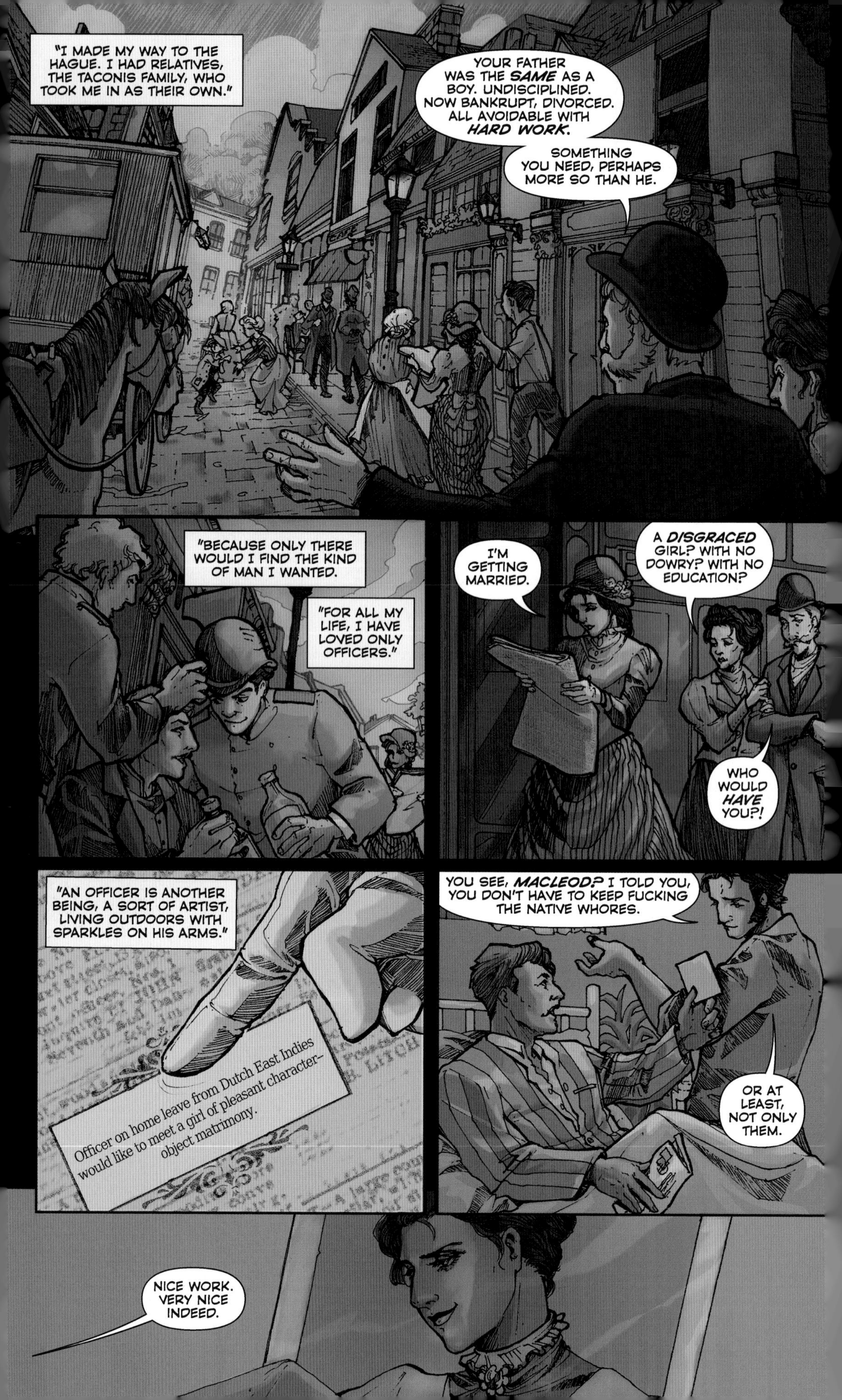
"I MADE MY WAY TO THE HAGUE. I HAD RELATIVES, THE TACONIS FAMILY, WHO TOOK ME IN AS THEIR OWN."
YOUR FATHER WAS THE SAME AS A BOY. UNDISCIPLINED. NOW BANKRUPT, DIVORCED. ALL AVOIDABLE WITH HARD WORK.
SOMETHING YOU NEED, PERHAPS MORE SO THAN HE.
"BECAUSE ONLY THERE WOULD I FIND THE KIND OF MAN I WANTED.
"FOR ALL MY LIFE, I HAVE LOVED ONLY OFFICERS."
I'M GETTING MARRIED.
A DISGRACED GIRL? WITH NO DOWRY? WITH NO EDUCATION?
WHO WOULD HAVE YOU?!
"AN OFFICER IS ANOTHER BEING, A SORT OF ARTIST, LIVING OUTDOORS WITH SPARKLES ON HIS ARMS."
Officer on home leave from Dutch East Indies would like to meet a girl of pleasant character-object matrimony.
YOU SEE, MACLEOD? I TOLD YOU, YOU DON'T HAVE TO KEEP FUCKING THE NATIVE WHORES.
OR AT LEAST, NOT ONLY THEM.
NICE WORK. VERY NICE INDEED.

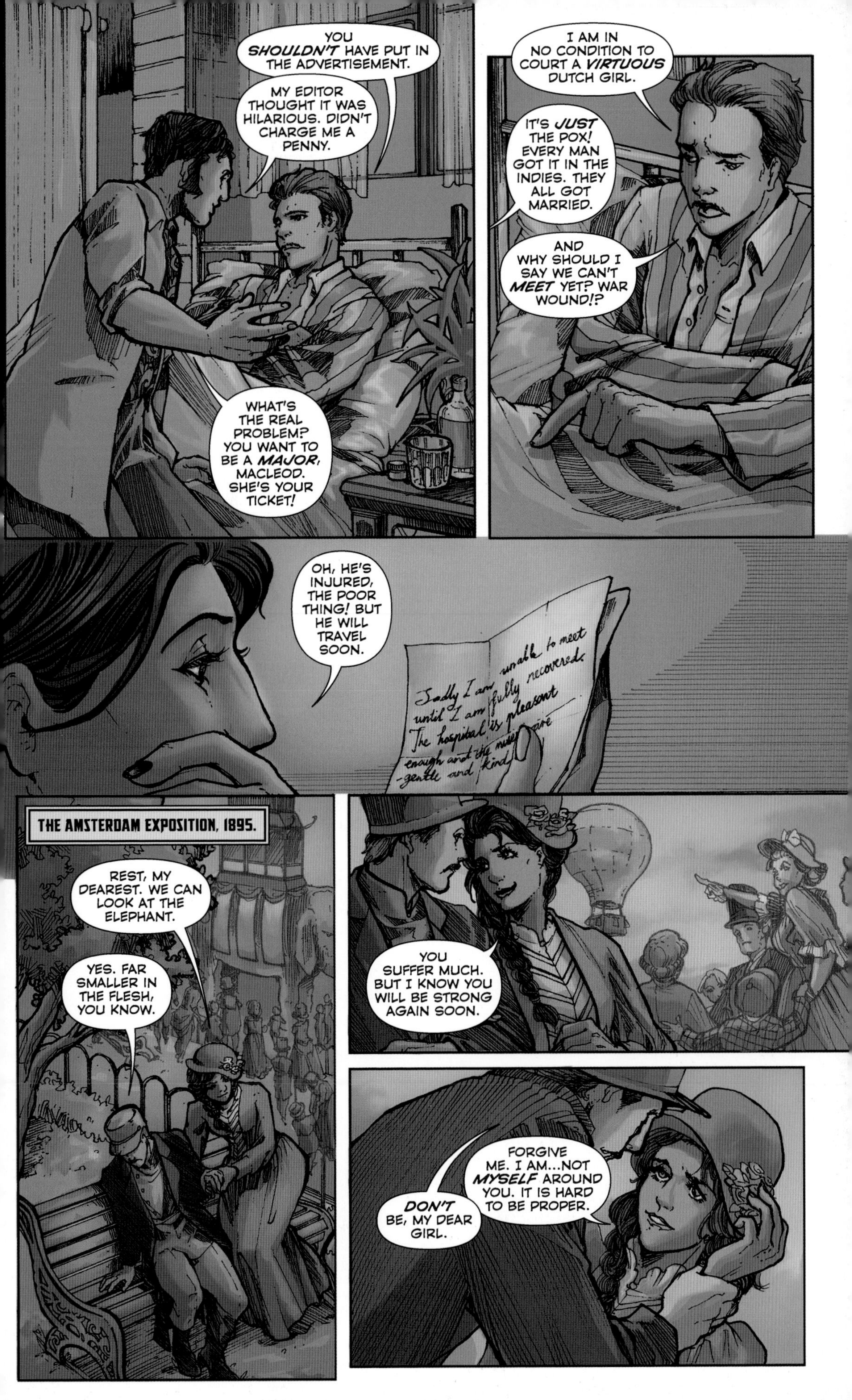
YOU SHOULDN'T HAVE PUT IN THE ADVERTISEMENT.
MY EDITOR THOUGHT IT WAS HILARIOUS. DIDN'T CHARGE ME A PENNY.
WHAT'S THE REAL PROBLEM? YOU WANT TO BE A MAJOR, MACLEOD. SHE'S YOUR TICKET!
I AM IN NO CONDITION TO COURT A VIRTUOUS DUTCH GIRL.
IT'S JUST THE POX! EVERY MAN GOT IT IN THE INDIES. THEY ALL GOT MARRIED.
AND WHY SHOULD I SAY WE CAN'T MEET YET? WAR WOUND!?
OH, HE'S INJURED, THE POOR THING! BUT HE WILL TRAVEL SOON.
Sadly I am unable to meet until I am fully recovered. The hospital is pleasant enough and the nurses are gentle and kind
THE AMSTERDAM EXPOSITION, 1895.
REST, MY DEAREST. WE CAN LOOK AT THE ELEPHANT.
YES. FAR SMALLER IN THE FLESH, YOU KNOW.
YOU SUFFER MUCH. BUT I KNOW YOU WILL BE STRONG AGAIN SOON.
FORGIVE ME. I AM...NOT MYSELF AROUND YOU. IT IS HARD TO BE PROPER.
DON'T BE, MY DEAR GIRL.

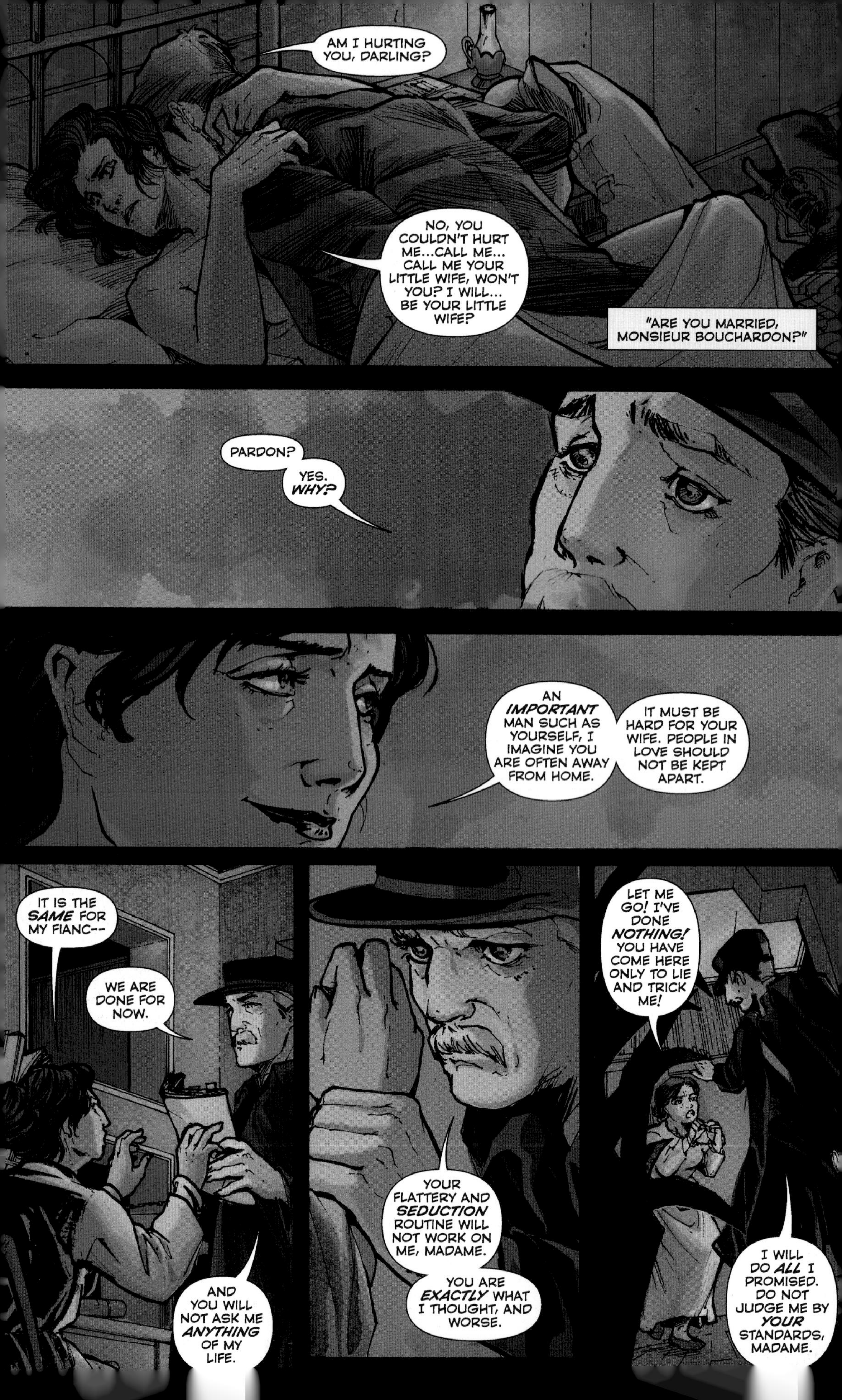
AM I HURTING YOU, DARLING?
NO, YOU COULDN'T HURT ME...CALL ME... CALL ME YOUR LITTLE WIFE, WON'T YOU? I WILL... BE YOUR LITTLE WIFE?
"ARE YOU MARRIED, MONSIEUR BOUCHARDON?"
PARDON?
YES. WHY?
AN IMPORTANT MAN SUCH AS YOURSELF, I IMAGINE YOU ARE OFTEN AWAY FROM HOME.
IT MUST BE HARD FOR YOUR WIFE. PEOPLE IN LOVE SHOULD NOT BE KEPT APART.
IT IS THE SAME FOR MY FIANC--
WE ARE DONE FOR NOW.
AND YOU WILL NOT ASK ME ANYTHING OF MY LIFE.
YOUR FLATTERY AND SEDUCTION ROUTINE WILL NOT WORK ON ME, MADAME.
YOU ARE EXACTLY WHAT I THOUGHT, AND WORSE.
LET ME GO! I'VE DONE NOTHING! YOU HAVE COME HERE ONLY TO LIE AND TRICK ME!
I WILL DO ALL I PROMISED. DO NOT JUDGE ME BY YOUR STANDARDS, MADAME.

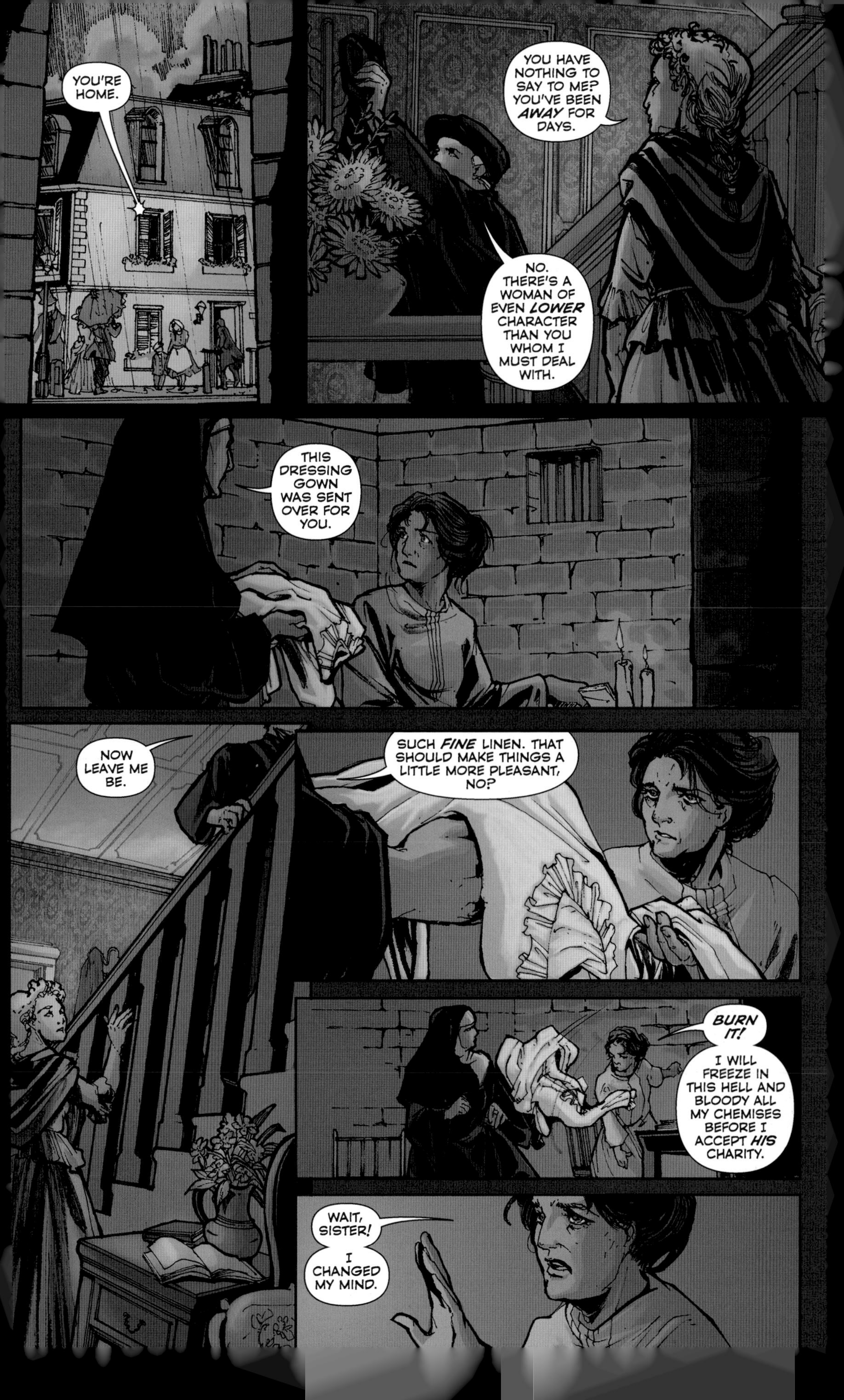
YOU'RE HOME.
YOU HAVE NOTHING TO SAY TO ME? YOU'VE BEEN AWAY FOR DAYS.
NO. THERE'S A WOMAN OF EVEN LOWER CHARACTER THAN YOU WHOM I MUST DEAL WITH.
THIS DRESSING GOWN WAS SENT OVER FOR YOU.
NOW LEAVE ME BE.
SUCH FINE LINEN. THAT SHOULD MAKE THINGS A LITTLE MORE PLEASANT, NO?
BURN IT!
I WILL FREEZE IN THIS HELL AND BLOODY ALL MY CHEMISES BEFORE I ACCEPT HIS CHARITY.
WAIT, SISTER!
I CHANGED MY MIND.

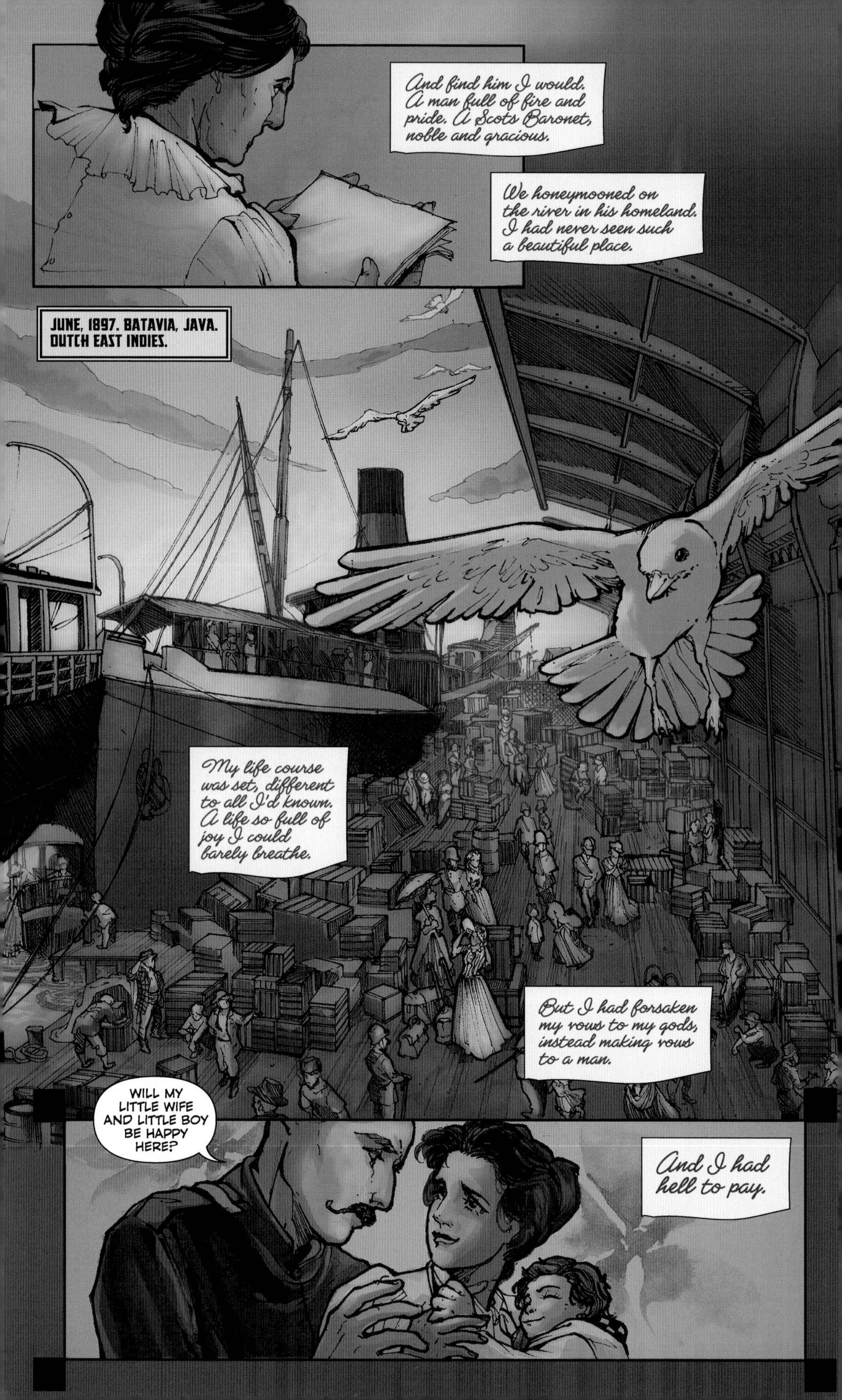

And find him I would. A man full of fire and pride. A Scots Baronet, noble and gracious.
We honeymooned on the river in his homeland. I had never seen such a beautiful place.
JUNE, 1897. BATAVIA, JAVA. DUTCH EAST INDIES.
My life course was set, different to all I'd known. A life so full of joy I could barely breathe.
But I had forsaken my vows to my gods, instead making vows to a man.
WILL MY LITTLE WIFE AND LITTLE BOY BE HAPPY HERE?
And I had hell to pay.

CHAPTER THREE
BARE·HEART

"I am athirst for thy beauty;
I am hungry for thy body;
and neither wine nor fruits can appease my desire.
Neither the floods nor the great waters
can quench my passion.
I was a princess, and thou didst scorn me.
I was a virgin, and thou didst take my virginity from me.
I was chaste, and thou didst fill my veins with fire..."

*SALOMÉ:
A TRAGEDY IN ONE ACT*
~ OSCAR WILDE ~

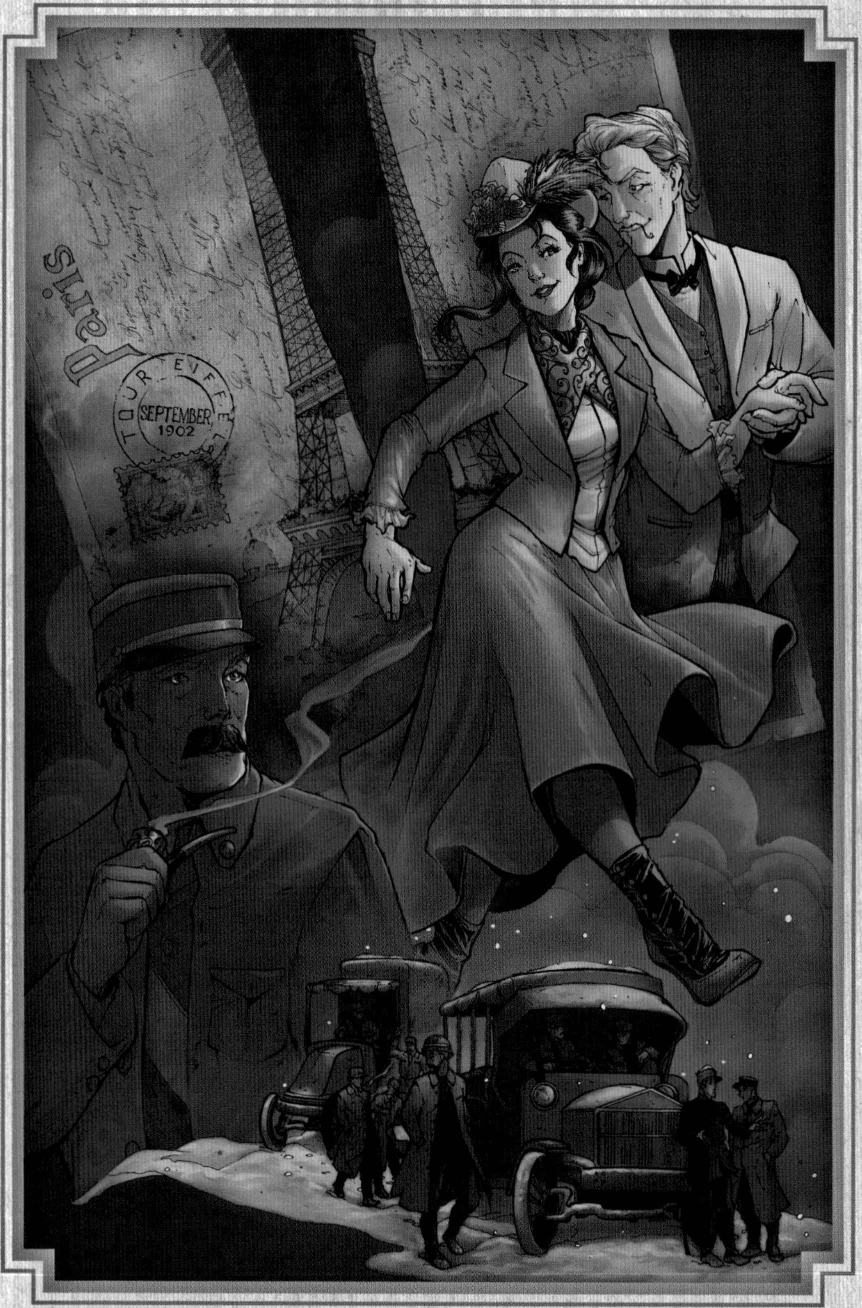
Paris
SEPTEMBER, 1902

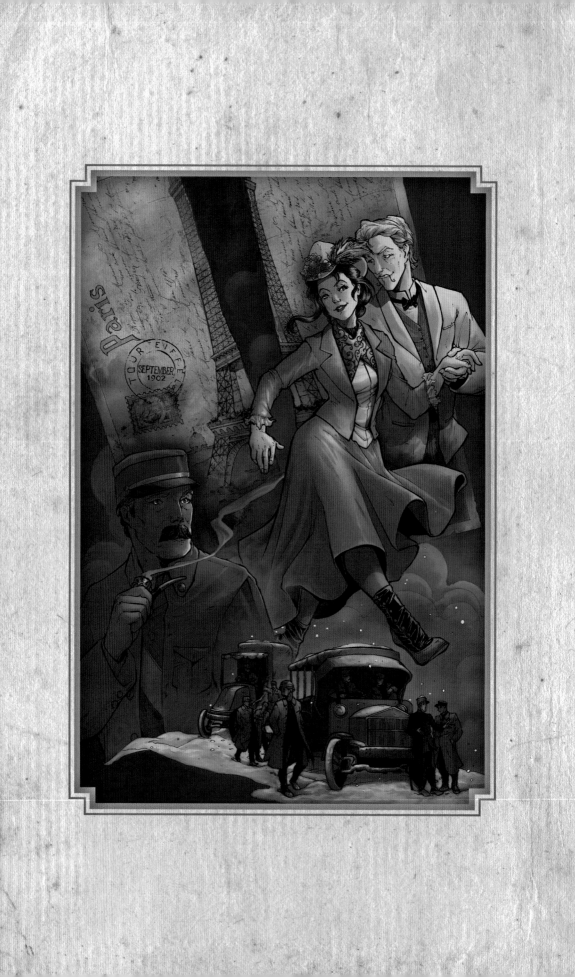

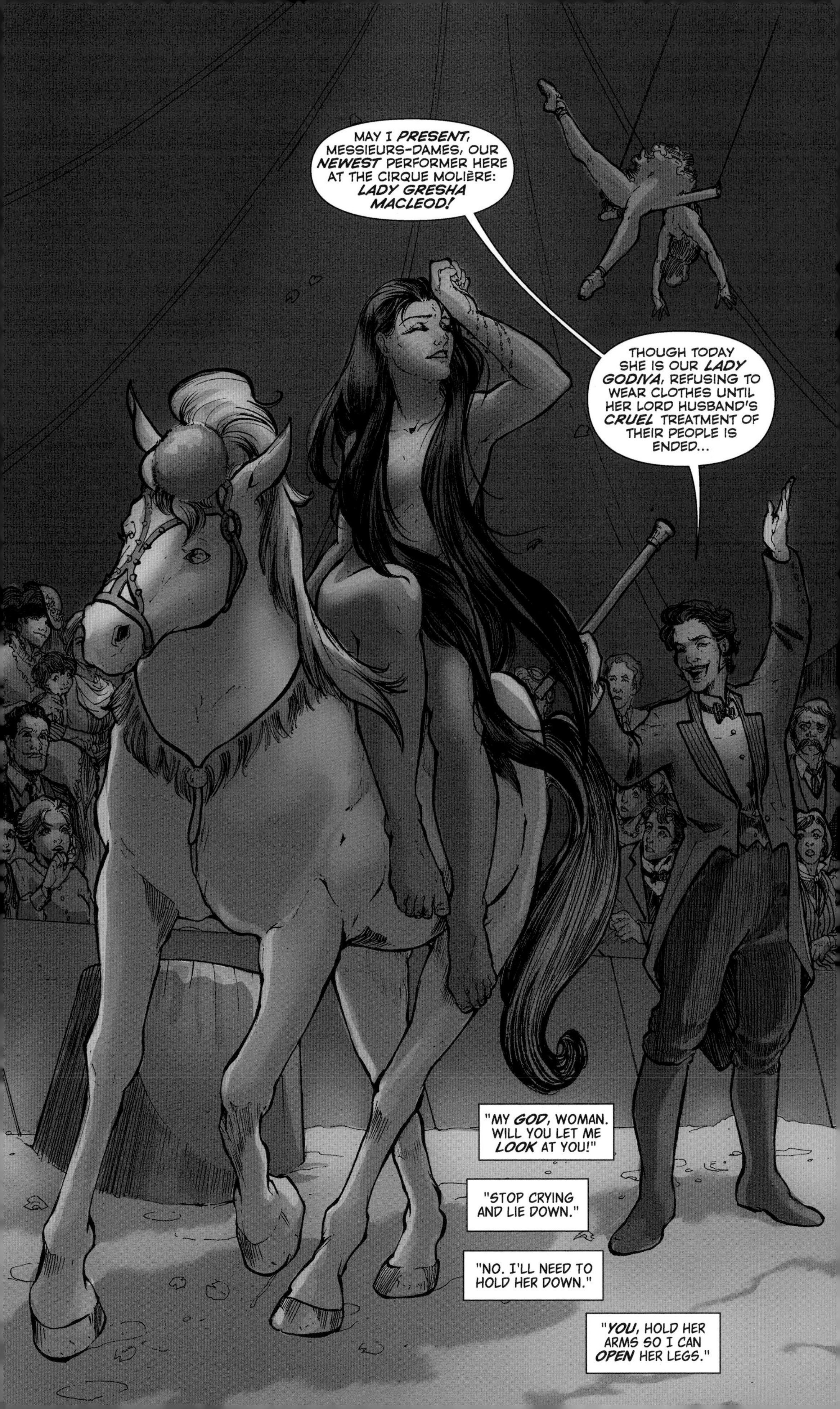

MAY I PRESENT, MESSIEURS-DAMES, OUR NEWEST PERFORMER HERE AT THE CIRQUE MOLIÈRE: LADY GRESHA MACLEOD!
THOUGH TODAY SHE IS OUR LADY GODIVA, REFUSING TO WEAR CLOTHES UNTIL HER LORD HUSBAND'S CRUEL TREATMENT OF THEIR PEOPLE IS ENDED...
"MY GOD, WOMAN. WILL YOU LET ME LOOK AT YOU!"
"STOP CRYING AND LIE DOWN."
"NO. I'LL NEED TO HOLD HER DOWN."
"YOU, HOLD HER ARMS SO I CAN OPEN HER LEGS."

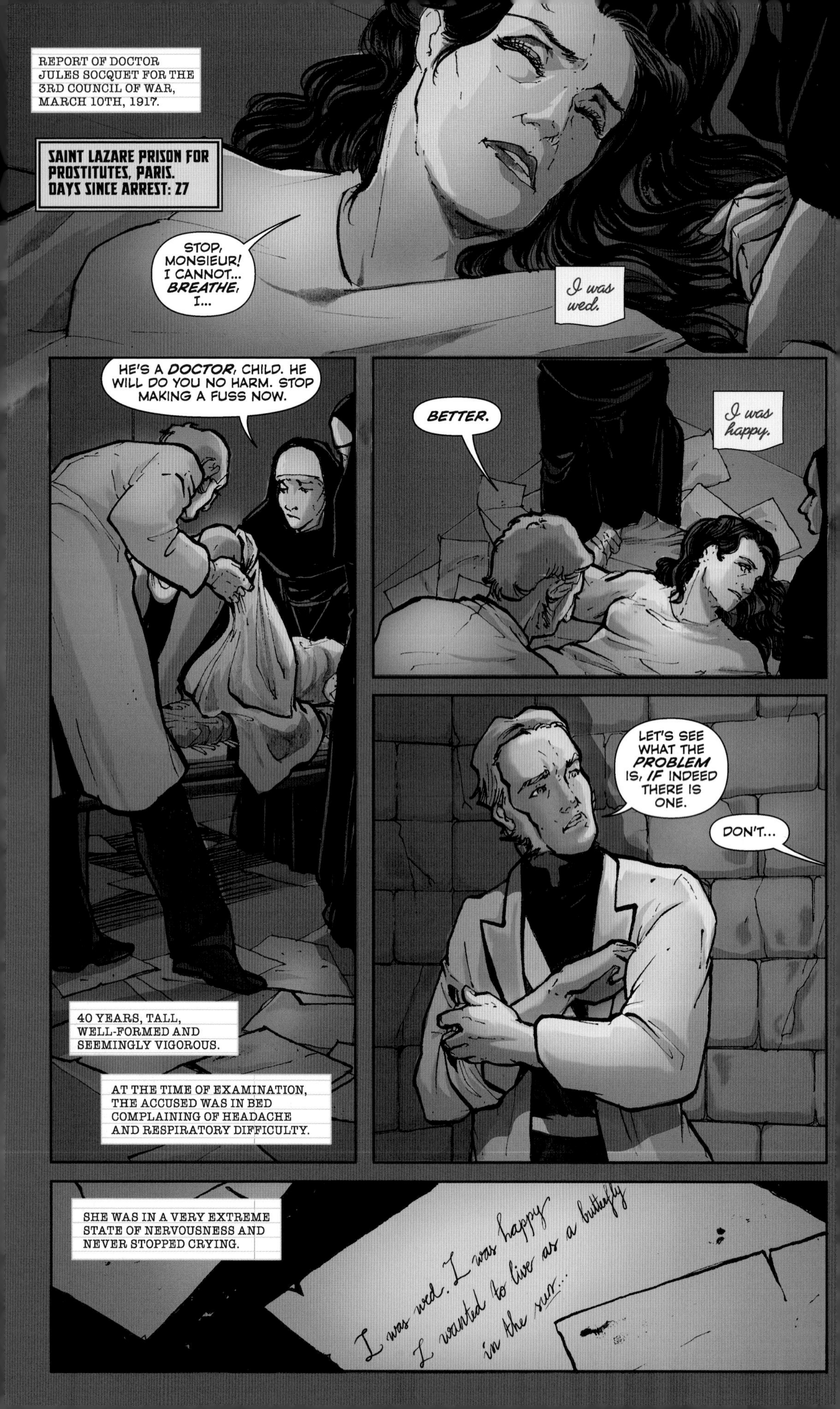
REPORT OF DOCTOR JULES SOCQUET FOR THE 3RD COUNCIL OF WAR, MARCH 10TH, 1917.
SAINT LAZARE PRISON FOR PROSTITUTES, PARIS. DAYS SINCE ARREST: 27
STOP, MONSIEUR! I CANNOT... BREATHE, I...
I was wed.
HE'S A DOCTOR, CHILD. HE WILL DO YOU NO HARM. STOP MAKING A FUSS NOW.
40 YEARS, TALL, WELL-FORMED AND SEEMINGLY VIGOROUS.
AT THE TIME OF EXAMINATION, THE ACCUSED WAS IN BED COMPLAINING OF HEADACHE AND RESPIRATORY DIFFICULTY.
BETTER.
I was happy.
LET'S SEE WHAT THE PROBLEM IS, IF INDEED THERE IS ONE.
DON'T...
SHE WAS IN A VERY EXTREME STATE OF NERVOUSNESS AND NEVER STOPPED CRYING.
I was wed. I was happy
I wanted to live as a butterfly
in the sun...

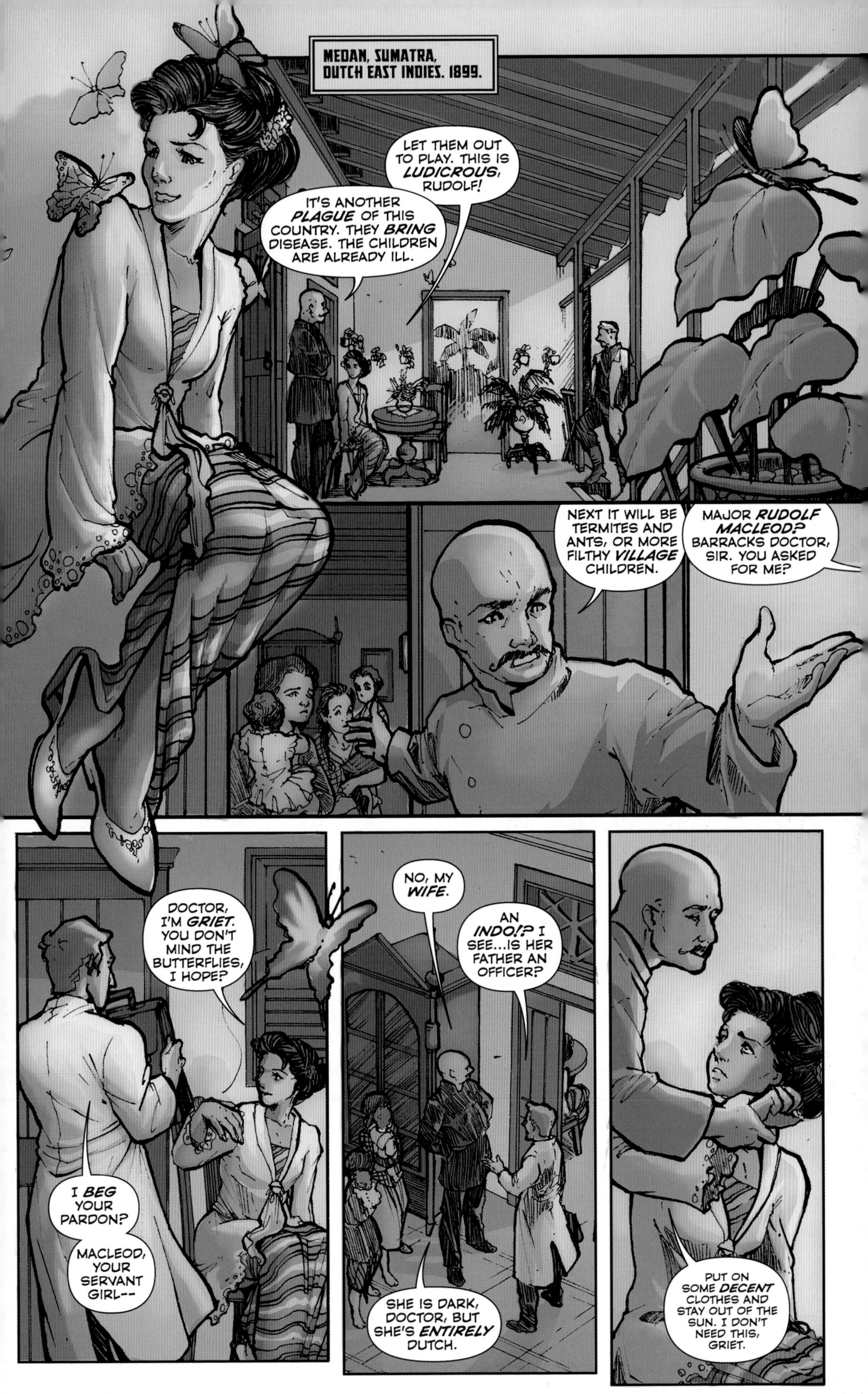
MEDAN, SUMATRA, DUTCH EAST INDIES. 1899.
LET THEM OUT TO PLAY. THIS IS LUDICROUS, RUDOLF!
IT'S ANOTHER PLAGUE OF THIS COUNTRY. THEY BRING DISEASE. THE CHILDREN ARE ALREADY ILL.
NEXT IT WILL BE TERMITES AND ANTS, OR MORE FILTHY VILLAGE CHILDREN.
MAJOR RUDOLF MACLEOD? BARRACKS DOCTOR, SIR. YOU ASKED FOR ME?
DOCTOR, I'M GRIET. YOU DON'T MIND THE BUTTERFLIES, I HOPE?
I BEG YOUR PARDON?
MACLEOD, YOUR SERVANT GIRL--
NO, MY WIFE.
AN INDO!? I SEE...IS HER FATHER AN OFFICER?
SHE IS DARK, DOCTOR, BUT SHE'S ENTIRELY DUTCH.
PUT ON SOME DECENT CLOTHES AND STAY OUT OF THE SUN. I DON'T NEED THIS, GRIET.

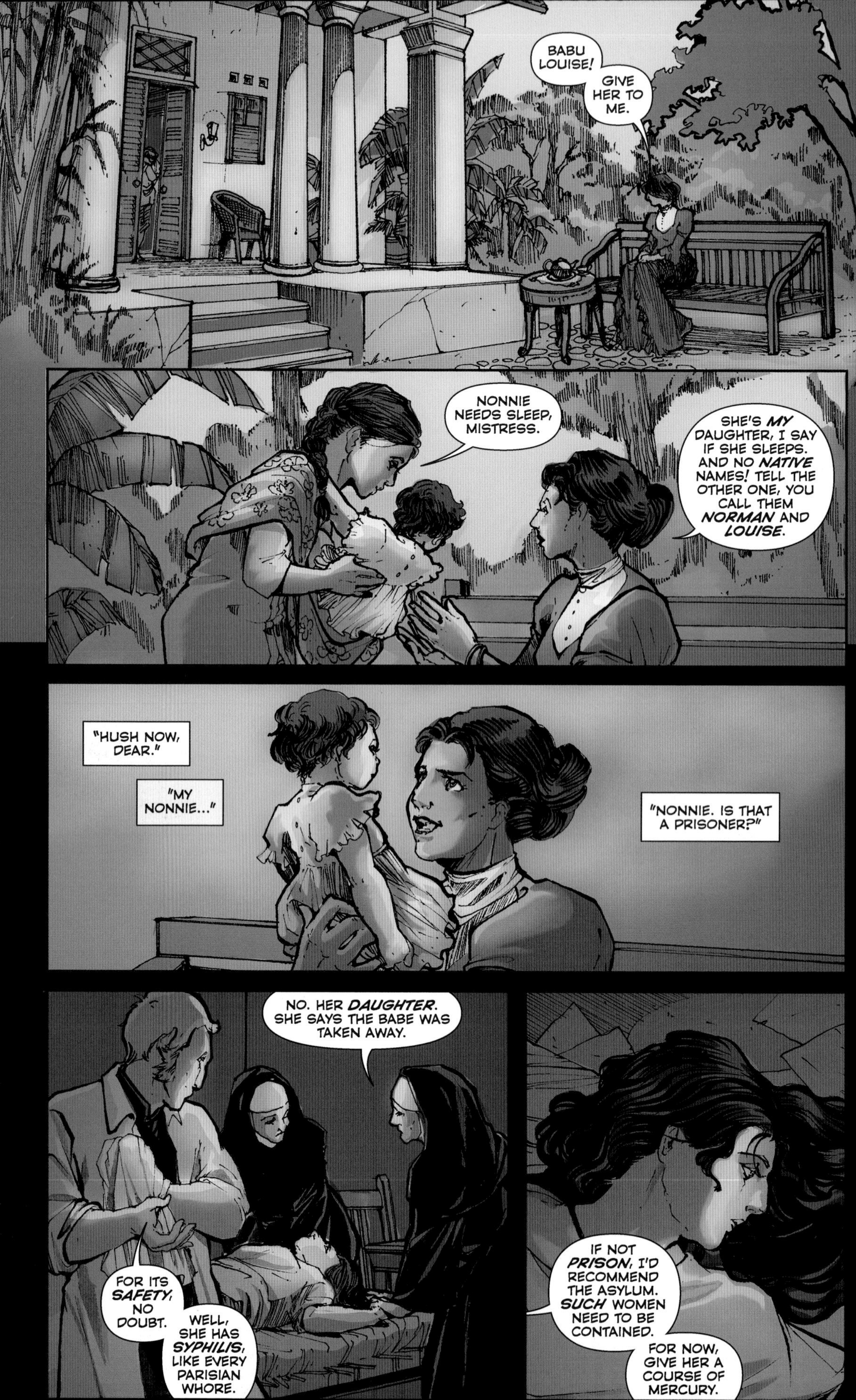
BABU LOUISE!
GIVE HER TO ME.
NONNIE NEEDS SLEEP, MISTRESS.
SHE'S MY DAUGHTER, I SAY IF SHE SLEEPS. AND NO NATIVE NAMES! TELL THE OTHER ONE, YOU CALL THEM NORMAN AND LOUISE.
"HUSH NOW, DEAR."
"MY NONNIE..."
"NONNIE. IS THAT A PRISONER?"
NO. HER DAUGHTER. SHE SAYS THE BABE WAS TAKEN AWAY.
FOR ITS SAFETY, NO DOUBT.
WELL, SHE HAS SYPHILIS, LIKE EVERY PARISIAN WHORE.
IF NOT PRISON, I'D RECOMMEND THE ASYLUM. SUCH WOMEN NEED TO BE CONTAINED.
FOR NOW, GIVE HER A COURSE OF MERCURY.

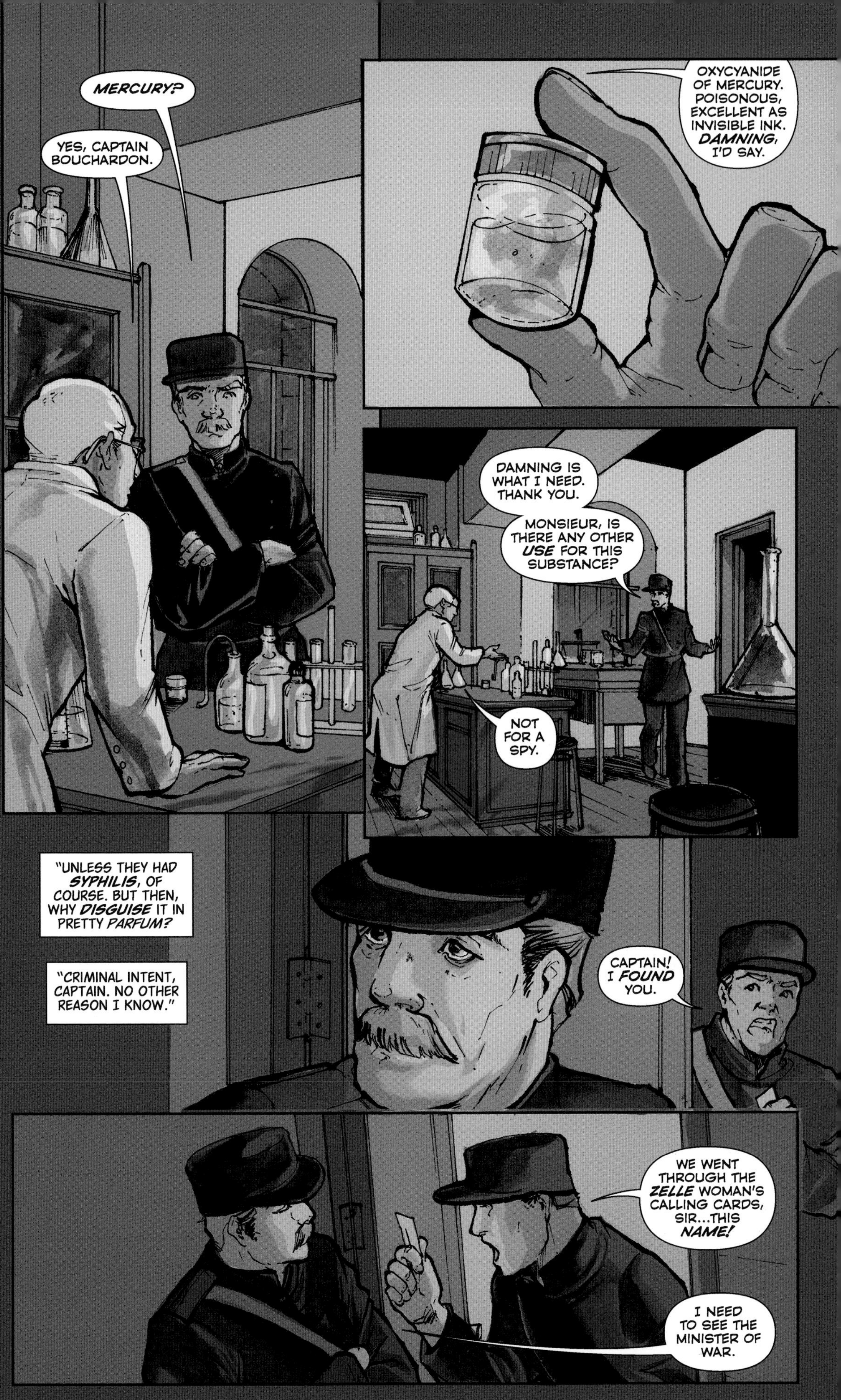
MERCURY?
YES, CAPTAIN BOUCHARDON.
OXYCYANIDE OF MERCURY. POISONOUS, EXCELLENT AS INVISIBLE INK. DAMNING, I'D SAY.
DAMNING IS WHAT I NEED. THANK YOU.
MONSIEUR, IS THERE ANY OTHER USE FOR THIS SUBSTANCE?
NOT FOR A SPY.
"UNLESS THEY HAD SYPHILIS, OF COURSE. BUT THEN, WHY DISGUISE IT IN PRETTY PARFUM?
"CRIMINAL INTENT, CAPTAIN. NO OTHER REASON I KNOW."
CAPTAIN! I FOUND YOU.
WE WENT THROUGH THE ZELLE WOMAN'S CALLING CARDS, SIR...THIS NAME!
I NEED TO SEE THE MINISTER OF WAR.

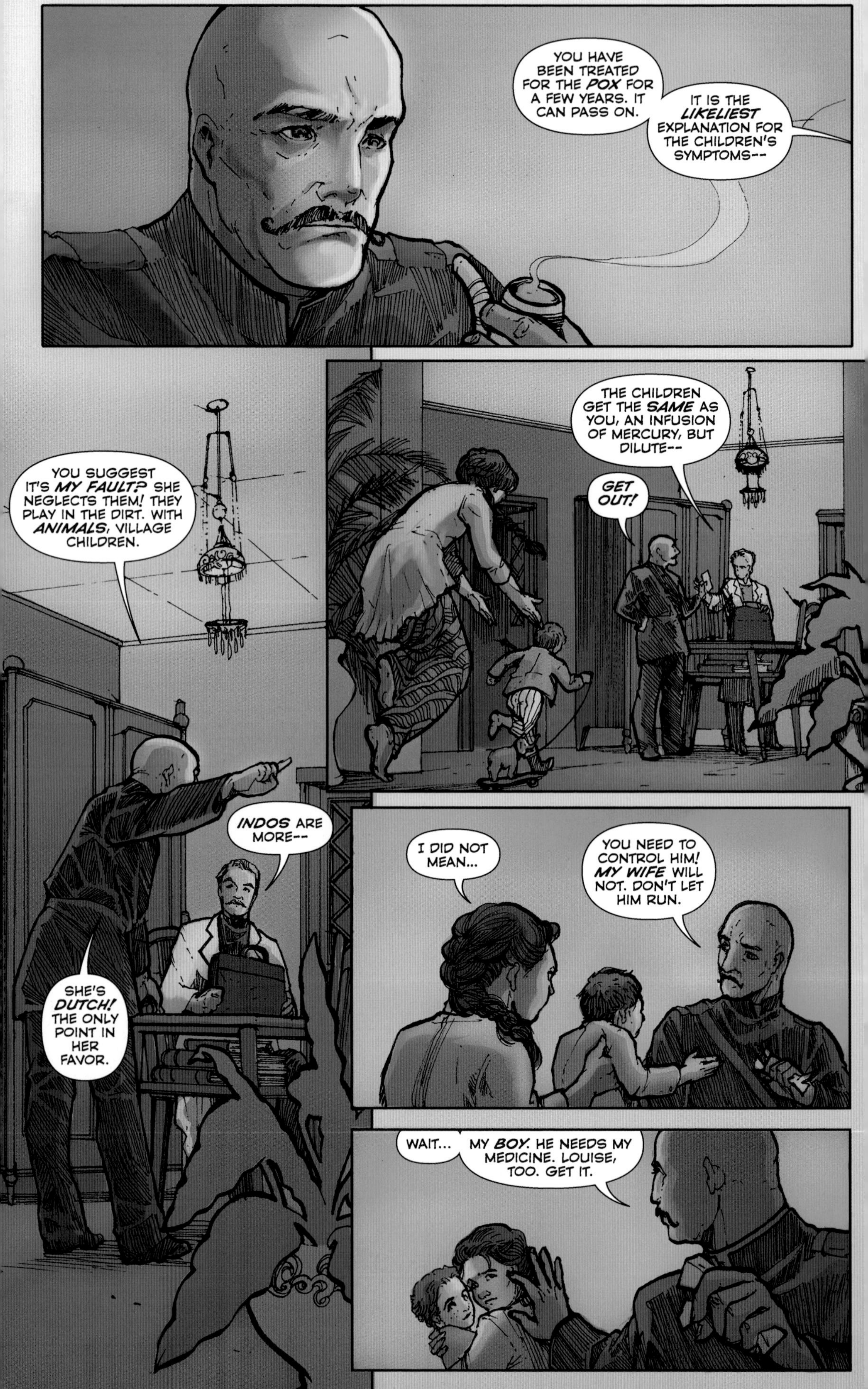
YOU HAVE BEEN TREATED FOR THE POX FOR A FEW YEARS. IT CAN PASS ON.
IT IS THE LIKELIEST EXPLANATION FOR THE CHILDREN'S SYMPTOMS--
YOU SUGGEST IT'S MY FAULT? SHE NEGLECTS THEM! THEY PLAY IN THE DIRT. WITH ANIMALS, VILLAGE CHILDREN.
THE CHILDREN GET THE SAME AS YOU, AN INFUSION OF MERCURY, BUT DILUTE--
GET OUT!
INDOS ARE MORE--
SHE'S DUTCH! THE ONLY POINT IN HER FAVOR.
I DID NOT MEAN...
YOU NEED TO CONTROL HIM! MY WIFE WILL NOT. DON'T LET HIM RUN.
WAIT...
MY BOY. HE NEEDS MY MEDICINE. LOUISE, TOO. GET IT.

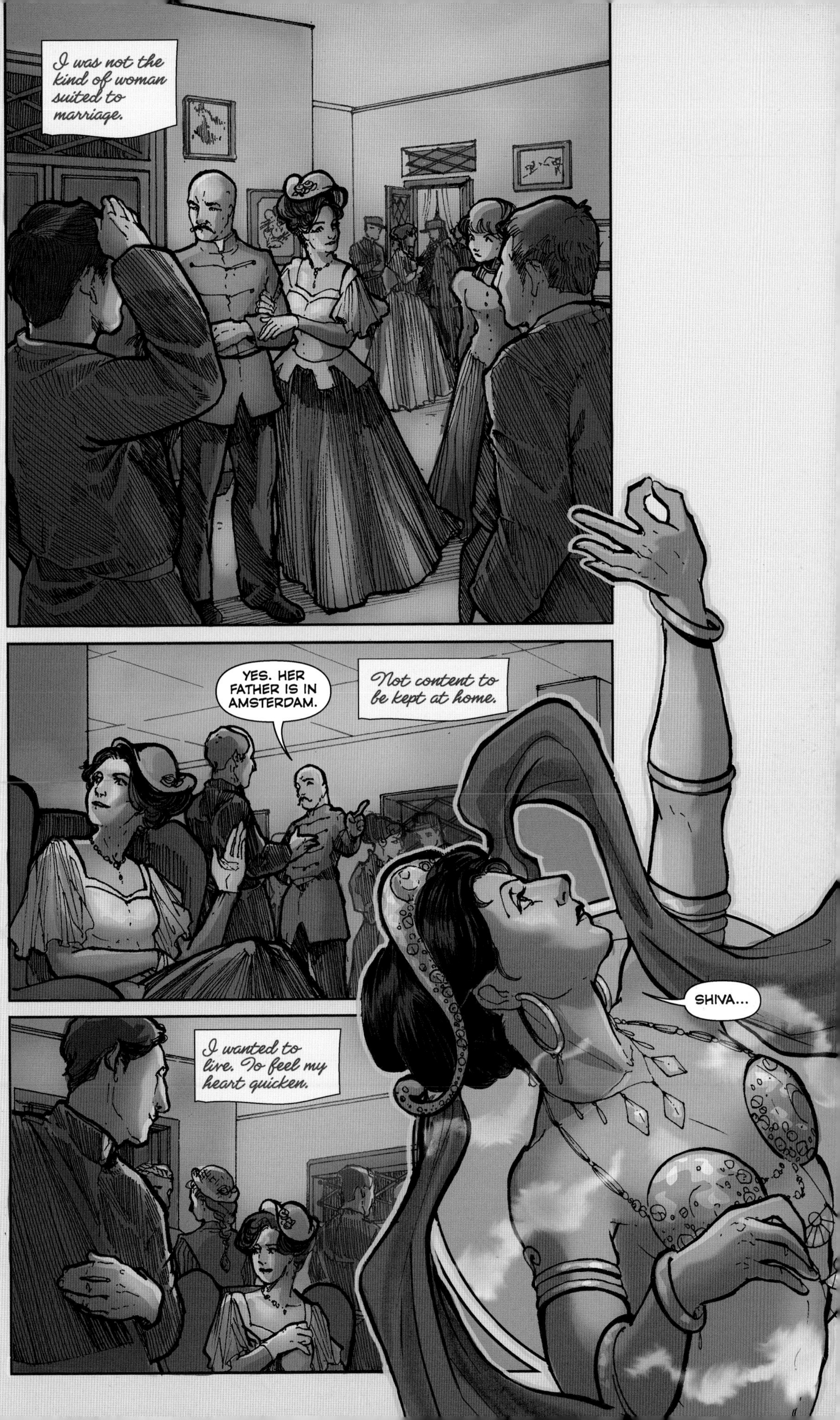
I was not the kind of woman suited to marriage.
YES. HER FATHER IS IN AMSTERDAM.
Not content to be kept at home.
SHIVA...
I wanted to live. To feel my heart quicken.

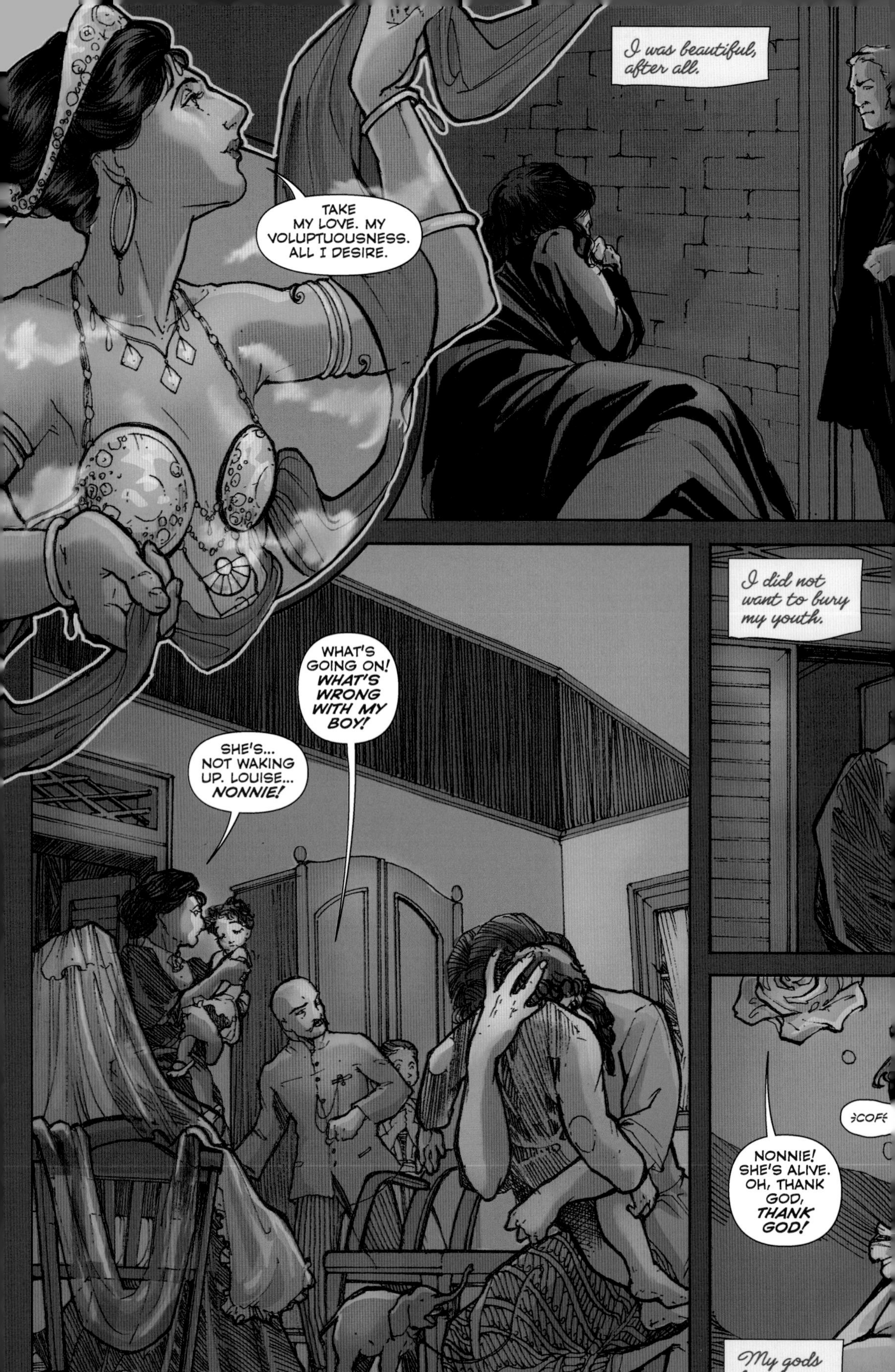
I was beautiful, after all.
TAKE MY LOVE. MY VOLUPTUOUSNESS. ALL I DESIRE.
I did not want to bury my youth.
WHAT'S GOING ON! WHAT'S WRONG WITH MY BOY!
SHE'S... NOT WAKING UP. LOUISE... NONNIE!
COF
NONNIE! SHE'S ALIVE. OH, THANK GOD, THANK GOD!
My gods heard me...

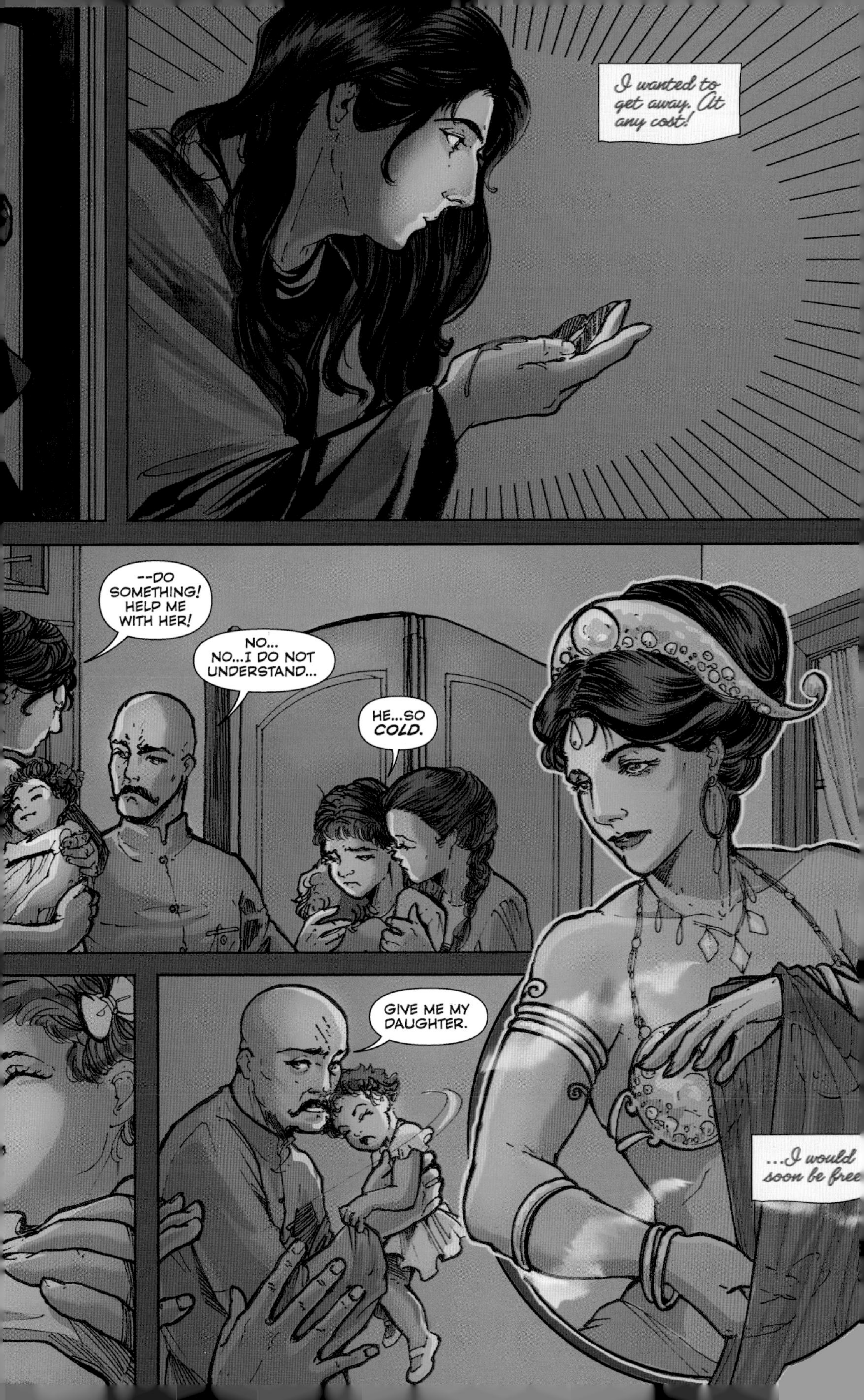

I wanted to get away. At any cost!
--DO SOMETHING! HELP ME WITH HER!
NO... NO...I DO NOT UNDERSTAND...
HE...SO COLD.
GIVE ME MY DAUGHTER.
...I would soon be free

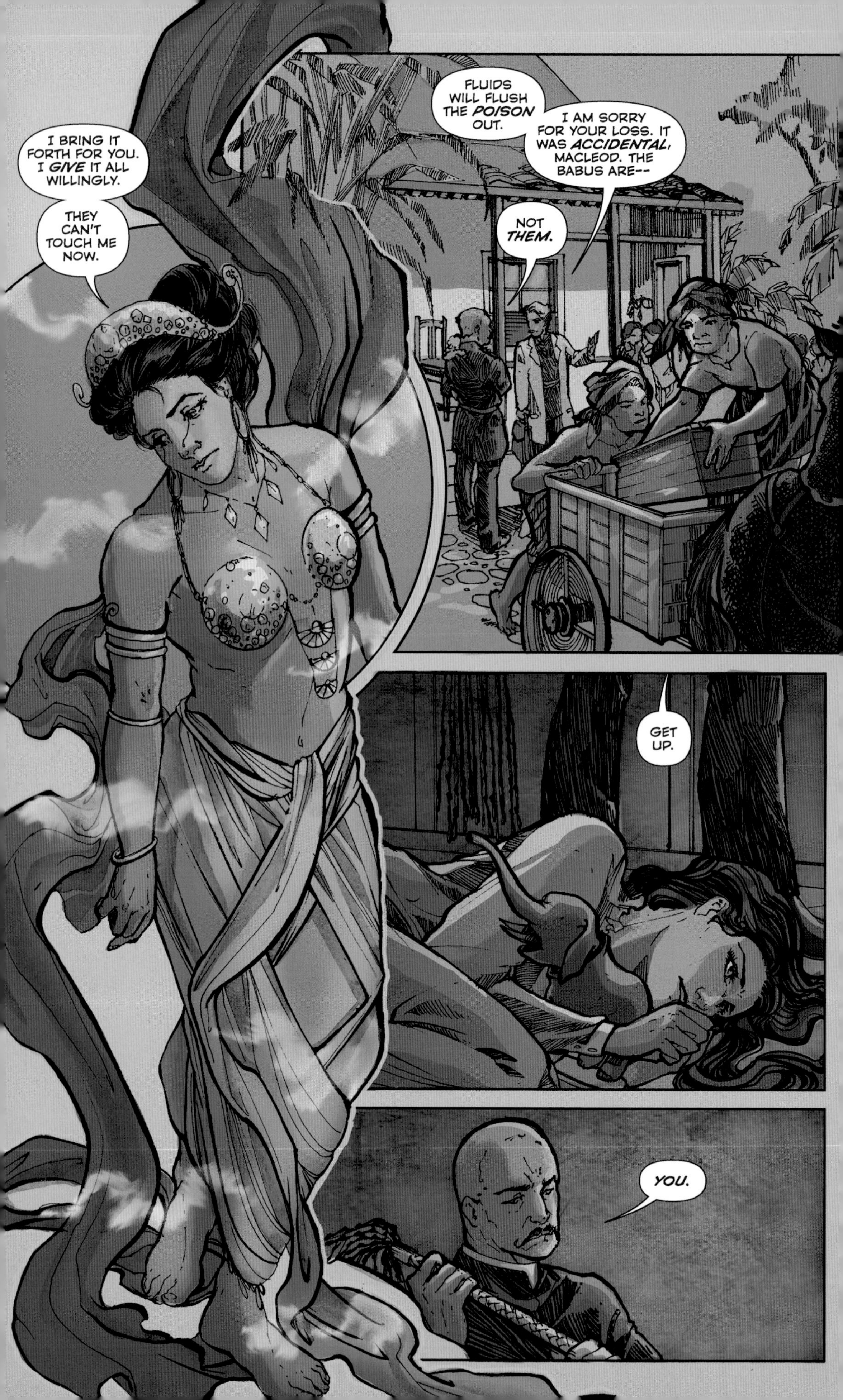
I BRING IT FORTH FOR YOU. I *GIVE* IT ALL WILLINGLY.
THEY CAN'T TOUCH ME NOW.
FLUIDS WILL FLUSH THE *POISON* OUT.
I AM SORRY FOR YOUR LOSS. IT WAS *ACCIDENTAL*, MACLEOD. THE BABUS ARE--
NOT *THEM*.
GET UP.
YOU.

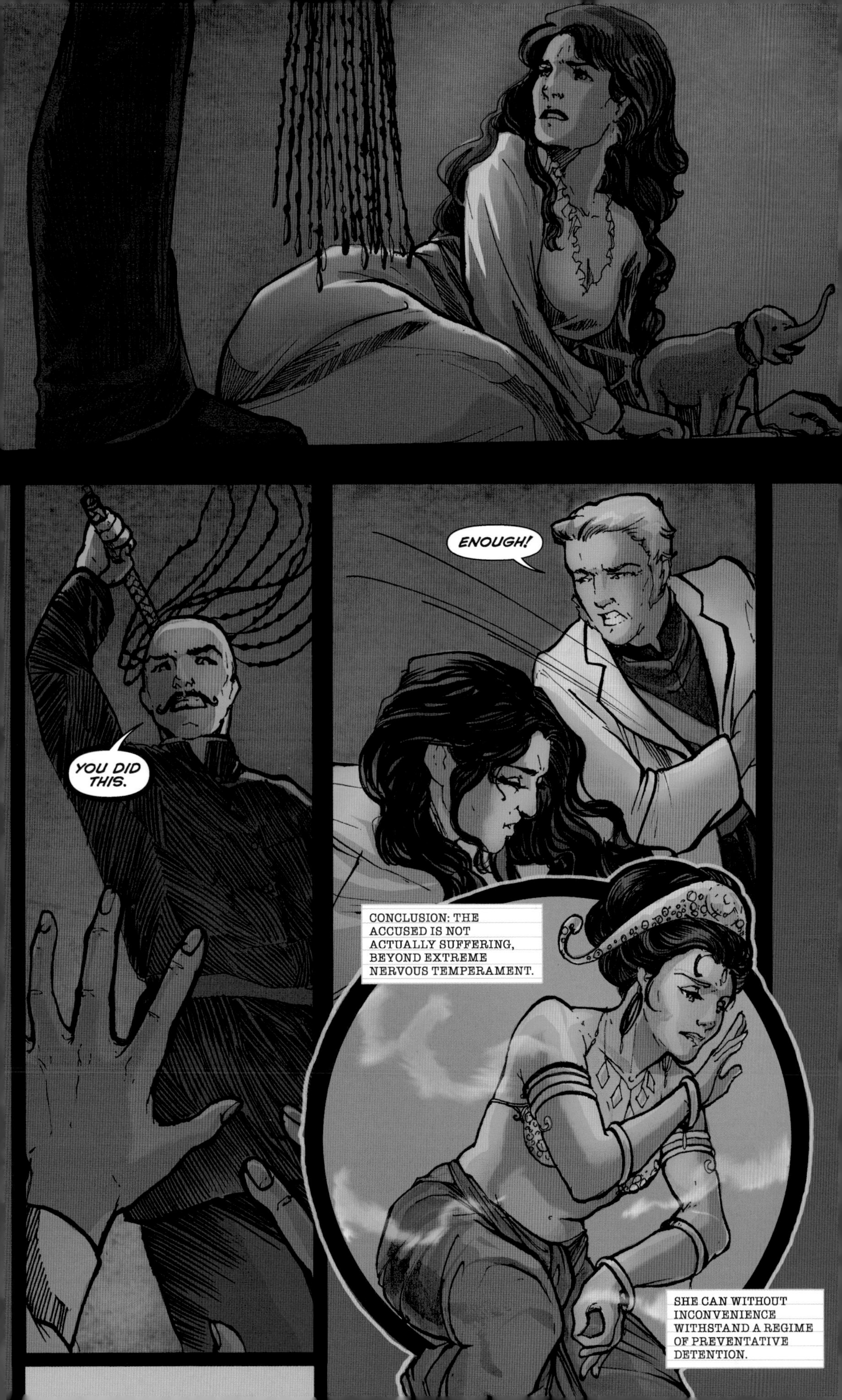
YOU DID THIS.
ENOUGH!
CONCLUSION: THE ACCUSED IS NOT ACTUALLY SUFFERING, BEYOND EXTREME NERVOUS TEMPERAMENT.
SHE CAN WITHOUT INCONVENIENCE WITHSTAND A REGIME OF PREVENTATIVE DETENTION.

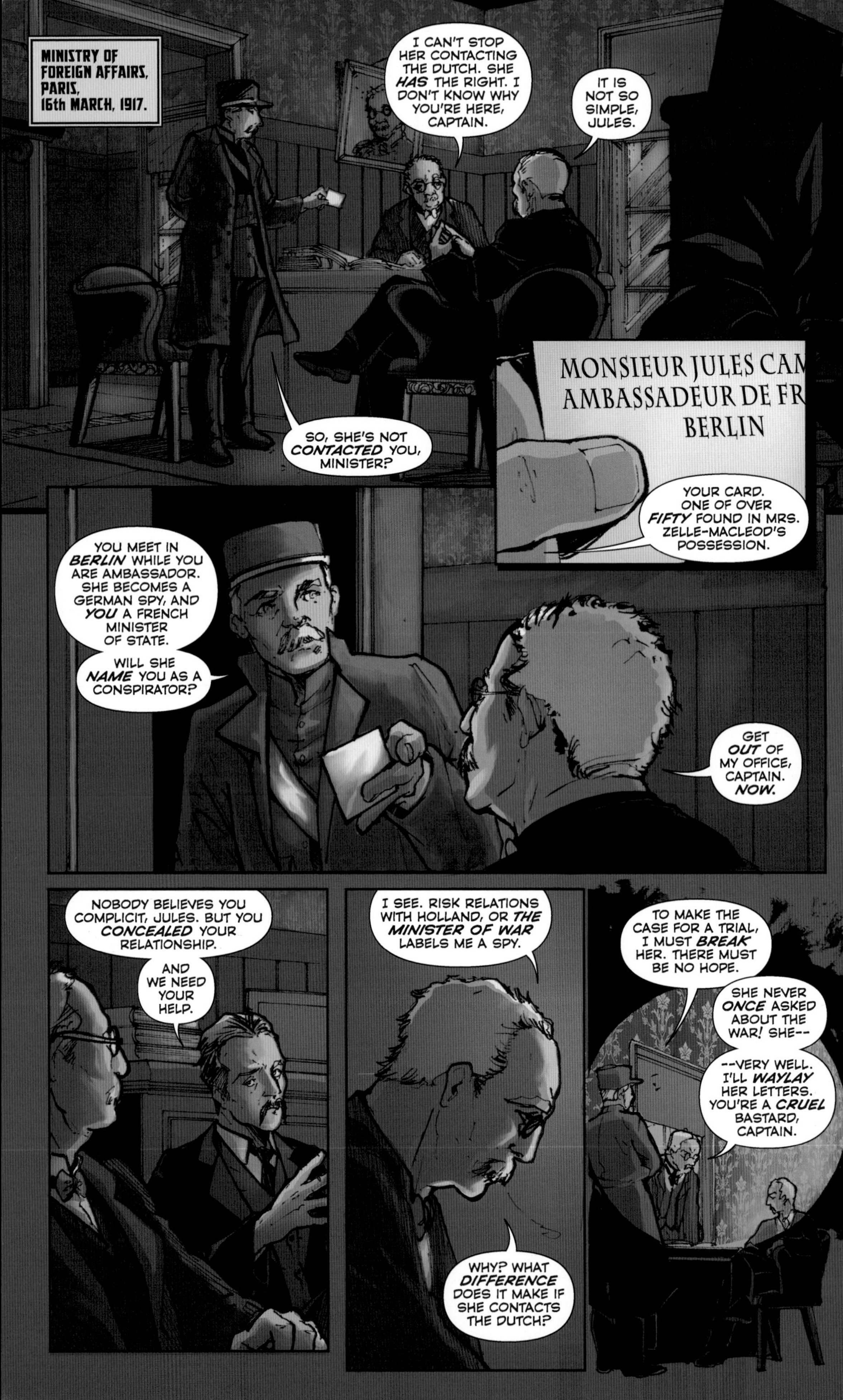
MINISTRY OF FOREIGN AFFAIRS, PARIS, 16th MARCH, 1917.
I CAN'T STOP HER CONTACTING THE DUTCH. SHE HAS THE RIGHT. I DON'T KNOW WHY YOU'RE HERE, CAPTAIN.
IT IS NOT SO SIMPLE, JULES.
SO, SHE'S NOT CONTACTED YOU, MINISTER?
MONSIEUR JULES CAM
AMBASSADEUR DE FR
BERLIN
YOUR CARD. ONE OF OVER FIFTY FOUND IN MRS. ZELLE-MACLEOD'S POSSESSION.
YOU MEET IN BERLIN WHILE YOU ARE AMBASSADOR. SHE BECOMES A GERMAN SPY, AND YOU A FRENCH MINISTER OF STATE.
WILL SHE NAME YOU AS A CONSPIRATOR?
GET OUT OF MY OFFICE, CAPTAIN. NOW.
NOBODY BELIEVES YOU COMPLICIT, JULES. BUT YOU CONCEALED YOUR RELATIONSHIP.
AND WE NEED YOUR HELP.
I SEE. RISK RELATIONS WITH HOLLAND, OR THE MINISTER OF WAR LABELS ME A SPY.
WHY? WHAT DIFFERENCE DOES IT MAKE IF SHE CONTACTS THE DUTCH?
TO MAKE THE CASE FOR A TRIAL, I MUST BREAK HER. THERE MUST BE NO HOPE.
SHE NEVER ONCE ASKED ABOUT THE WAR! SHE--
--VERY WELL. I'LL WAYLAY HER LETTERS. YOU'RE A CRUEL BASTARD, CAPTAIN.

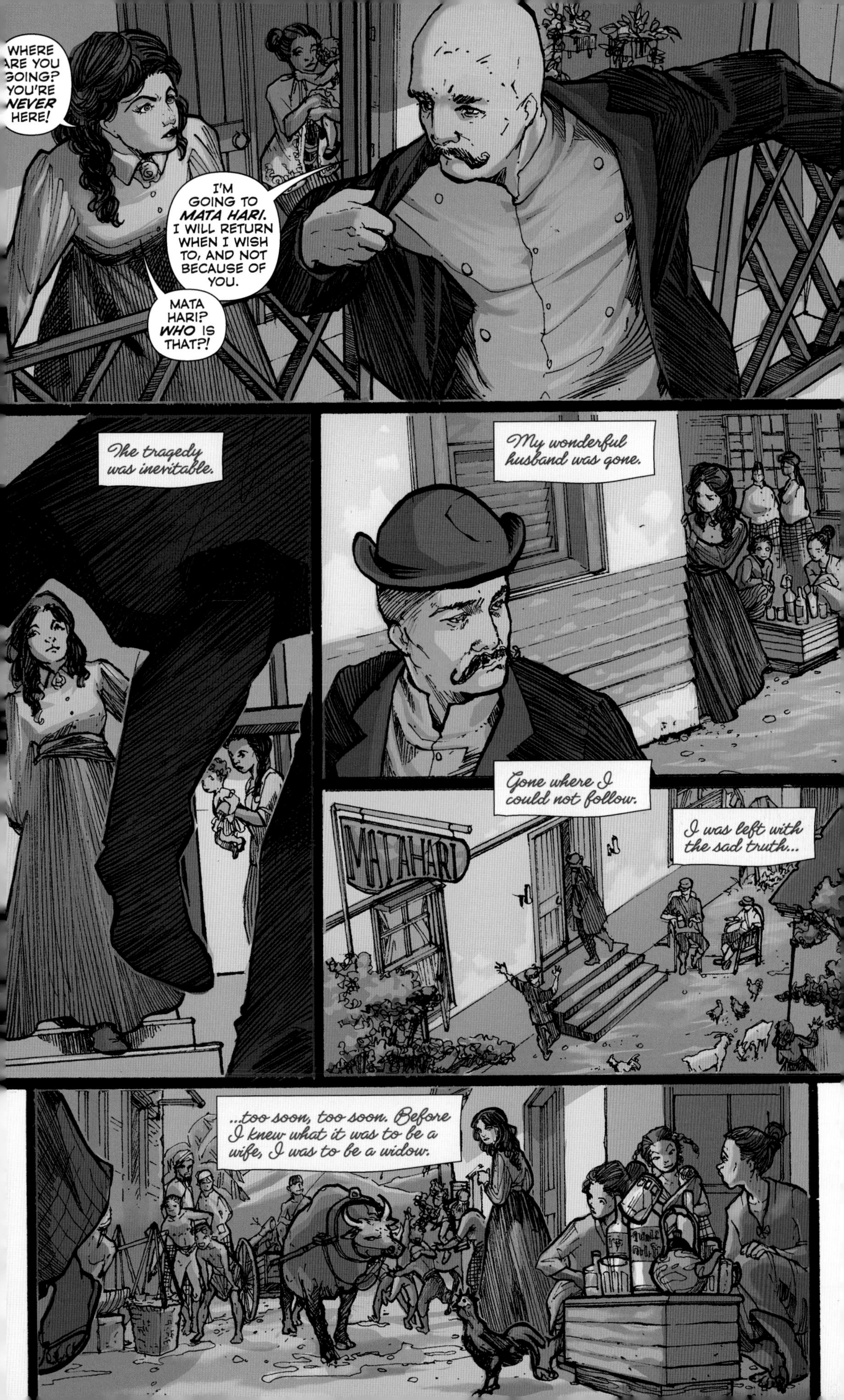
WHERE ARE YOU GOING? YOU'RE NEVER HERE!
I'M GOING TO MATA HARI. I WILL RETURN WHEN I WISH TO, AND NOT BECAUSE OF YOU.
MATA HARI? WHO IS THAT?!
The tragedy was inevitable.
My wonderful husband was gone.
Gone where I could not follow.
MATAHARI
I was left with the sad truth...
...too soon, too soon. Before I knew what it was to be a wife, I was to be a widow.

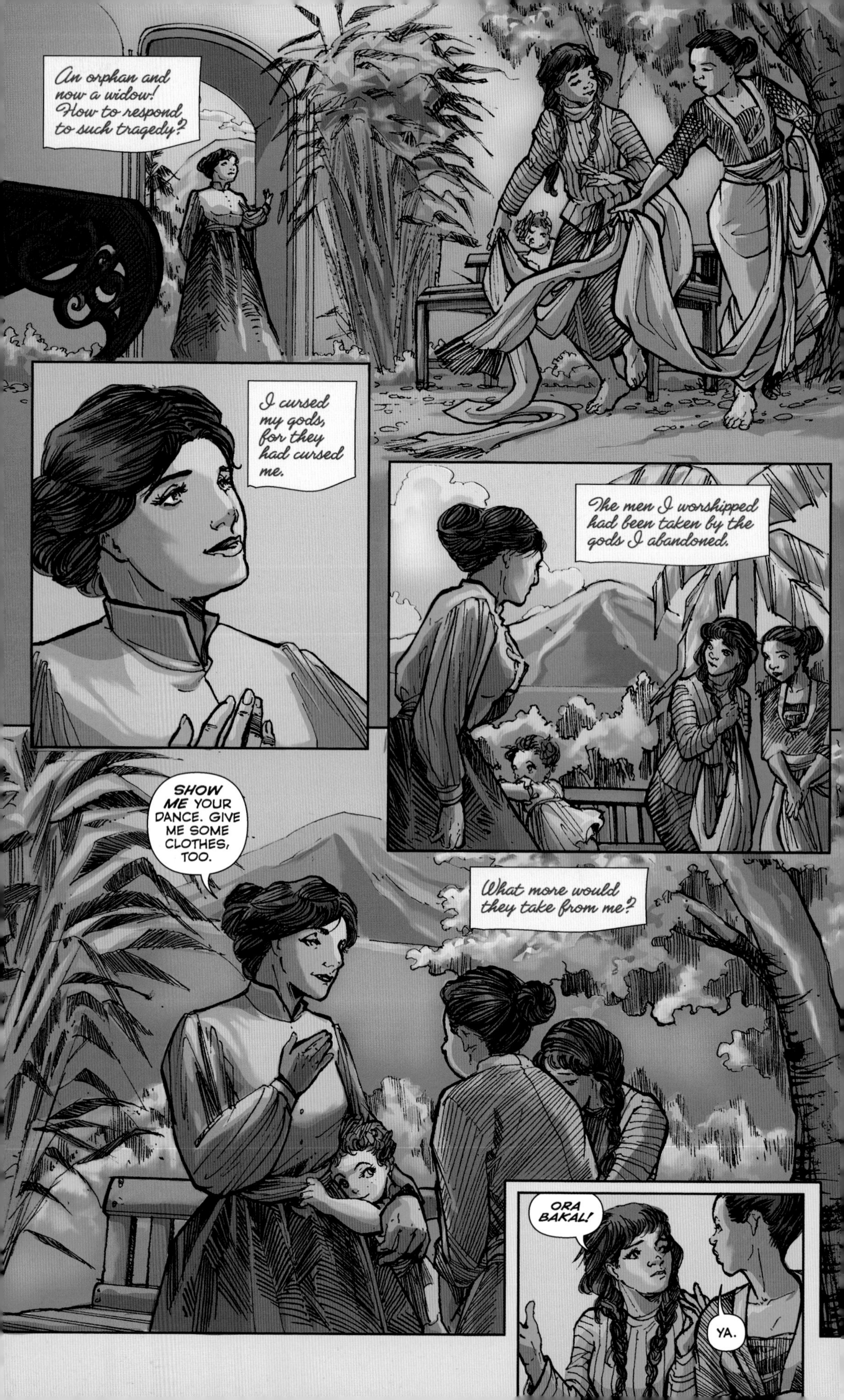
An orphan and now a widow! How to respond to such tragedy?
I cursed my gods, for they had cursed me.
The men I worshipped had been taken by the gods I abandoned.
SHOW ME YOUR DANCE. GIVE ME SOME CLOTHES, TOO.
What more would they take from me?
ORA BAKAL!
YA.

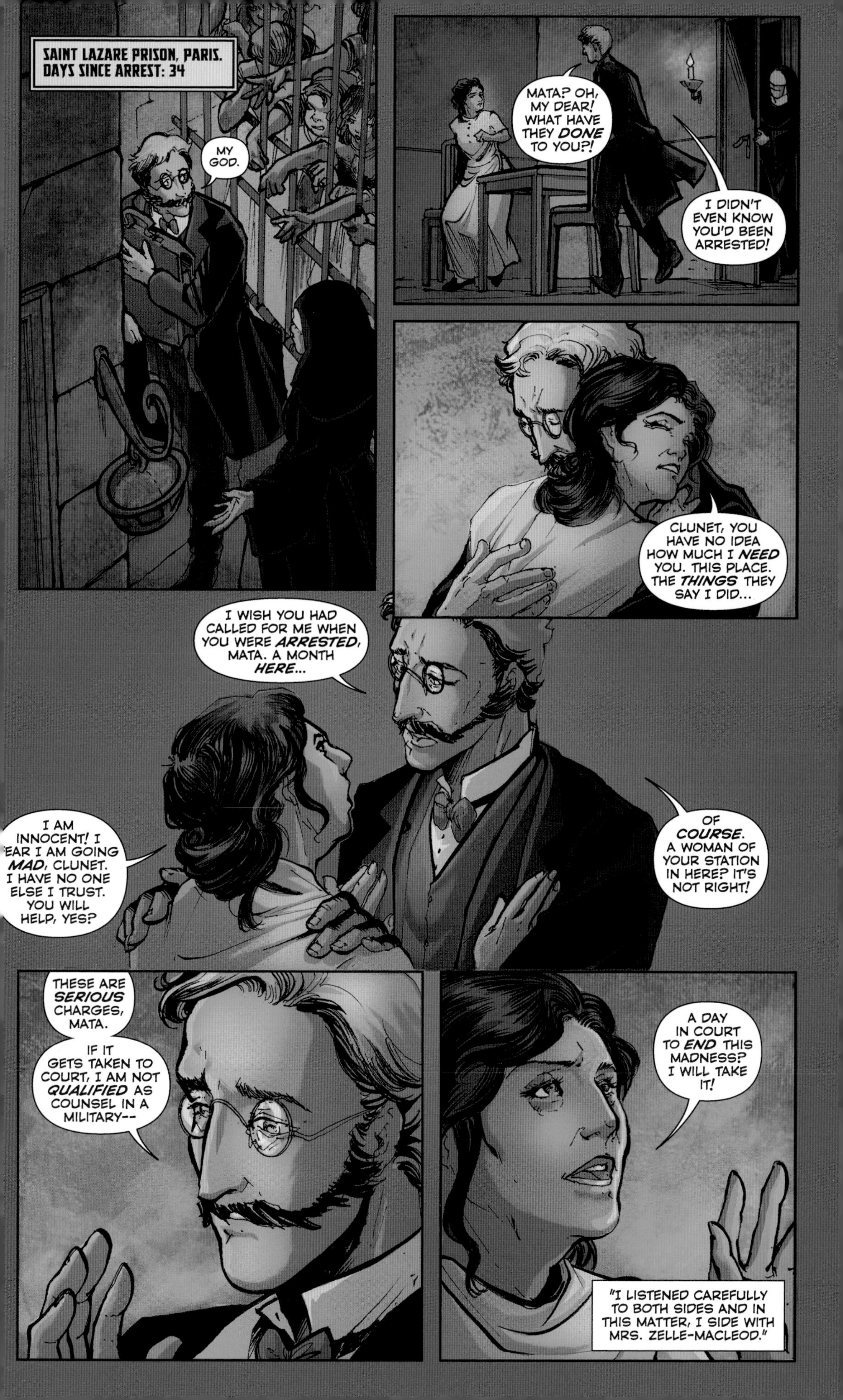
SAINT LAZARE PRISON, PARIS.
DAYS SINCE ARREST: 34
MY GOD.
MATA? OH, MY DEAR! WHAT HAVE THEY DONE TO YOU?!
I DIDN'T EVEN KNOW YOU'D BEEN ARRESTED!
CLUNET, YOU HAVE NO IDEA HOW MUCH I NEED YOU. THIS PLACE. THE THINGS THEY SAY I DID...
I WISH YOU HAD CALLED FOR ME WHEN YOU WERE ARRESTED, MATA. A MONTH HERE...
I AM INNOCENT! I FEAR I AM GOING MAD, CLUNET. I HAVE NO ONE ELSE I TRUST. YOU WILL HELP, YES?
OF COURSE. A WOMAN OF YOUR STATION IN HERE? IT'S NOT RIGHT!
THESE ARE SERIOUS CHARGES, MATA.
IF IT GETS TAKEN TO COURT, I AM NOT QUALIFIED AS COUNSEL IN A MILITARY--
A DAY IN COURT TO END THIS MADNESS? I WILL TAKE IT!
"I LISTENED CAREFULLY TO BOTH SIDES AND IN THIS MATTER, I SIDE WITH MRS. ZELLE-MACLEOD."

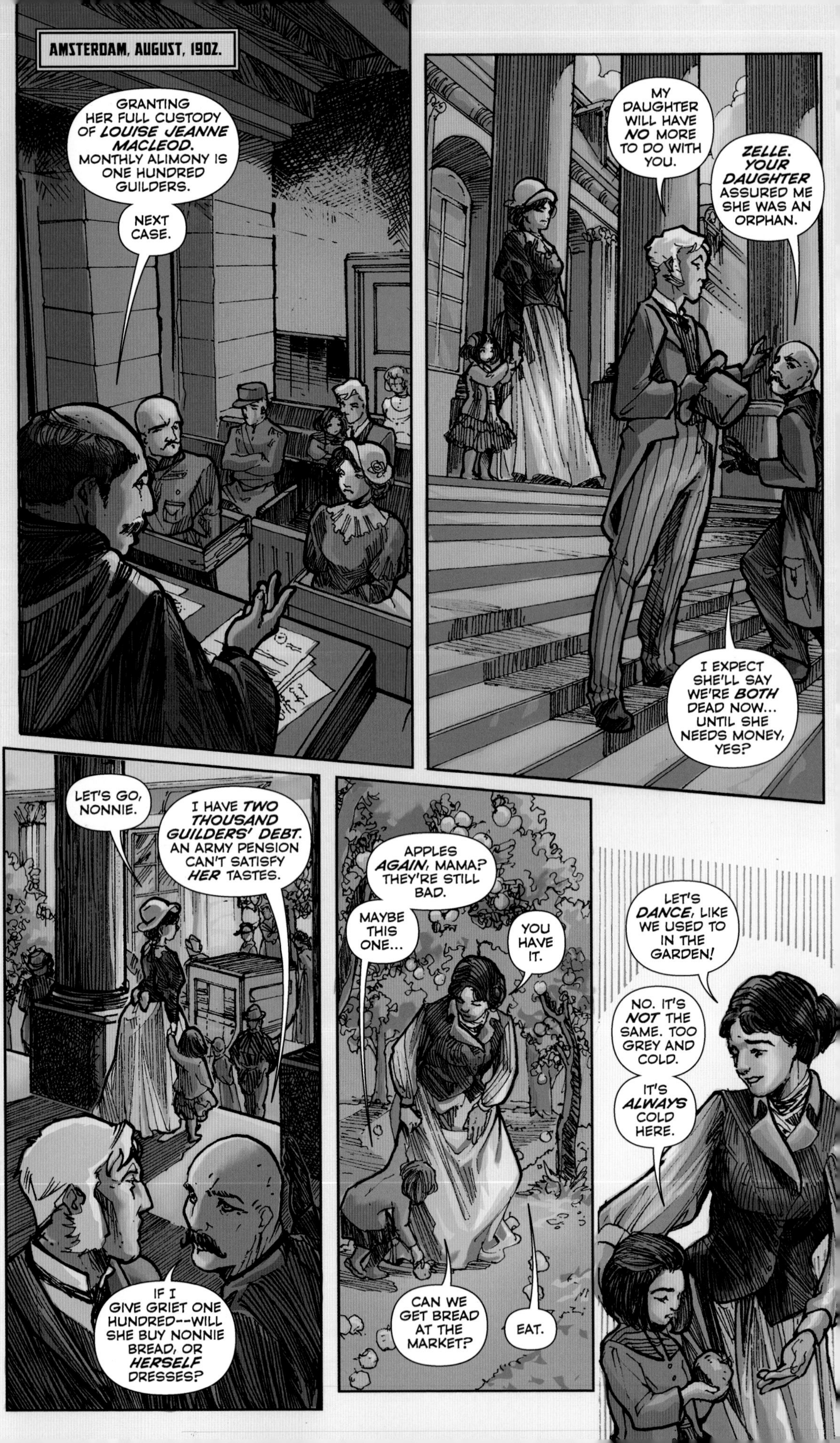
AMSTERDAM, AUGUST, 1902.
GRANTING HER FULL CUSTODY OF LOUISE JEANNE MACLEOD. MONTHLY ALIMONY IS ONE HUNDRED GUILDERS.
NEXT CASE.
MY DAUGHTER WILL HAVE NO MORE TO DO WITH YOU.
ZELLE. YOUR DAUGHTER ASSURED ME SHE WAS AN ORPHAN.
I EXPECT SHE'LL SAY WE'RE BOTH DEAD NOW... UNTIL SHE NEEDS MONEY, YES?
LET'S GO, NONNIE.
I HAVE TWO THOUSAND GUILDERS' DEBT. AN ARMY PENSION CAN'T SATISFY HER TASTES.
IF I GIVE GRIET ONE HUNDRED--WILL SHE BUY NONNIE BREAD, OR HERSELF DRESSES?
APPLES AGAIN, MAMA? THEY'RE STILL BAD.
MAYBE THIS ONE...
YOU HAVE IT.
CAN WE GET BREAD AT THE MARKET?
EAT.
LET'S DANCE, LIKE WE USED TO IN THE GARDEN!
NO. IT'S NOT THE SAME. TOO GREY AND COLD.
IT'S ALWAYS COLD HERE.

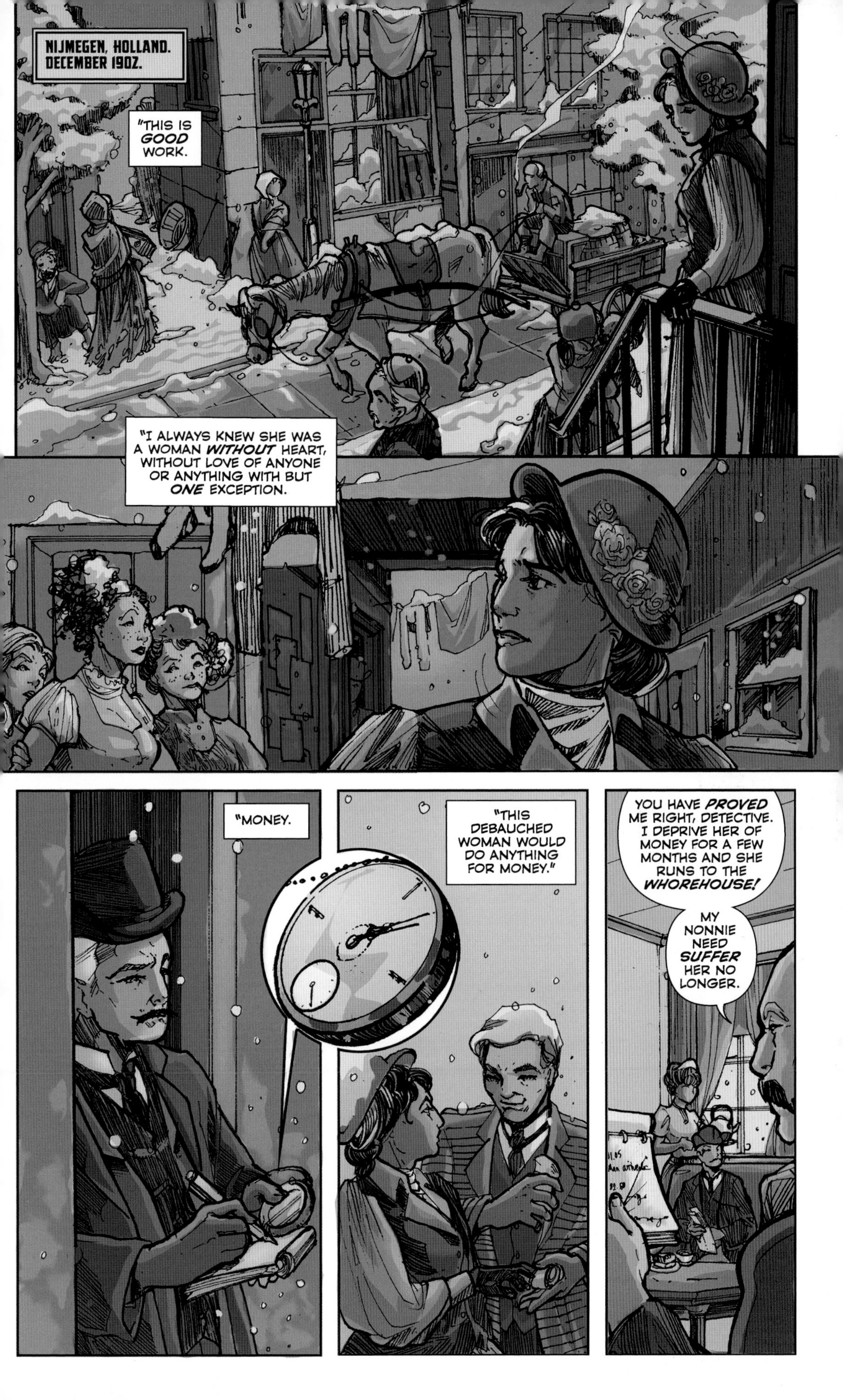
NIJMEGEN, HOLLAND. DECEMBER 1902.
"THIS IS GOOD WORK.
"I ALWAYS KNEW SHE WAS A WOMAN WITHOUT HEART, WITHOUT LOVE OF ANYONE OR ANYTHING WITH BUT ONE EXCEPTION.
"MONEY.
"THIS DEBAUCHED WOMAN WOULD DO ANYTHING FOR MONEY."
YOU HAVE PROVED ME RIGHT, DETECTIVE. I DEPRIVE HER OF MONEY FOR A FEW MONTHS AND SHE RUNS TO THE WHOREHOUSE!
MY NONNIE NEED SUFFER HER NO LONGER.

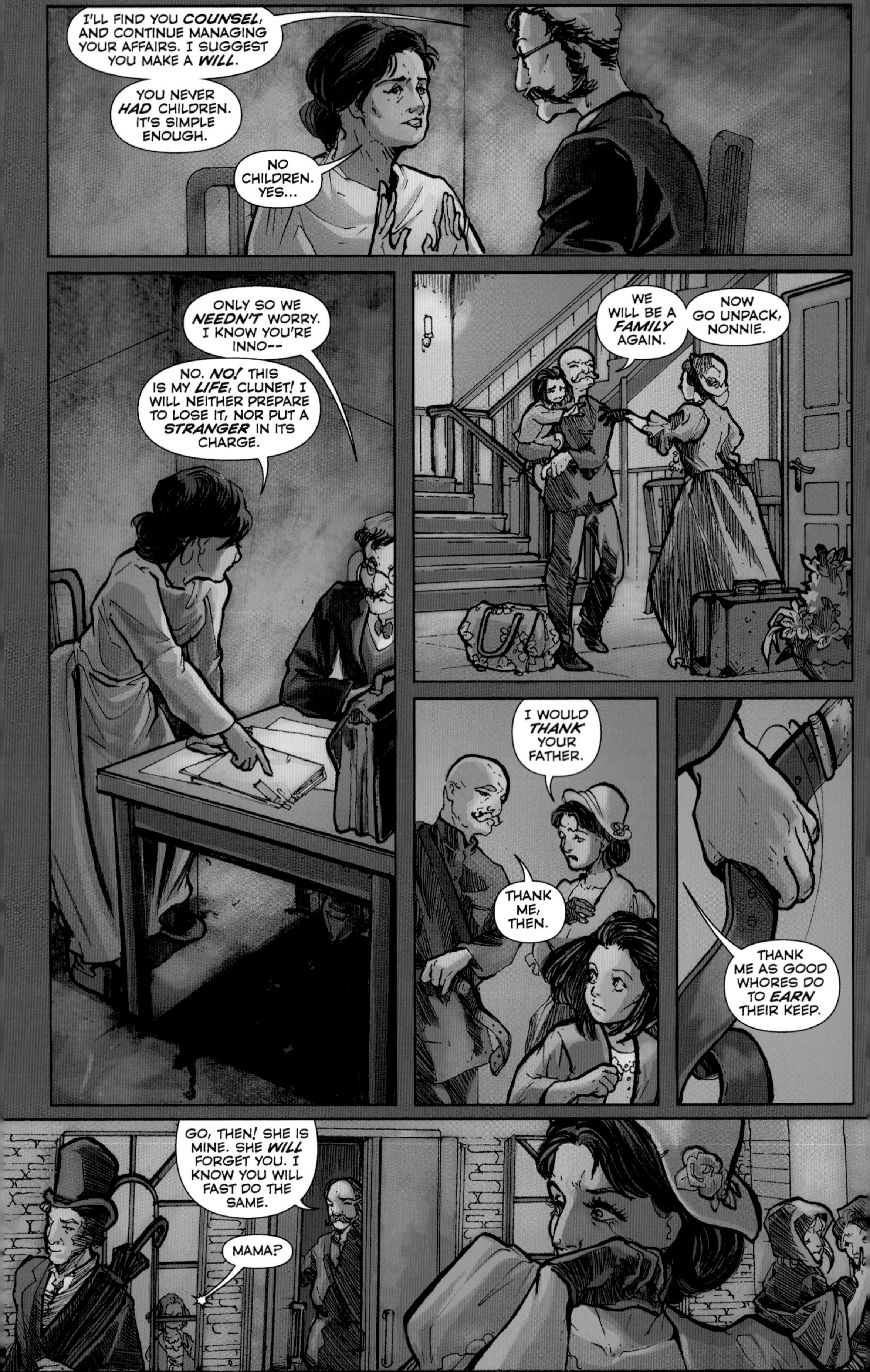
I'LL FIND YOU COUNSEL, AND CONTINUE MANAGING YOUR AFFAIRS. I SUGGEST YOU MAKE A WILL.
YOU NEVER HAD CHILDREN. IT'S SIMPLE ENOUGH.
NO CHILDREN. YES...
ONLY SO WE NEEDN'T WORRY. I KNOW YOU'RE INNO--
NO. NO! THIS IS MY LIFE, CLUNET! I WILL NEITHER PREPARE TO LOSE IT, NOR PUT A STRANGER IN ITS CHARGE.
WE WILL BE A FAMILY AGAIN.
NOW GO UNPACK, NONNIE.
I WOULD THANK YOUR FATHER.
THANK ME, THEN.
THANK ME AS GOOD WHORES DO TO EARN THEIR KEEP.
GO, THEN! SHE IS MINE. SHE WILL FORGET YOU. I KNOW YOU WILL FAST DO THE SAME.
MAMA?

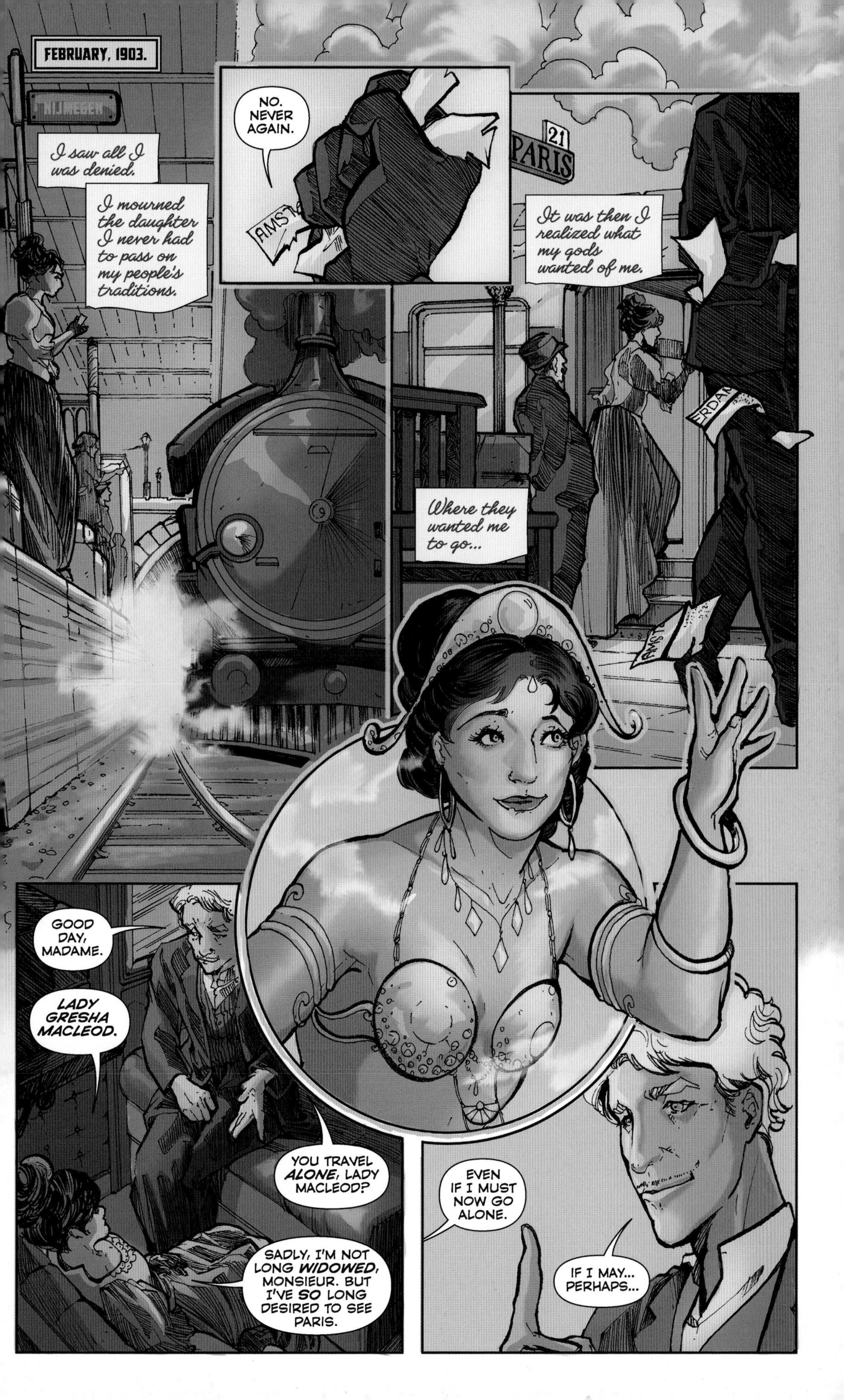
FEBRUARY, 1903.
NIJMEGEN
I saw all I was denied.
I mourned the daughter I never had to pass on my people's traditions.
NO. NEVER AGAIN.
21 PARIS
It was then I realized what my gods wanted of me.
Where they wanted me to go...
GOOD DAY, MADAME.
LADY GRESHA MACLEOD.
YOU TRAVEL ALONE, LADY MACLEOD?
SADLY, I'M NOT LONG WIDOWED, MONSIEUR. BUT I'VE SO LONG DESIRED TO SEE PARIS.
EVEN IF I MUST NOW GO ALONE.
IF I MAY... PERHAPS...

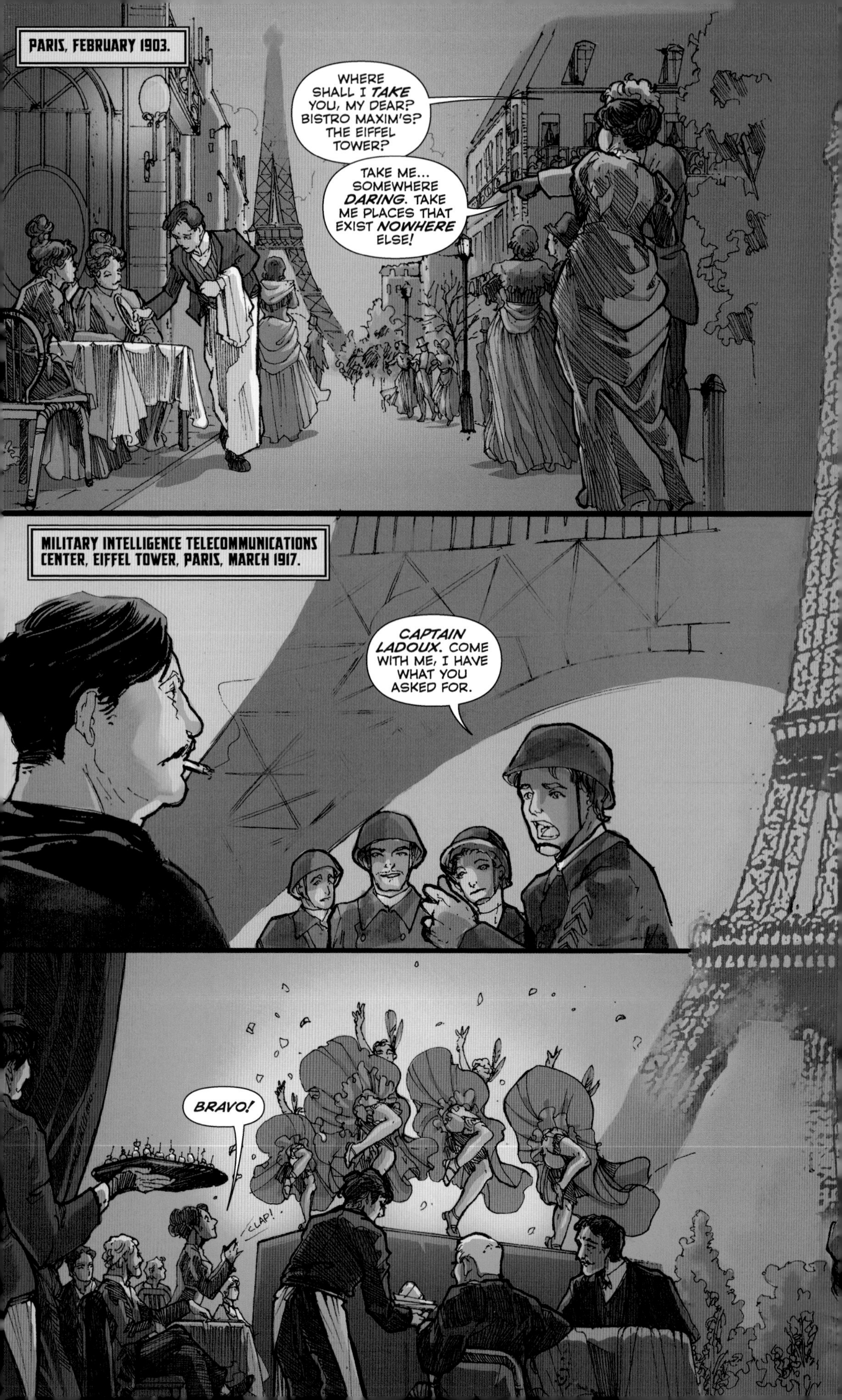
PARIS, FEBRUARY 1903.
WHERE SHALL I TAKE YOU, MY DEAR? BISTRO MAXIM'S? THE EIFFEL TOWER?
TAKE ME... SOMEWHERE DARING. TAKE ME PLACES THAT EXIST NOWHERE ELSE!
MILITARY INTELLIGENCE TELECOMMUNICATIONS CENTER, EIFFEL TOWER, PARIS, MARCH 1917.
CAPTAIN LADOUX. COME WITH ME, I HAVE WHAT YOU ASKED FOR.
BRAVO!
CLAP!

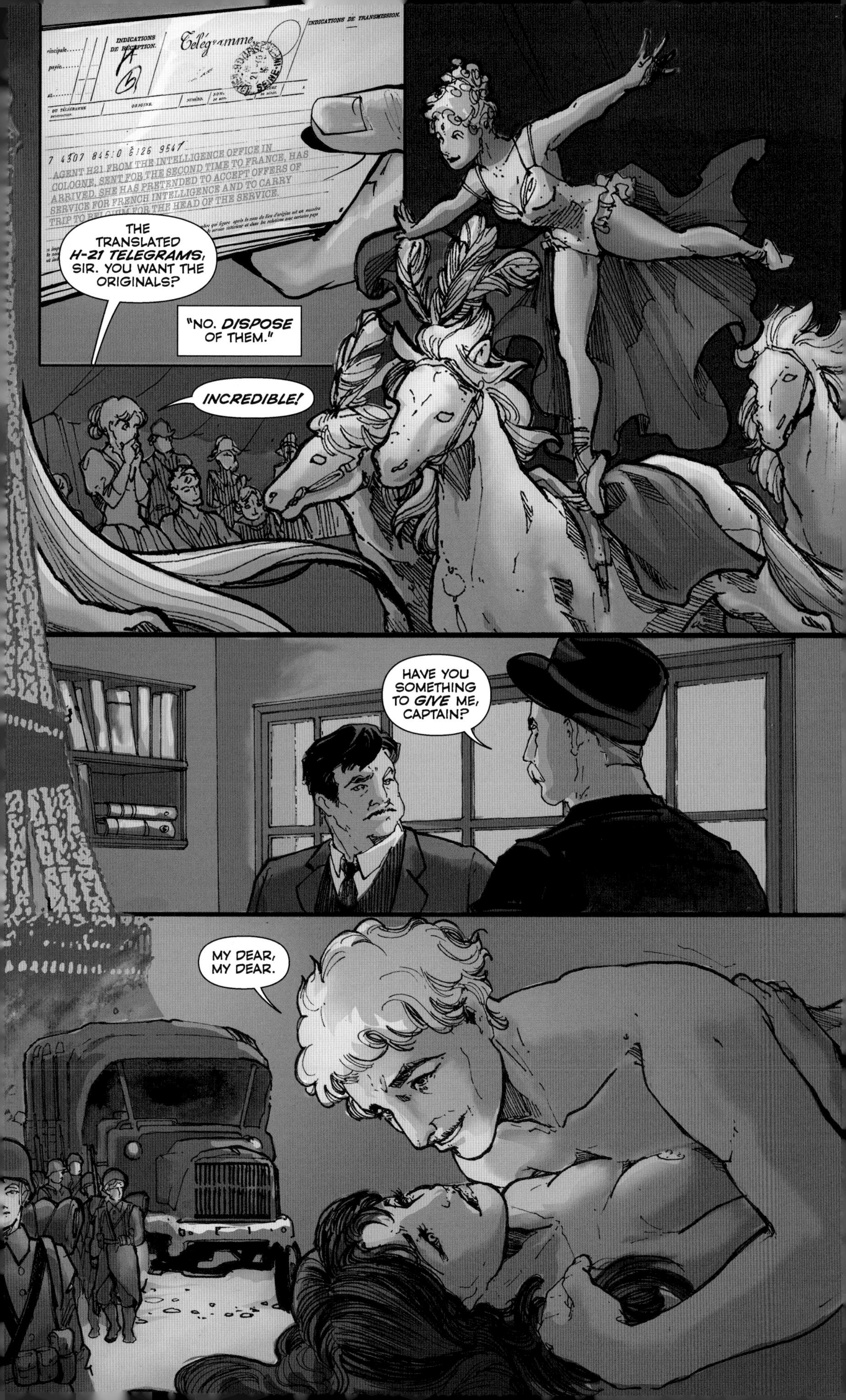
INDICATIONS DE TRANSMISSION.
INDICATIONS DE RÉCEPTION.
Télégramme
7 4307 845:0 6126 9547
AGENT H21 FROM THE INTELLIGENCE OFFICE IN
COLOGNE, SENT FOR THE SECOND TIME TO FRANCE, HAS
ARRIVED. SHE HAS PRETENDED TO ACCEPT OFFERS OF
SERVICE FOR FRENCH INTELLIGENCE AND TO CARRY
TRIP TO BELGIUM FOR THE HEAD OF THE SERVICE.
THE TRANSLATED *H-21 TELEGRAMS*, SIR. YOU WANT THE ORIGINALS?
"NO. *DISPOSE* OF THEM."
INCREDIBLE!
HAVE YOU SOMETHING TO *GIVE* ME, CAPTAIN?
MY DEAR, MY DEAR.

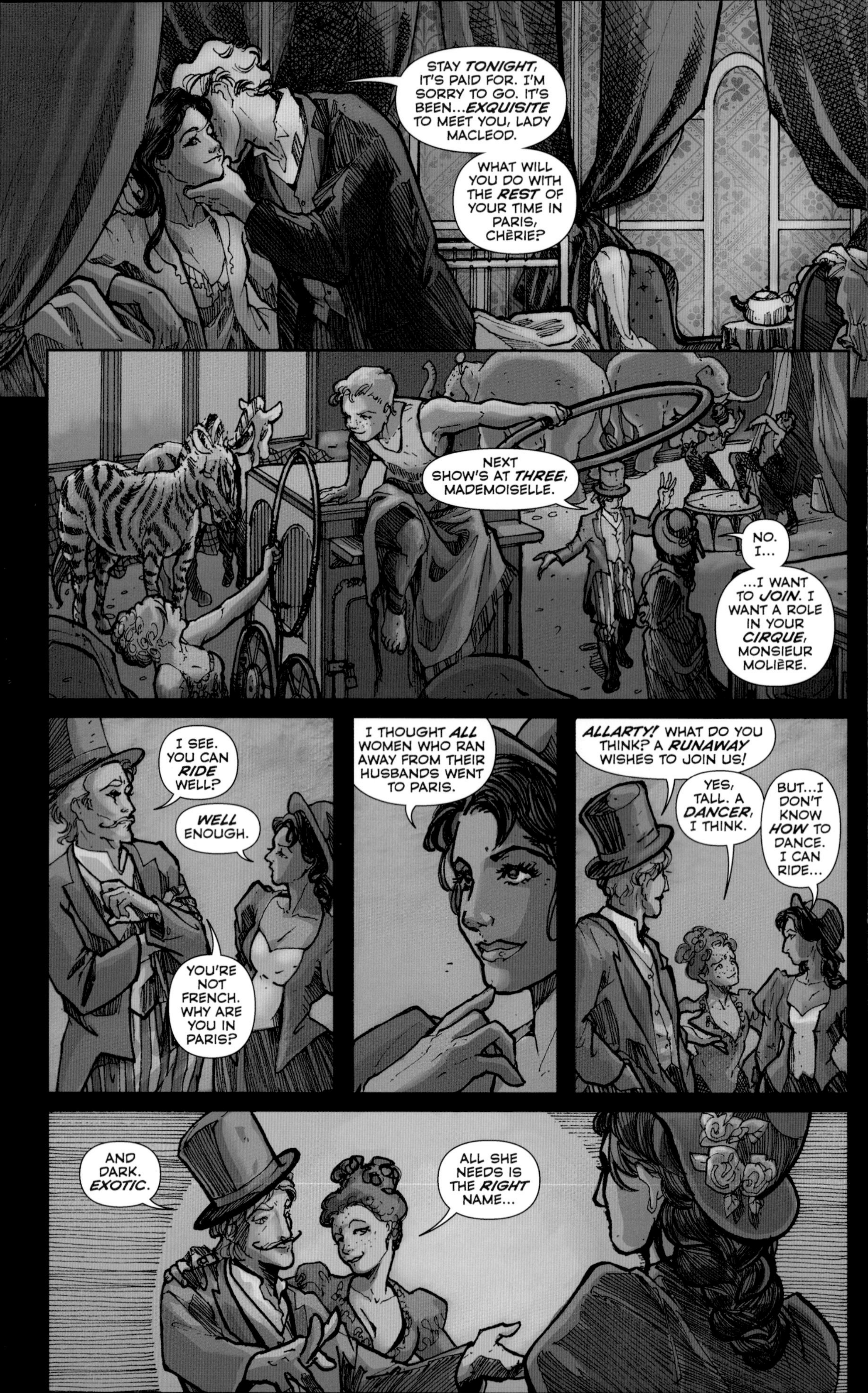
STAY TONIGHT, IT'S PAID FOR. I'M SORRY TO GO. IT'S BEEN...EXQUISITE TO MEET YOU, LADY MACLEOD.
WHAT WILL YOU DO WITH THE REST OF YOUR TIME IN PARIS, CHÈRIE?
NEXT SHOW'S AT THREE, MADEMOISELLE.
NO. I...
...I WANT TO JOIN. I WANT A ROLE IN YOUR CIRQUE, MONSIEUR MOLIÈRE.
I SEE. YOU CAN RIDE WELL?
WELL ENOUGH.
YOU'RE NOT FRENCH. WHY ARE YOU IN PARIS?
I THOUGHT ALL WOMEN WHO RAN AWAY FROM THEIR HUSBANDS WENT TO PARIS.
ALLARTY! WHAT DO YOU THINK? A RUNAWAY WISHES TO JOIN US!
YES, TALL. A DANCER, I THINK.
BUT...I DON'T KNOW HOW TO DANCE. I CAN RIDE...
AND DARK. EXOTIC.
ALL SHE NEEDS IS THE RIGHT NAME...

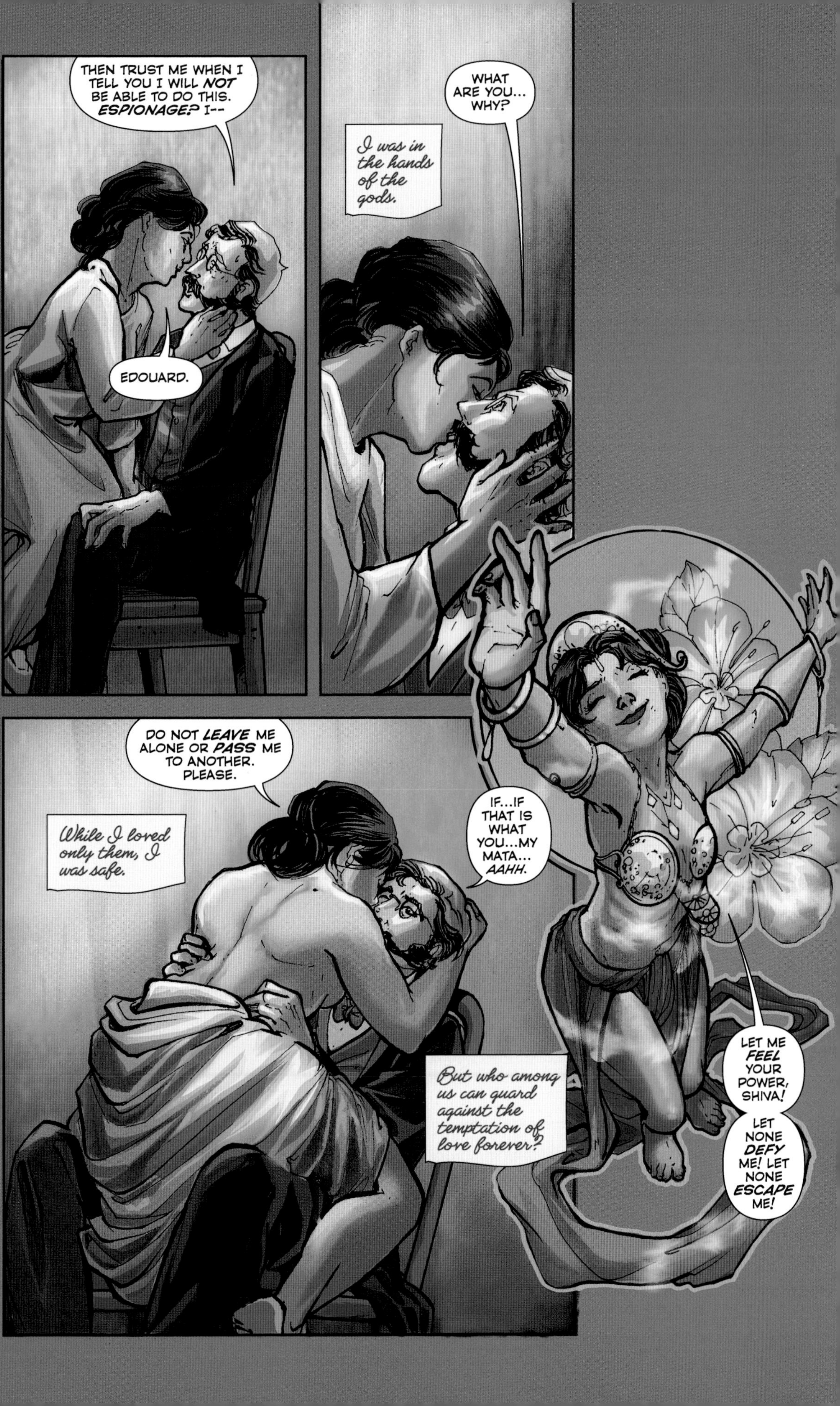
THEN TRUST ME WHEN I TELL YOU I WILL NOT BE ABLE TO DO THIS. ESPIONAGE? I--
EDOUARD.
WHAT ARE YOU... WHY?
I was in the hands of the gods.
DO NOT LEAVE ME ALONE OR PASS ME TO ANOTHER. PLEASE.
While I loved only them, I was safe.
IF...IF THAT IS WHAT YOU...MY MATA... AAHH.
But who among us can guard against the temptation of love forever?
LET ME FEEL YOUR POWER, SHIVA!
LET NONE DEFY ME! LET NONE ESCAPE ME!

CHAPTER FOUR
BARE·TEETH

"Salomé, Salomé, dance for me...
Dance for me, Salomé, I beseech you.
If you dance for me you may ask of me what you will,
and I will give it you...
...even unto half of my kingdom.."
I was a virgin, and thou didst take my virginity from me.
I was chaste, and thou didst fill my veins with fire..."

SALOMÉ:
A TRAGEDY IN ONE ACT
~ Oscar Wilde ~

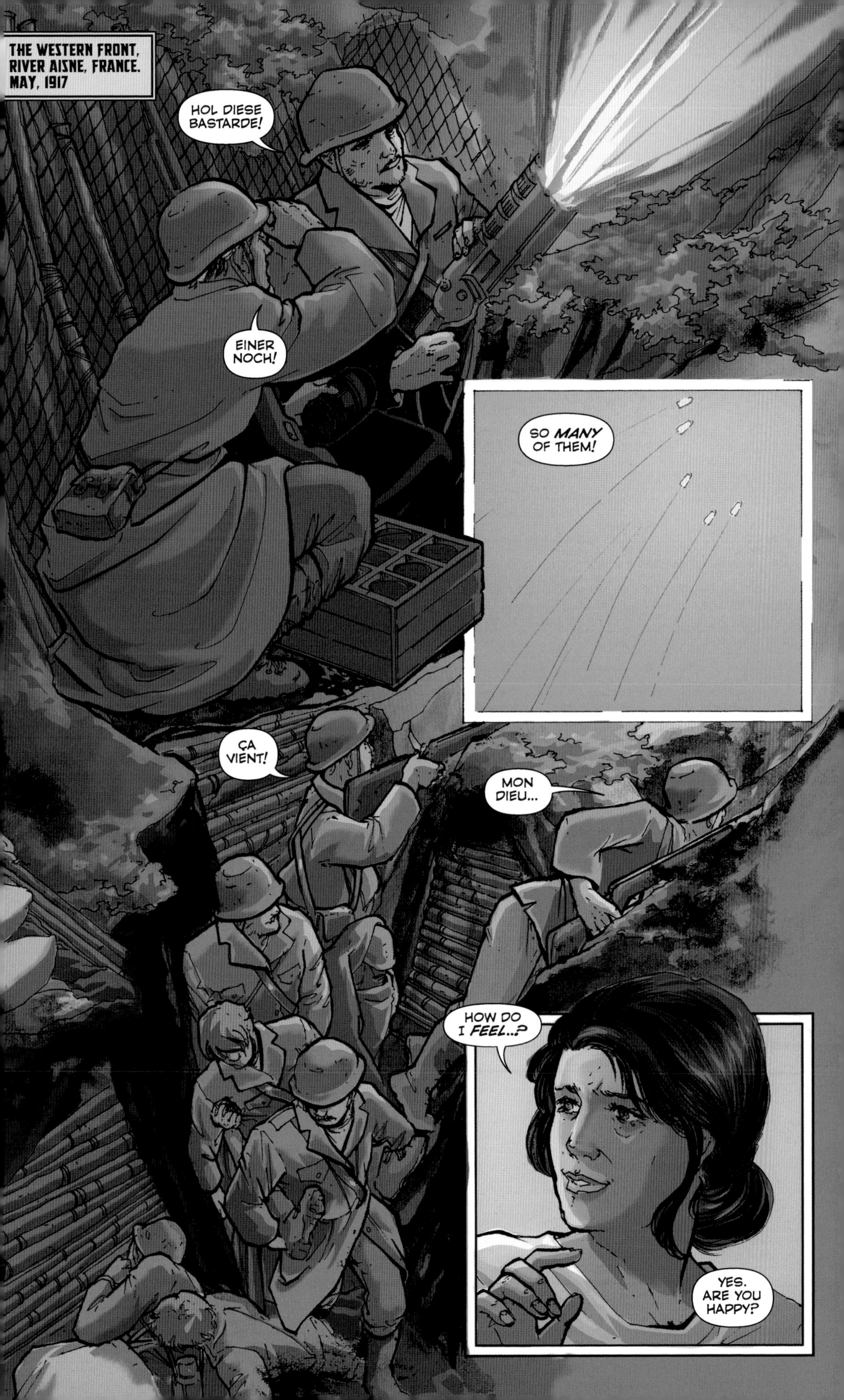
THE WESTERN FRONT, RIVER AISNE, FRANCE. MAY, 1917
HOL DIESE BASTARDE!
EINER NOCH!
SO *MANY* OF THEM!
ÇA VIENT!
MON DIEU...
HOW DO I *FEEL*...?
YES. ARE YOU HAPPY?

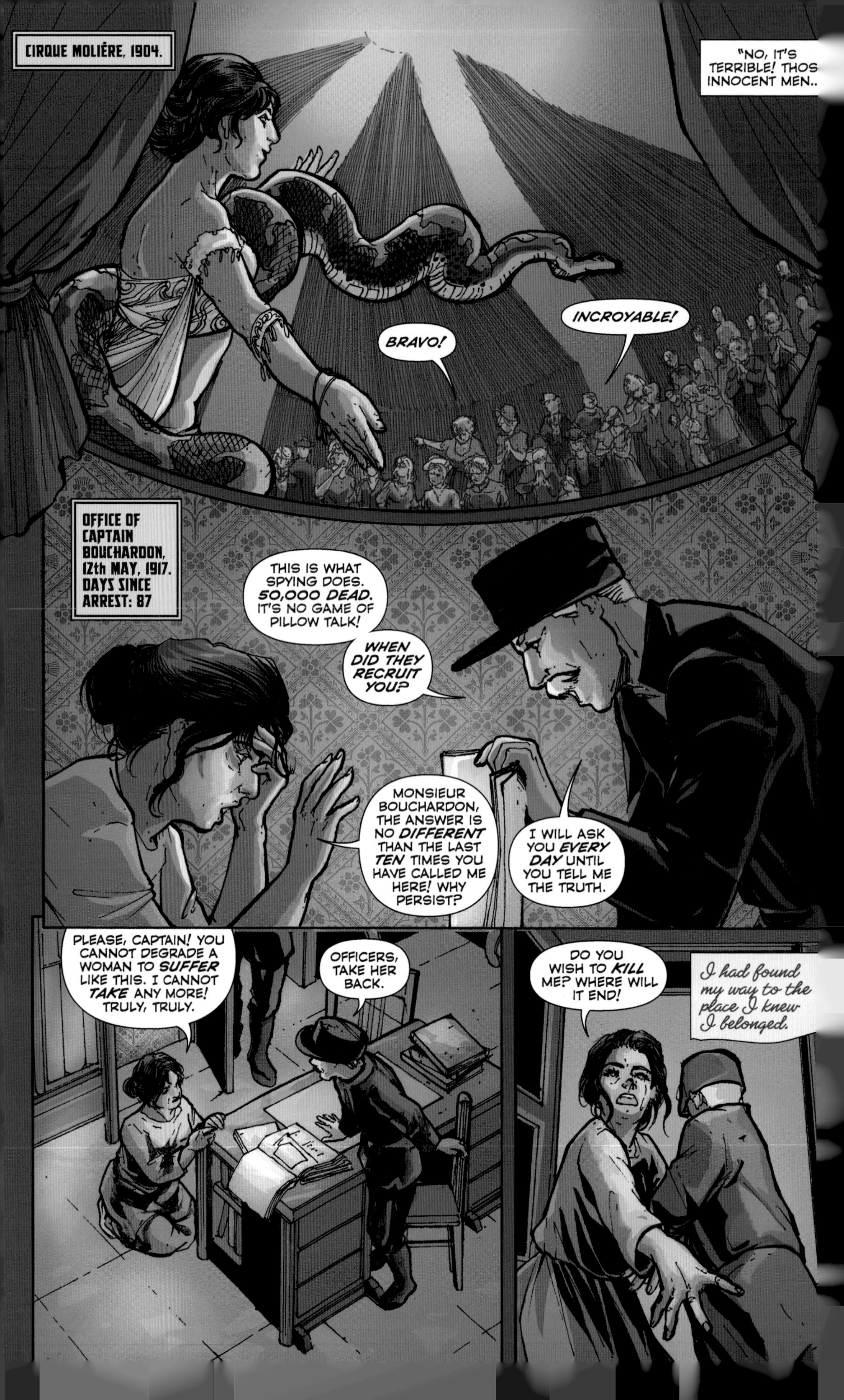
CIRQUE MOLIÈRE, 1904.
"NO, IT'S TERRIBLE! THOS INNOCENT MEN..
BRAVO!
INCROYABLE!
OFFICE OF CAPTAIN BOUCHARDON, 12th MAY, 1917. DAYS SINCE ARREST: 87
THIS IS WHAT SPYING DOES. 50,000 DEAD. IT'S NO GAME OF PILLOW TALK!
WHEN DID THEY RECRUIT YOU?
MONSIEUR BOUCHARDON, THE ANSWER IS NO DIFFERENT THAN THE LAST TEN TIMES YOU HAVE CALLED ME HERE! WHY PERSIST?
I WILL ASK YOU EVERY DAY UNTIL YOU TELL ME THE TRUTH.
PLEASE, CAPTAIN! YOU CANNOT DEGRADE A WOMAN TO SUFFER LIKE THIS. I CANNOT TAKE ANY MORE! TRULY, TRULY.
OFFICERS, TAKE HER BACK.
DO YOU WISH TO KILL ME? WHERE WILL IT END!
I had found my way to the place I knew I belonged.

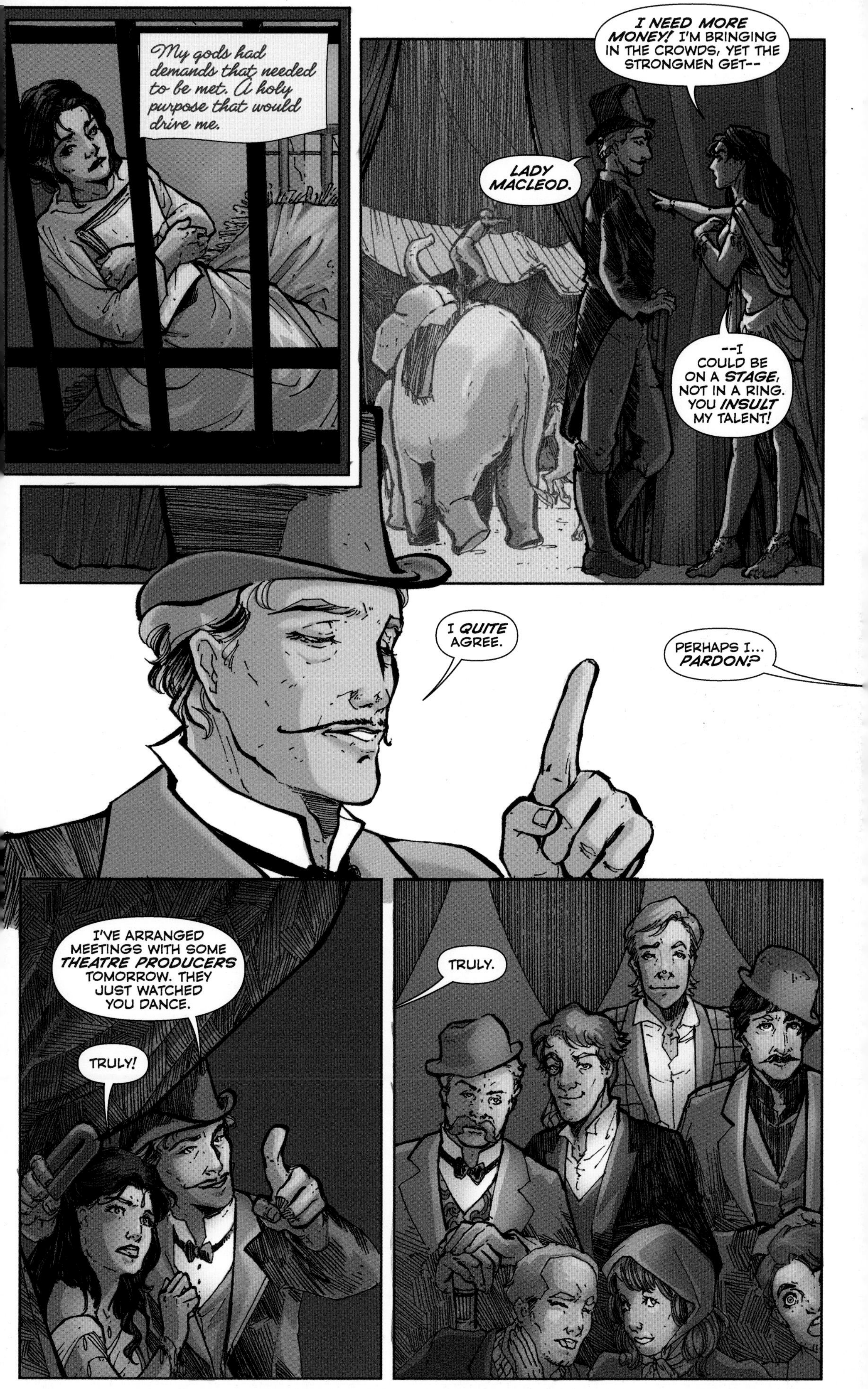
My gods had demands that needed to be met. A holy purpose that would drive me.
I NEED MORE MONEY! I'M BRINGING IN THE CROWDS, YET THE STRONGMEN GET--
LADY MACLEOD.
--I COULD BE ON A STAGE, NOT IN A RING. YOU INSULT MY TALENT!
I QUITE AGREE.
PERHAPS I... PARDON?
I'VE ARRANGED MEETINGS WITH SOME THEATRE PRODUCERS TOMORROW. THEY JUST WATCHED YOU DANCE.
TRULY!
TRULY.

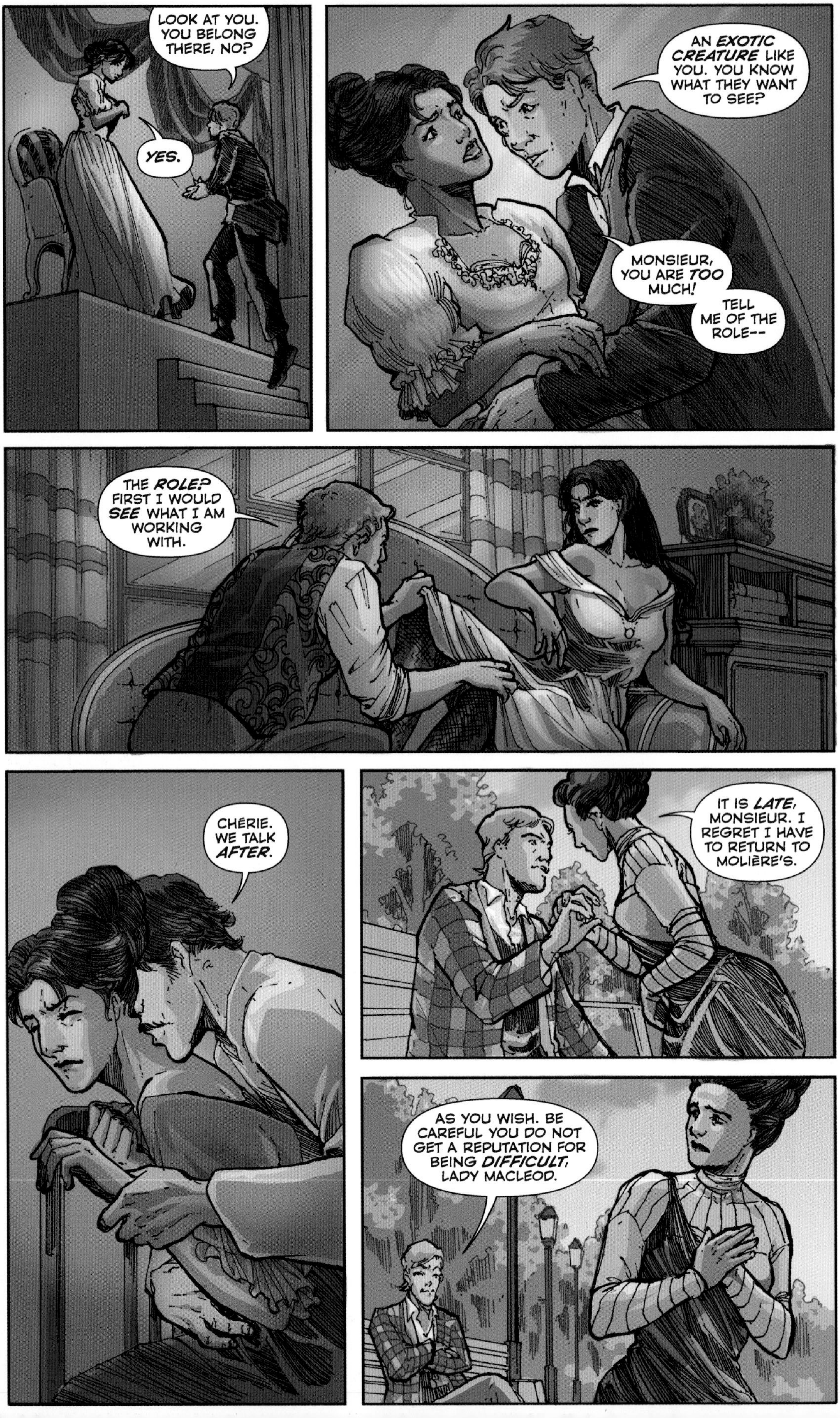
LOOK AT YOU. YOU BELONG THERE, NO?
YES.
AN EXOTIC CREATURE LIKE YOU. YOU KNOW WHAT THEY WANT TO SEE?
MONSIEUR, YOU ARE TOO MUCH!
TELL ME OF THE ROLE--
THE ROLE? FIRST I WOULD SEE WHAT I AM WORKING WITH.
CHÉRIE. WE TALK AFTER.
IT IS LATE, MONSIEUR. I REGRET I HAVE TO RETURN TO MOLIÈRE'S.
AS YOU WISH. BE CAREFUL YOU DO NOT GET A REPUTATION FOR BEING DIFFICULT, LADY MACLEOD.

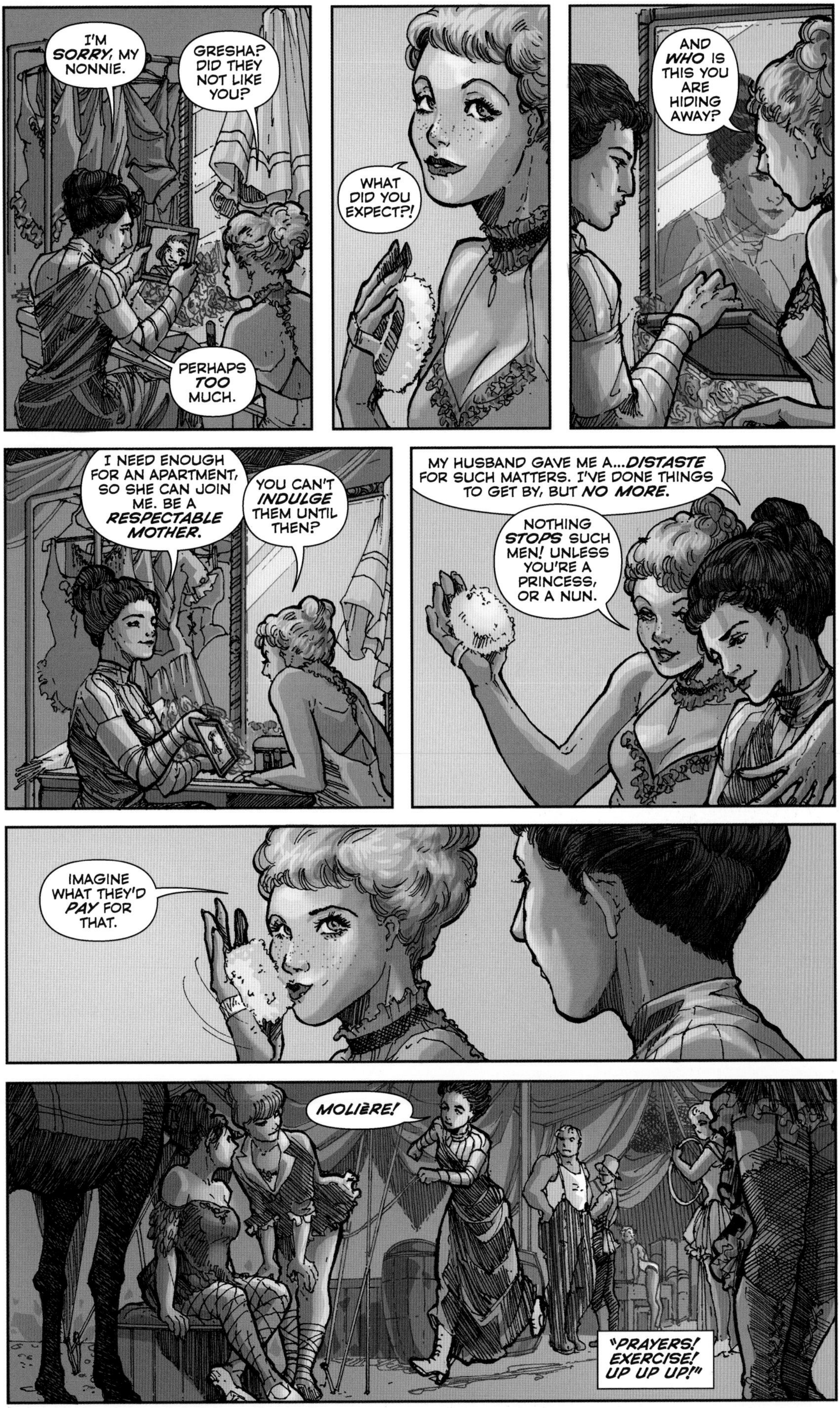

I'M SORRY, MY NONNIE.
GRESHA? DID THEY NOT LIKE YOU?
PERHAPS TOO MUCH.
WHAT DID YOU EXPECT?!
AND WHO IS THIS YOU ARE HIDING AWAY?
I NEED ENOUGH FOR AN APARTMENT, SO SHE CAN JOIN ME. BE A RESPECTABLE MOTHER.
YOU CAN'T INDULGE THEM UNTIL THEN?
MY HUSBAND GAVE ME A...DISTASTE FOR SUCH MATTERS. I'VE DONE THINGS TO GET BY, BUT NO MORE.
NOTHING STOPS SUCH MEN! UNLESS YOU'RE A PRINCESS, OR A NUN.
IMAGINE WHAT THEY'D PAY FOR THAT.
MOLIÈRE!
"PRAYERS! EXERCISE! UP UP UP!"

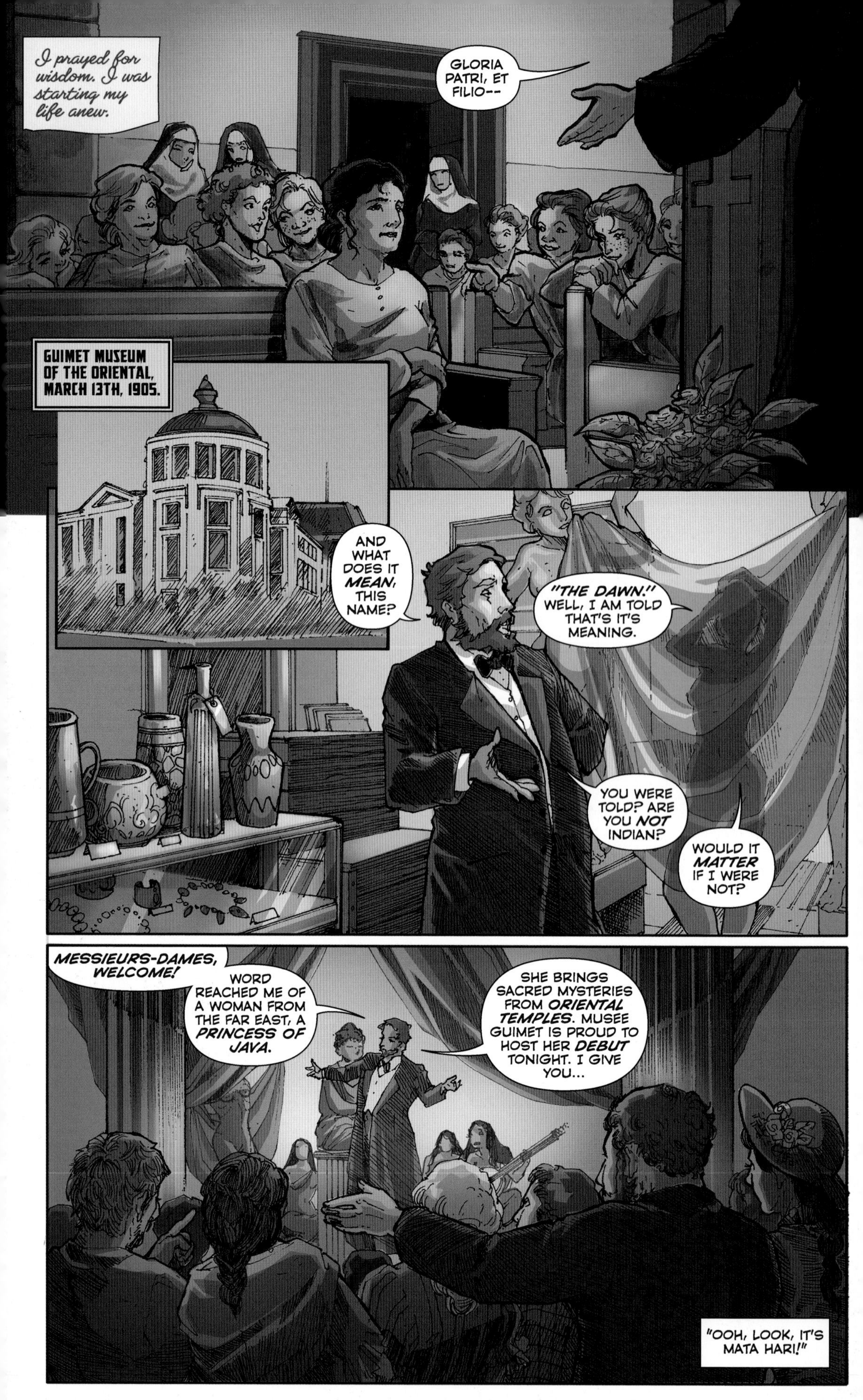
I prayed for wisdom. I was starting my life anew.
GLORIA PATRI, ET FILIO--
GUIMET MUSEUM OF THE ORIENTAL, MARCH 13TH, 1905.
AND WHAT DOES IT MEAN, THIS NAME?
"THE DAWN." WELL, I AM TOLD THAT'S IT'S MEANING.
YOU WERE TOLD? ARE YOU NOT INDIAN?
WOULD IT MATTER IF I WERE NOT?
MESSIEURS-DAMES, WELCOME!
WORD REACHED ME OF A WOMAN FROM THE FAR EAST, A PRINCESS OF JAVA.
SHE BRINGS SACRED MYSTERIES FROM ORIENTAL TEMPLES. MUSEE GUIMET IS PROUD TO HOST HER DEBUT TONIGHT. I GIVE YOU...
"OOH, LOOK, IT'S MATA HARI!"

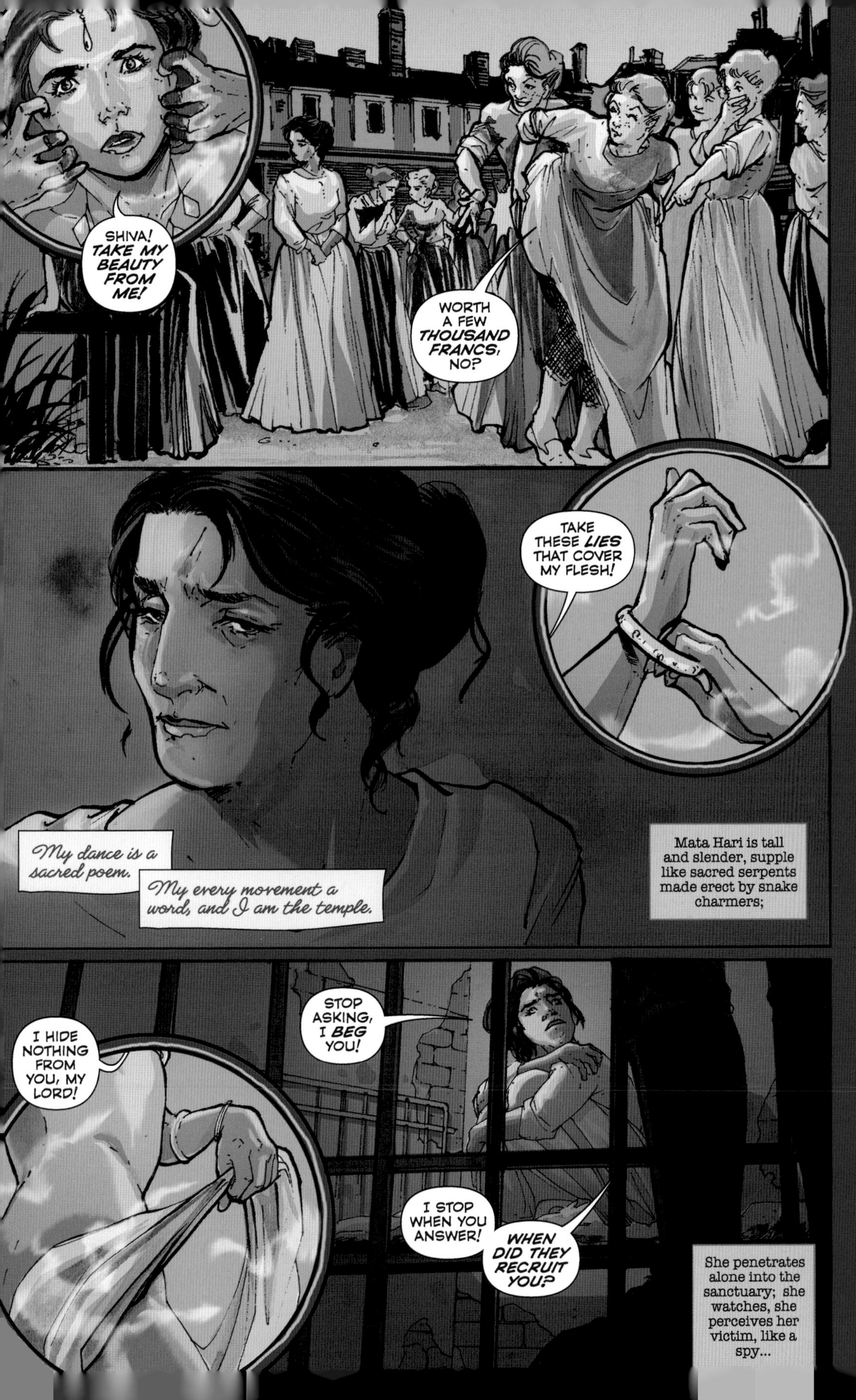
SHIVA! TAKE MY BEAUTY FROM ME!
WORTH A FEW THOUSAND FRANCS, NO?
TAKE THESE LIES THAT COVER MY FLESH!
My dance is a sacred poem.
My every movement a word, and I am the temple.
Mata Hari is tall and slender, supple like sacred serpents made erect by snake charmers;
I HIDE NOTHING FROM YOU, MY LORD!
STOP ASKING, I BEG YOU!
I STOP WHEN YOU ANSWER!
WHEN DID THEY RECRUIT YOU?
She penetrates alone into the sanctuary; she watches, she perceives her victim, like a spy...

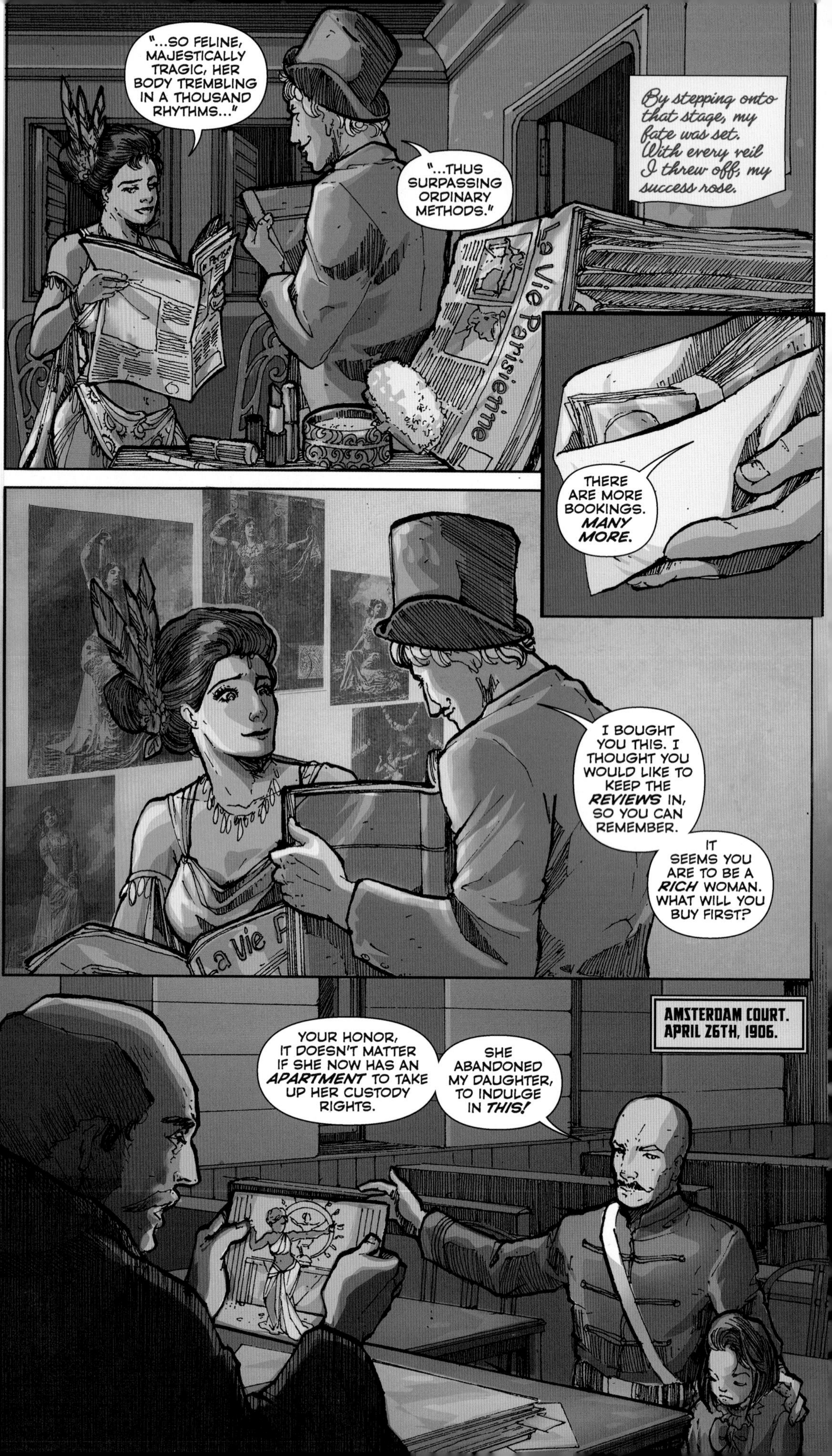

"...SO FELINE, MAJESTICALLY TRAGIC, HER BODY TREMBLING IN A THOUSAND RHYTHMS..."
"...THUS SURPASSING ORDINARY METHODS."
By stepping onto that stage, my fate was set. With every veil I threw off, my success rose.
La Vie Parisienne
THERE ARE MORE BOOKINGS. MANY MORE.
I BOUGHT YOU THIS. I THOUGHT YOU WOULD LIKE TO KEEP THE REVIEWS IN, SO YOU CAN REMEMBER.
IT SEEMS YOU ARE TO BE A RICH WOMAN. WHAT WILL YOU BUY FIRST?
La Vie P
AMSTERDAM COURT. APRIL 26TH, 1906.
YOUR HONOR, IT DOESN'T MATTER IF SHE NOW HAS AN APARTMENT TO TAKE UP HER CUSTODY RIGHTS.
SHE ABANDONED MY DAUGHTER, TO INDULGE IN THIS!

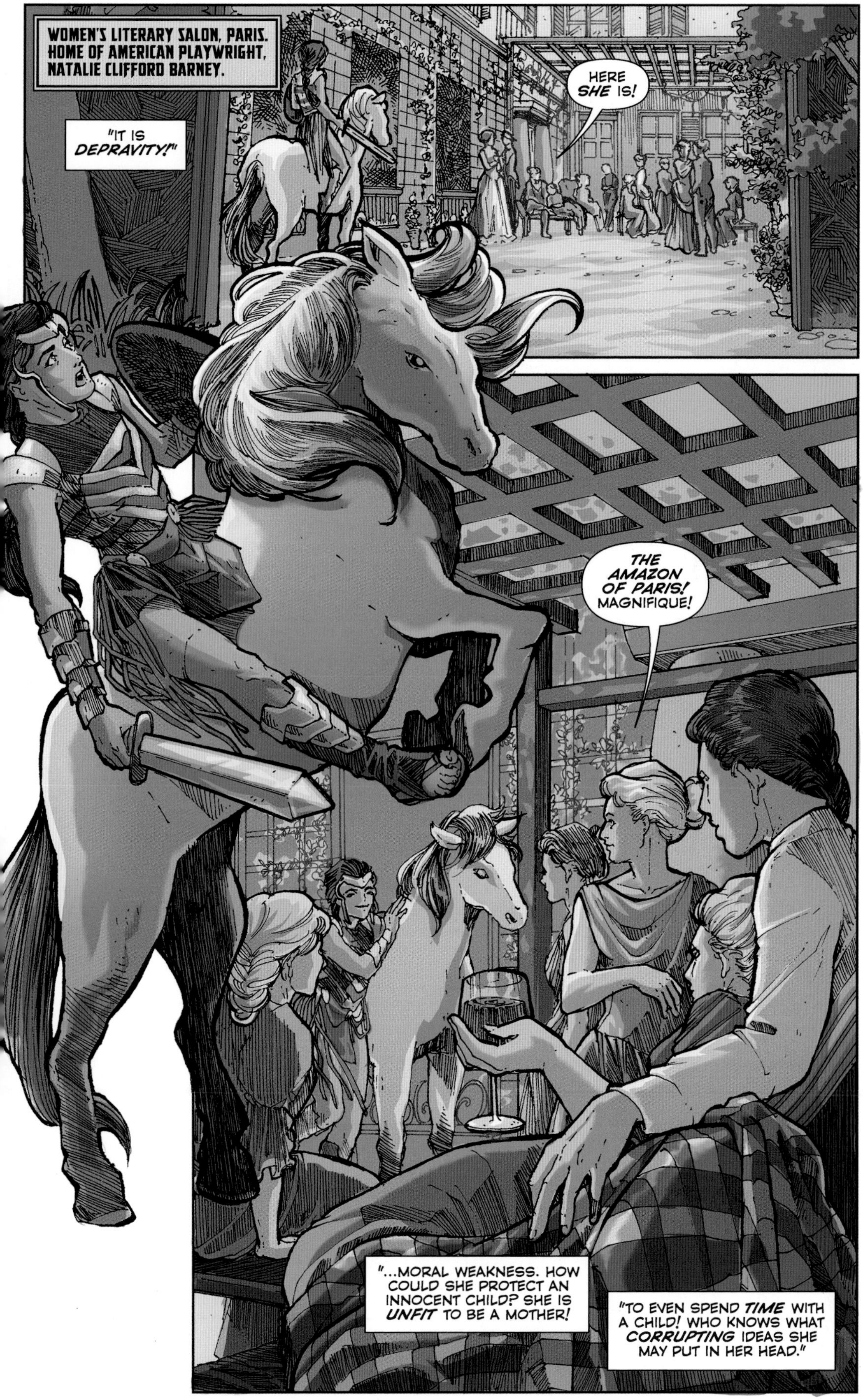
WOMEN'S LITERARY SALON, PARIS. HOME OF AMERICAN PLAYWRIGHT, NATALIE CLIFFORD BARNEY.
"IT IS DEPRAVITY!"
HERE SHE IS!
THE AMAZON OF PARIS! MAGNIFIQUE!
"...MORAL WEAKNESS. HOW COULD SHE PROTECT AN INNOCENT CHILD? SHE IS UNFIT TO BE A MOTHER!
"TO EVEN SPEND TIME WITH A CHILD! WHO KNOWS WHAT CORRUPTING IDEAS SHE MAY PUT IN HER HEAD."

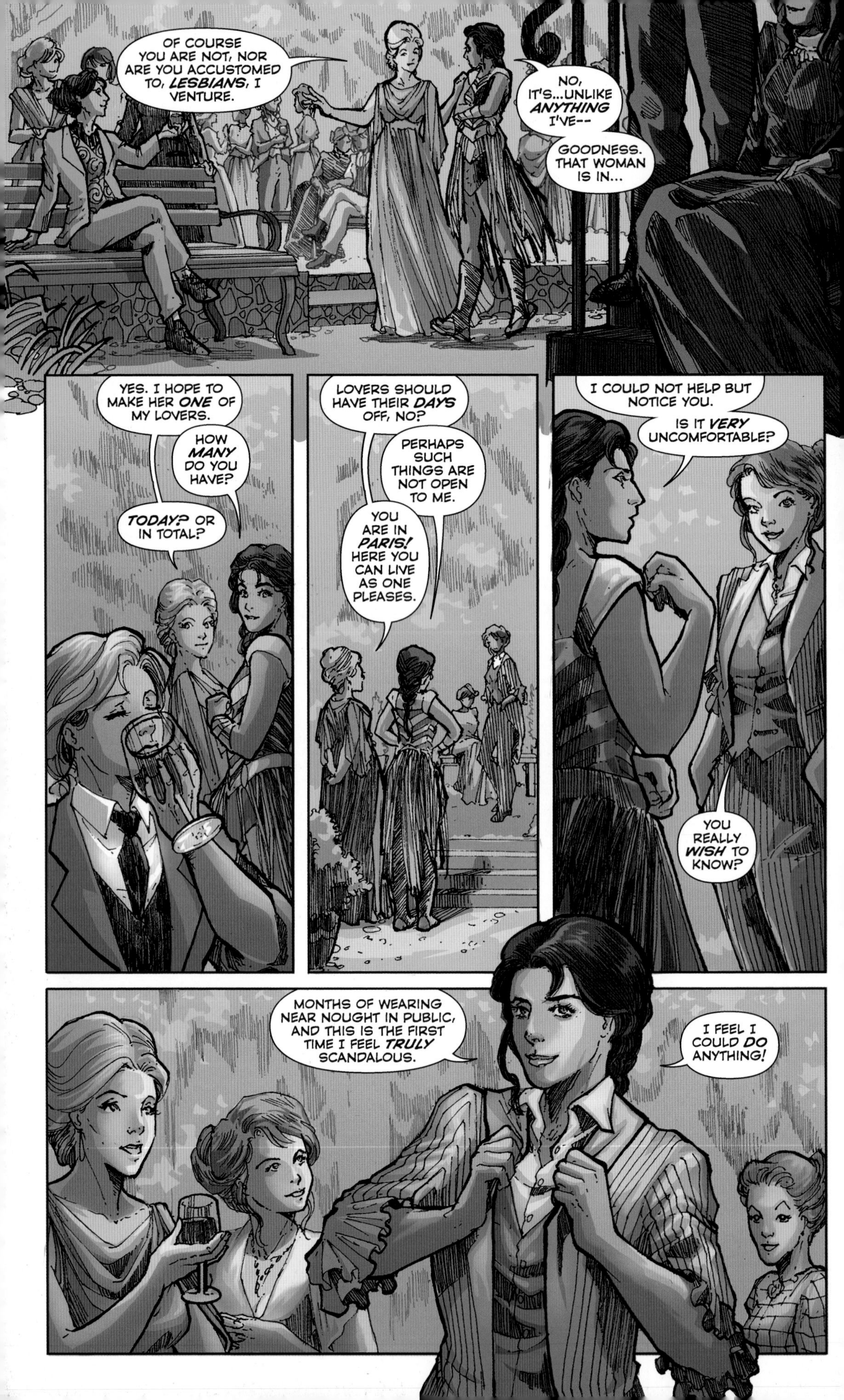
OF COURSE YOU ARE NOT, NOR ARE YOU ACCUSTOMED TO, *LESBIANS*, I VENTURE.
NO, IT'S...UNLIKE *ANYTHING* I'VE--
GOODNESS. THAT WOMAN IS IN...
YES. I HOPE TO MAKE HER *ONE* OF MY LOVERS.
HOW *MANY* DO YOU HAVE?
TODAY? OR IN TOTAL?
LOVERS SHOULD HAVE THEIR *DAYS* OFF, NO?
PERHAPS SUCH THINGS ARE NOT OPEN TO ME.
YOU ARE IN *PARIS!* HERE YOU CAN LIVE AS ONE PLEASES.
I COULD NOT HELP BUT NOTICE YOU.
IS IT *VERY* UNCOMFORTABLE?
YOU REALLY *WISH* TO KNOW?
MONTHS OF WEARING NEAR NOUGHT IN PUBLIC, AND THIS IS THE FIRST TIME I FEEL *TRULY* SCANDALOUS.
I FEEL I COULD *DO* ANYTHING!

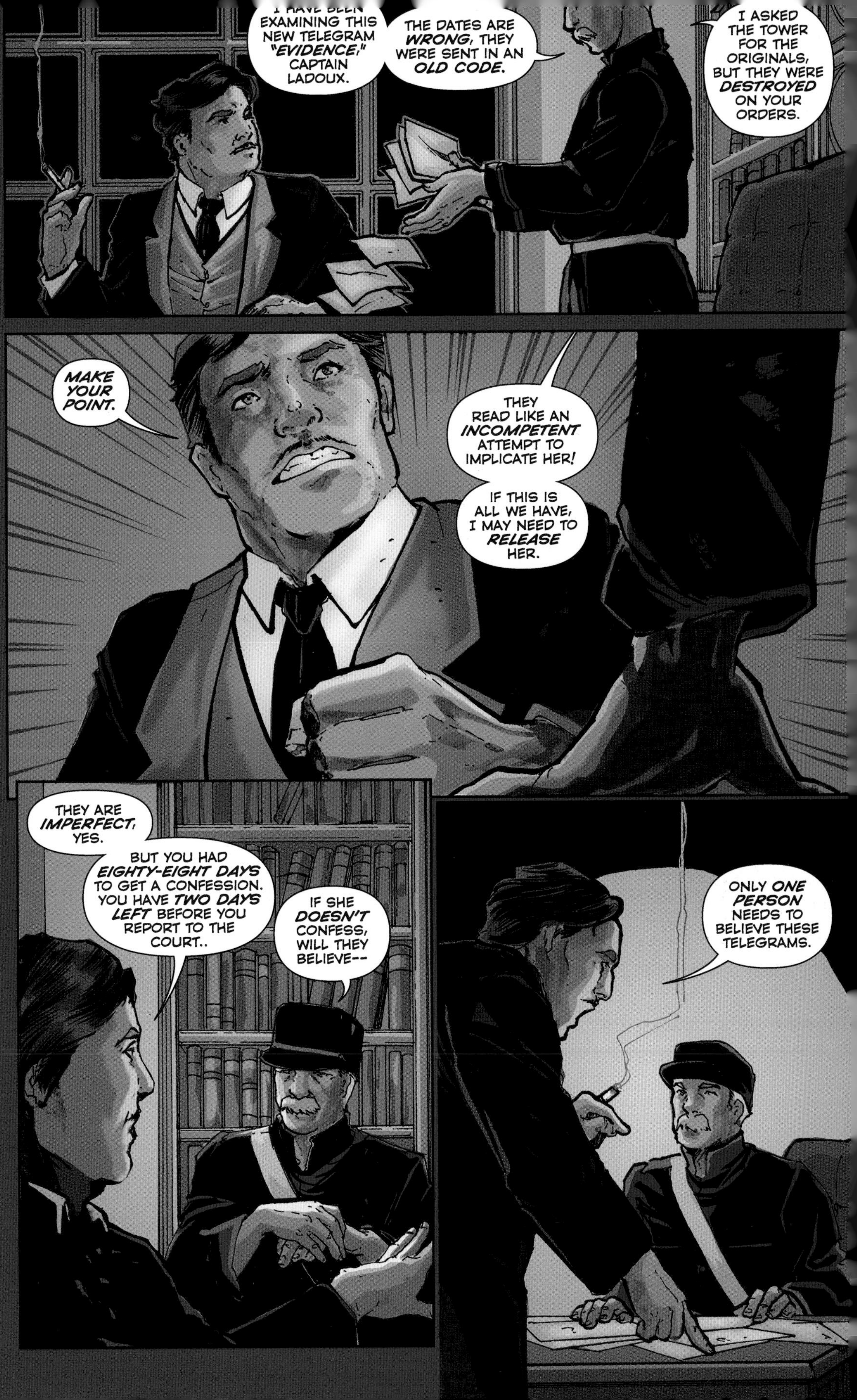
EXAMINING THIS NEW TELEGRAM "EVIDENCE," CAPTAIN LADOUX.
THE DATES ARE WRONG, THEY WERE SENT IN AN OLD CODE.
I ASKED THE TOWER FOR THE ORIGINALS, BUT THEY WERE DESTROYED ON YOUR ORDERS.
MAKE YOUR POINT.
THEY READ LIKE AN INCOMPETENT ATTEMPT TO IMPLICATE HER!
IF THIS IS ALL WE HAVE, I MAY NEED TO RELEASE HER.
THEY ARE IMPERFECT, YES.
BUT YOU HAD EIGHTY-EIGHT DAYS TO GET A CONFESSION. YOU HAVE TWO DAYS LEFT BEFORE YOU REPORT TO THE COURT..
IF SHE DOESN'T CONFESS, WILL THEY BELIEVE--
ONLY ONE PERSON NEEDS TO BELIEVE THESE TELEGRAMS.

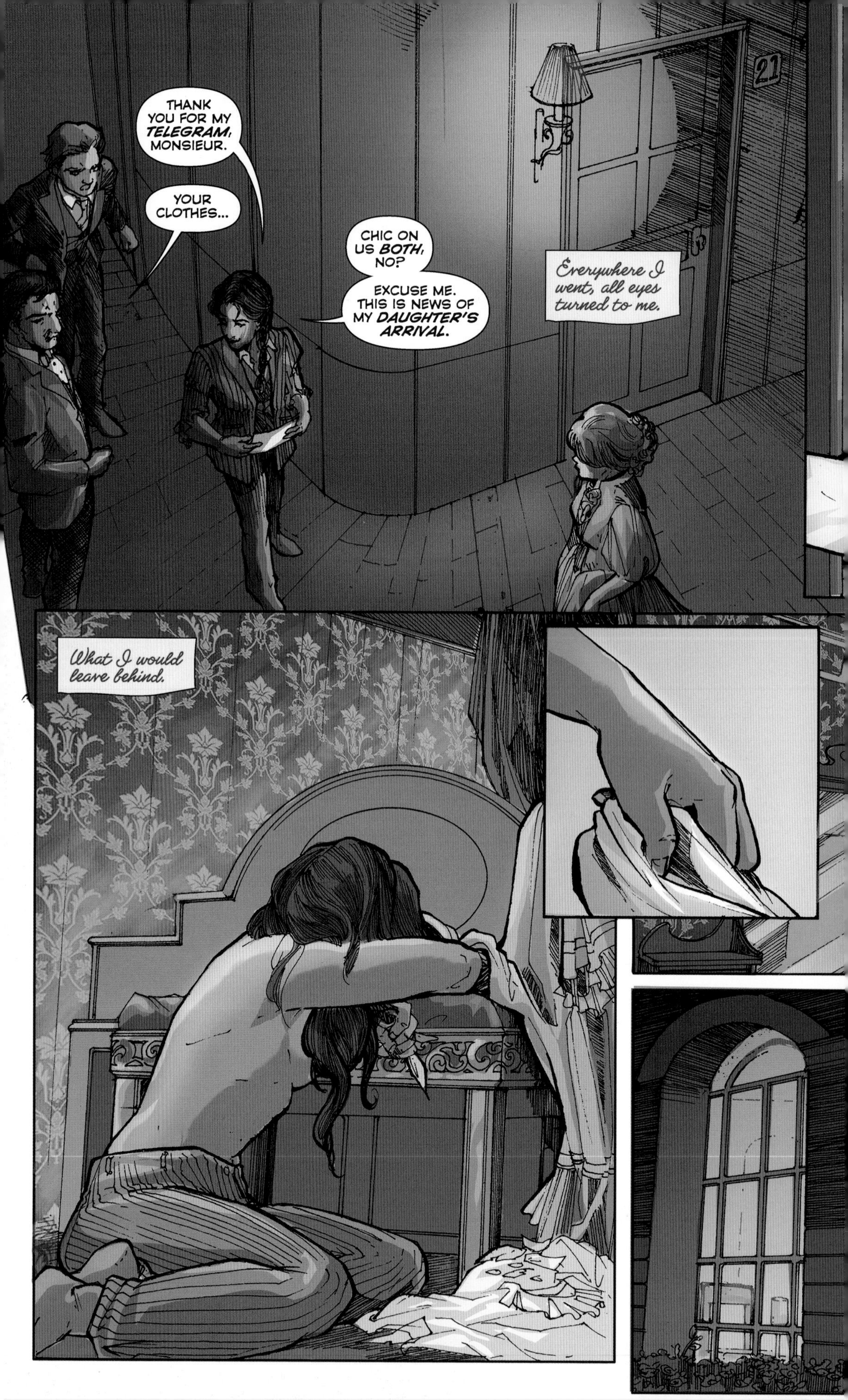
THANK YOU FOR MY *TELEGRAM*, MONSIEUR.
YOUR CLOTHES...
CHIC ON US *BOTH*, NO?
EXCUSE ME. THIS IS NEWS OF MY *DAUGHTER'S ARRIVAL*.
Everywhere I went, all eyes turned to me.
What I would leave behind.

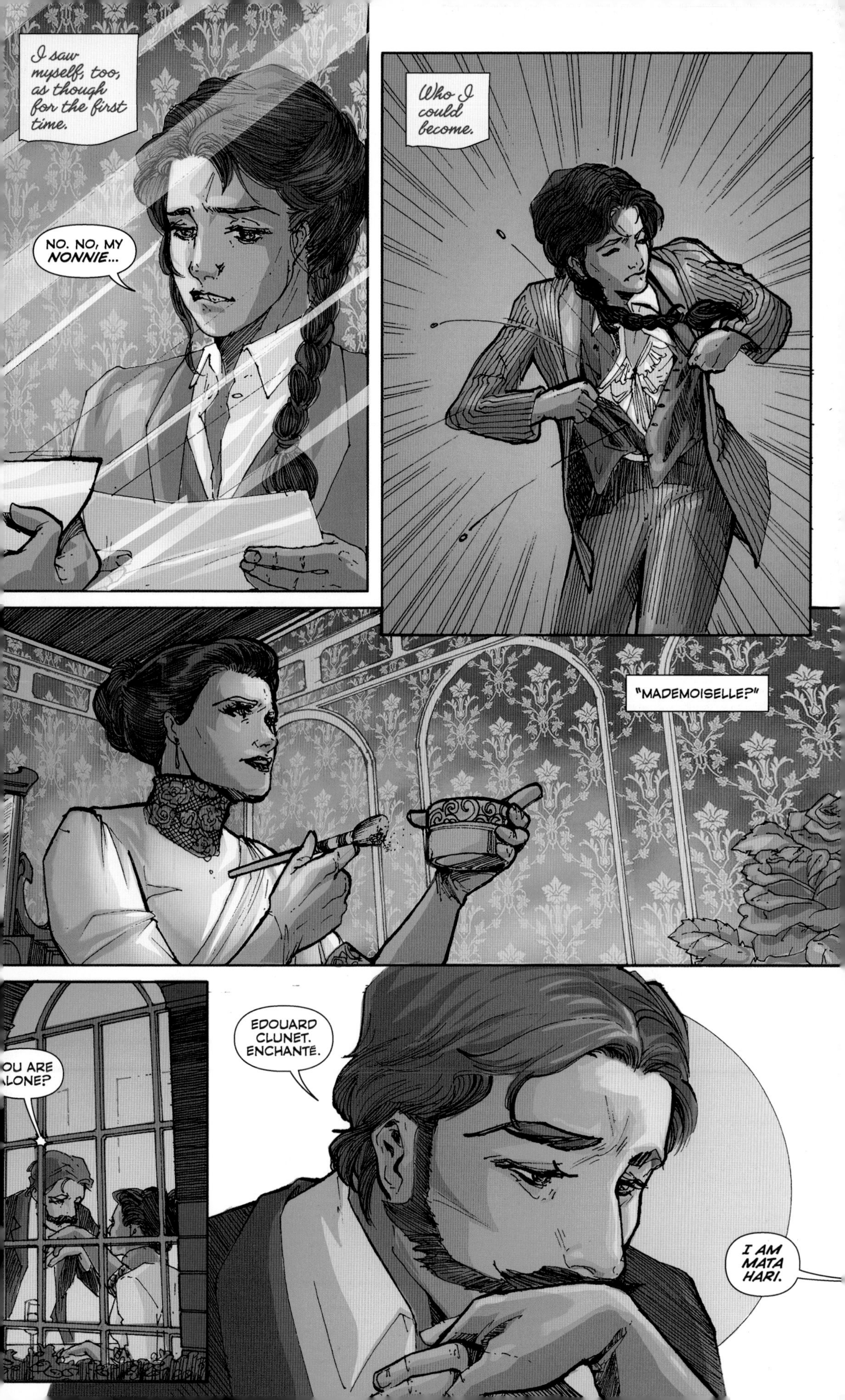
I saw myself, too, as though for the first time.
NO. NO, MY NONNIE...
Who I could become.
"MADEMOISELLE?"
OU ARE
LONE?
EDOUARD CLUNET. ENCHANTÉ.
I AM MATA HARI.

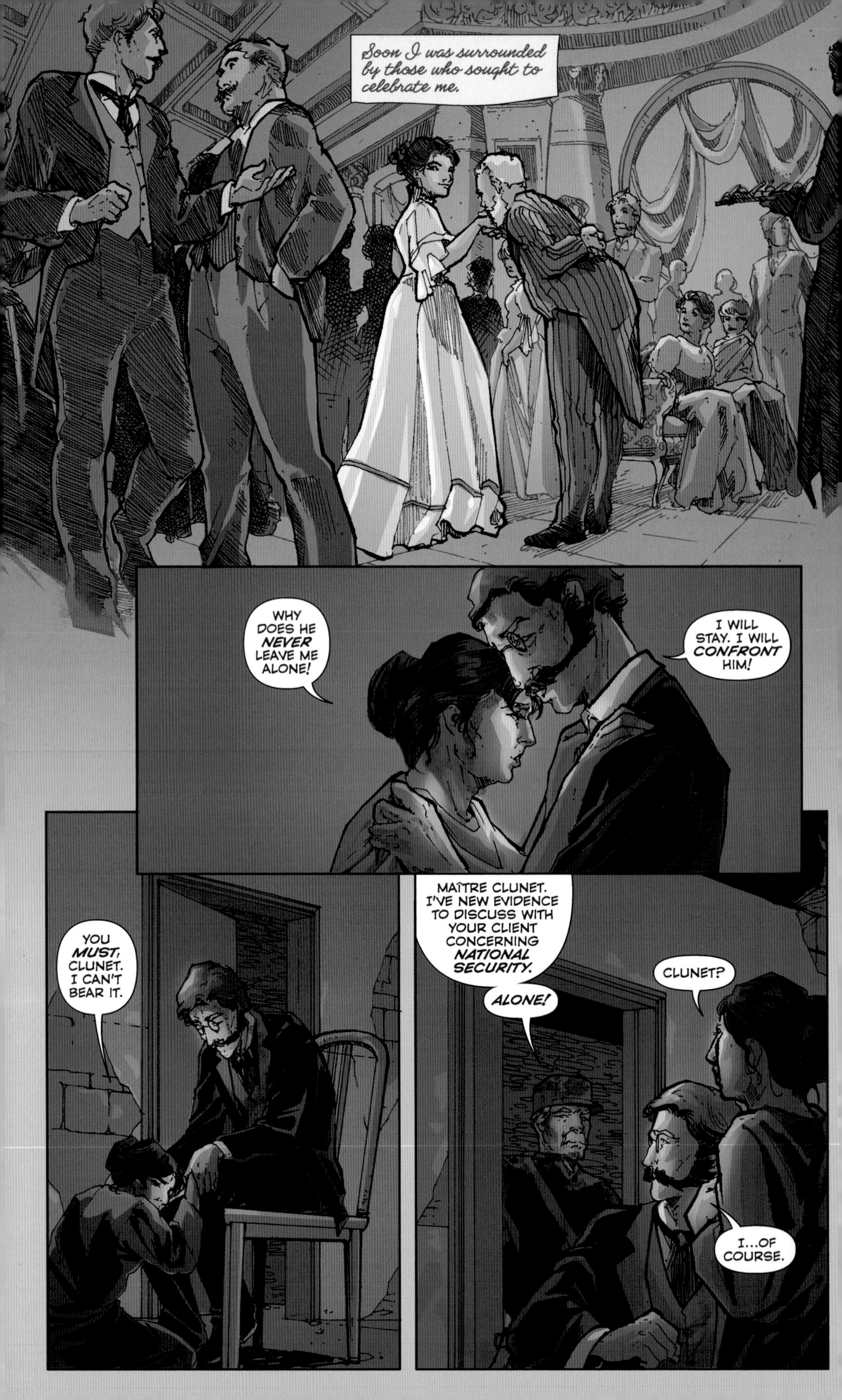
Soon I was surrounded by those who sought to celebrate me.
WHY DOES HE *NEVER* LEAVE ME ALONE!
I WILL STAY. I WILL *CONFRONT* HIM!
YOU *MUST*, CLUNET. I CAN'T BEAR IT.
MAÎTRE CLUNET. I'VE NEW EVIDENCE TO DISCUSS WITH YOUR CLIENT CONCERNING *NATIONAL SECURITY.*
ALONE!
CLUNET?
I...OF COURSE.

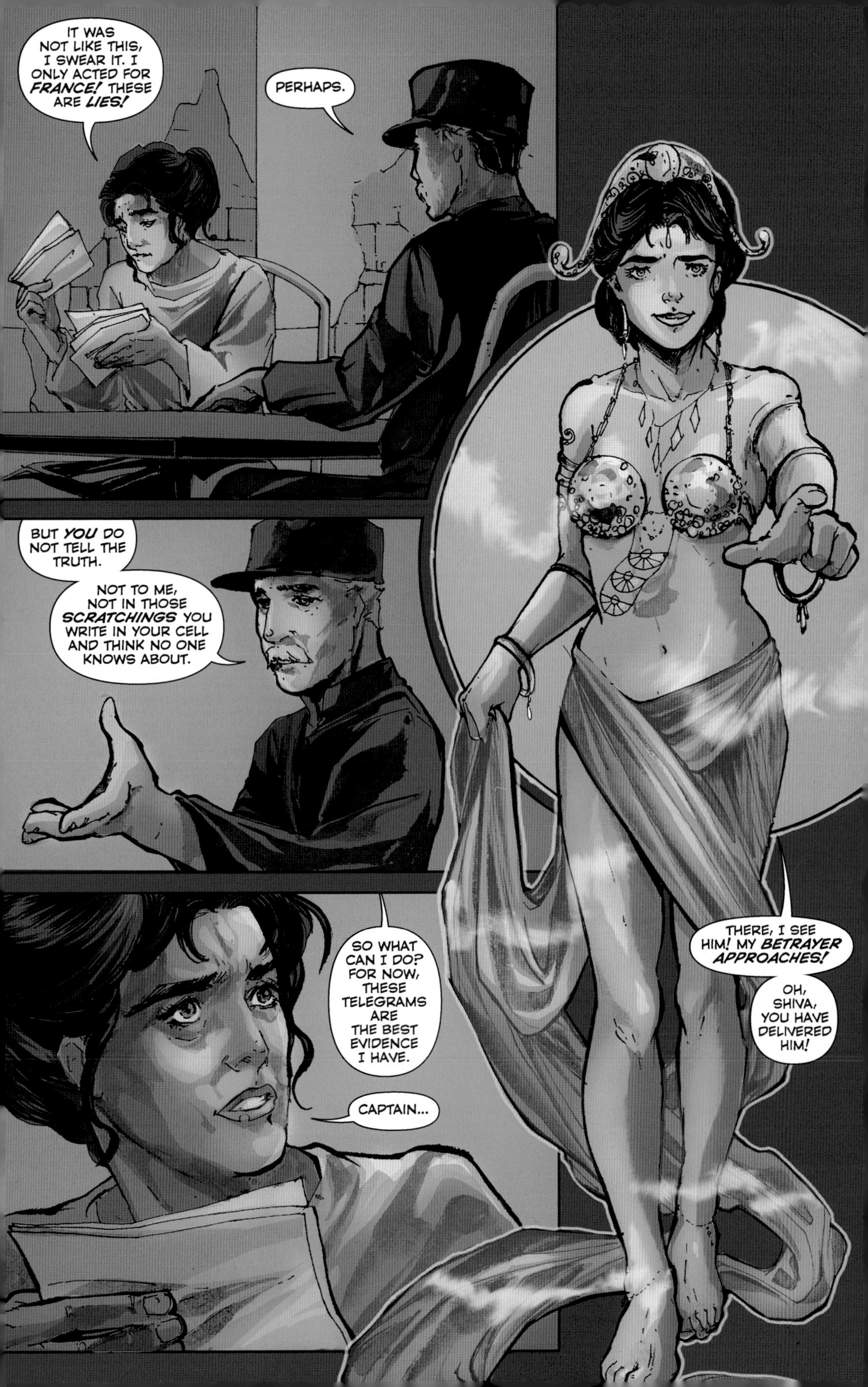
IT WAS NOT LIKE THIS, I SWEAR IT. I ONLY ACTED FOR *FRANCE!* THESE ARE *LIES!*
PERHAPS.
BUT *YOU* DO NOT TELL THE TRUTH.
NOT TO ME, NOT IN THOSE *SCRATCHINGS* YOU WRITE IN YOUR CELL AND THINK NO ONE KNOWS ABOUT.
SO WHAT CAN I DO? FOR NOW, THESE TELEGRAMS ARE THE BEST EVIDENCE I HAVE.
CAPTAIN...
THERE, I SEE HIM! MY *BETRAYER APPROACHES!*
OH, SHIVA, YOU HAVE DELIVERED HIM!

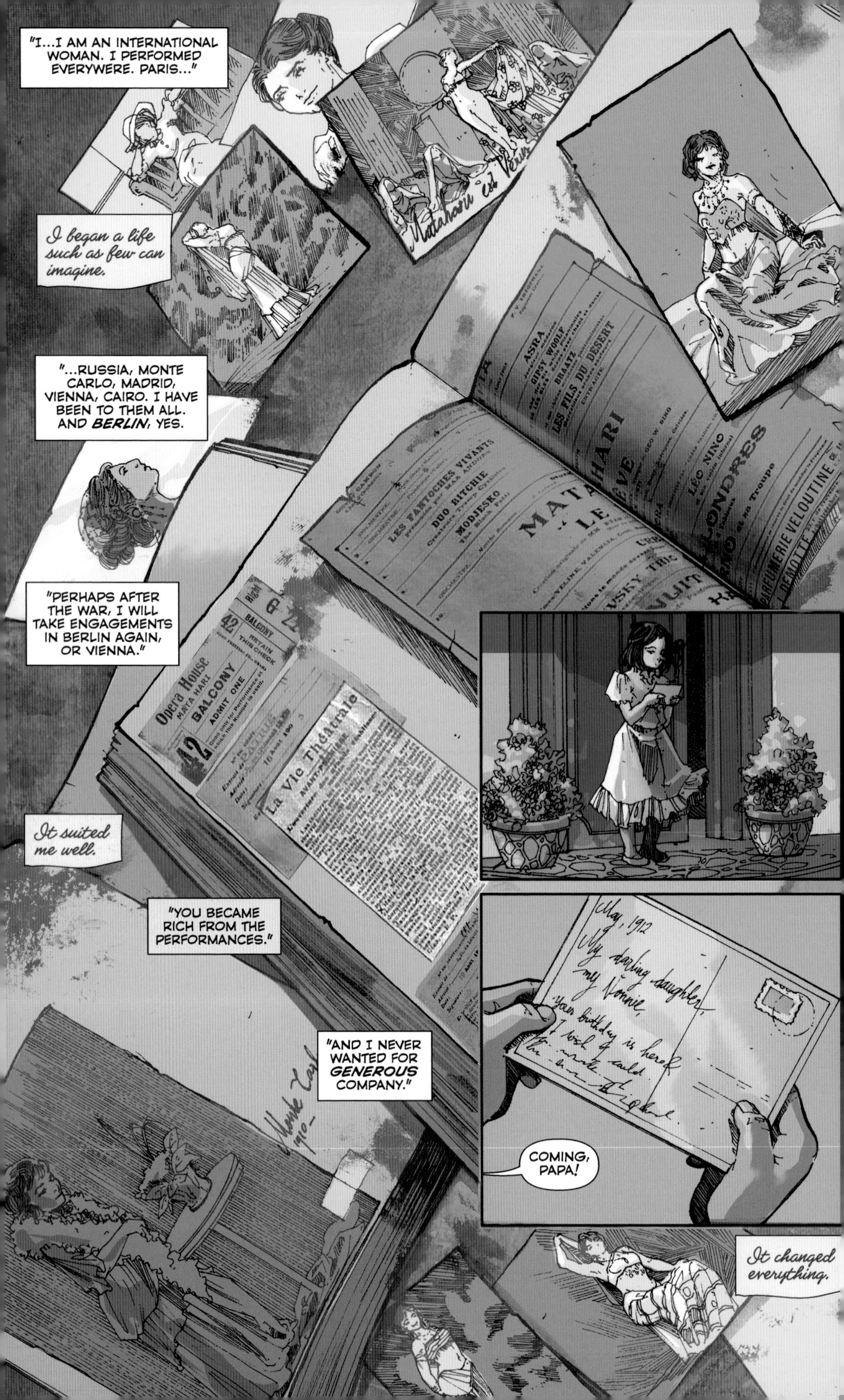
"I...I AM AN INTERNATIONAL WOMAN. I PERFORMED EVERYWERE. PARIS..."
I began a life such as few can imagine.
"...RUSSIA, MONTE CARLO, MADRID, VIENNA, CAIRO. I HAVE BEEN TO THEM ALL. AND BERLIN, YES.
"PERHAPS AFTER THE WAR, I WILL TAKE ENGAGEMENTS IN BERLIN AGAIN, OR VIENNA."
It suited me well.
"YOU BECAME RICH FROM THE PERFORMANCES."
"AND I NEVER WANTED FOR GENEROUS COMPANY."
May, 1912
My darling daughter,
my Nonnie,
Your birthday is here
COMING, PAPA!
It changed everything.

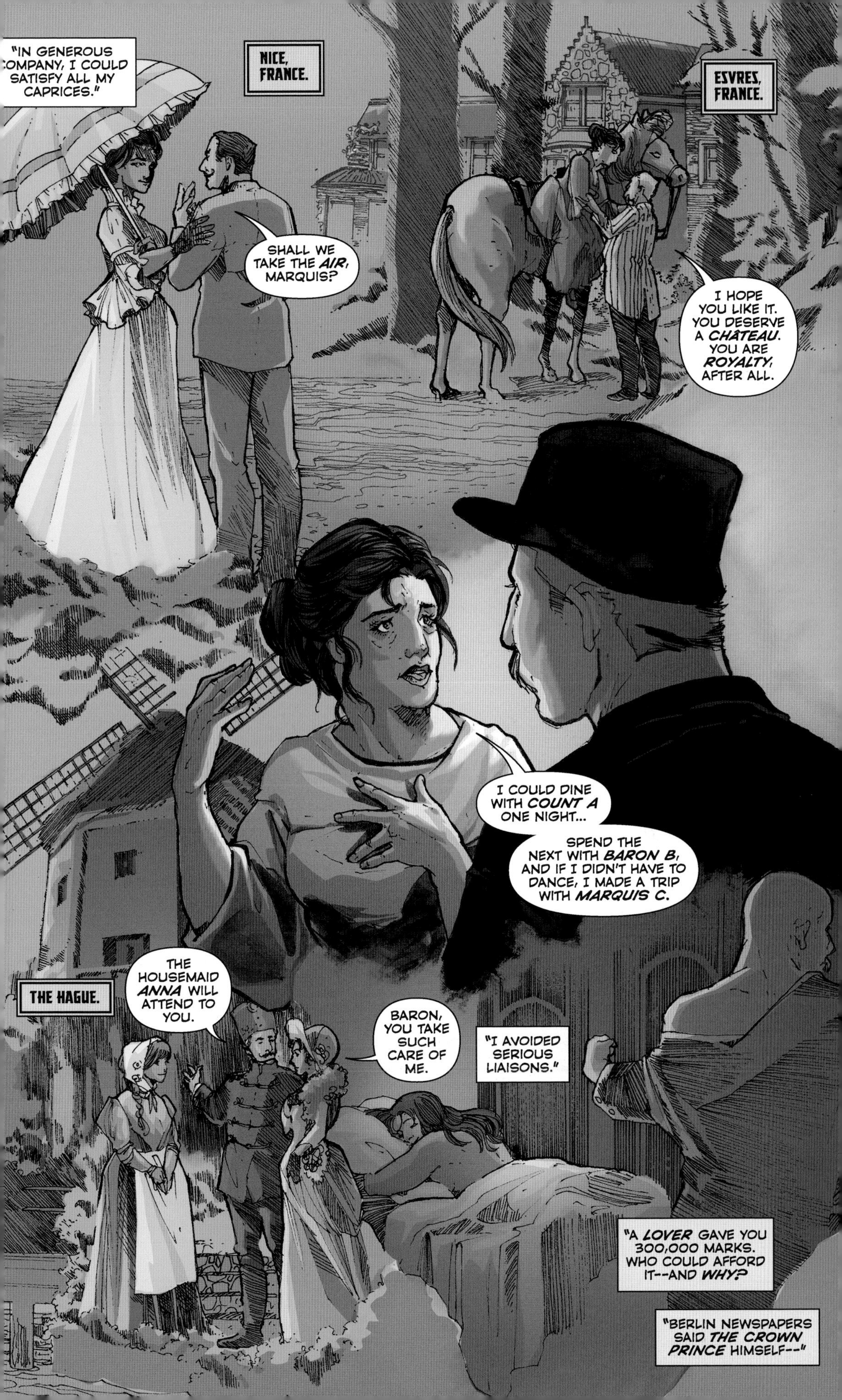
"IN GENEROUS COMPANY, I COULD SATISFY ALL MY CAPRICES."
NICE, FRANCE.
SHALL WE TAKE THE AIR, MARQUIS?
ESVRES, FRANCE.
I HOPE YOU LIKE IT. YOU DESERVE A CHÂTEAU. YOU ARE ROYALTY, AFTER ALL.
I COULD DINE WITH COUNT A ONE NIGHT...
SPEND THE NEXT WITH BARON B, AND IF I DIDN'T HAVE TO DANCE, I MADE A TRIP WITH MARQUIS C.
THE HAGUE.
THE HOUSEMAID ANNA WILL ATTEND TO YOU.
BARON, YOU TAKE SUCH CARE OF ME.
"I AVOIDED SERIOUS LIAISONS."
"A LOVER GAVE YOU 300,000 MARKS. WHO COULD AFFORD IT--AND WHY?
"BERLIN NEWSPAPERS SAID THE CROWN PRINCE HIMSELF--"

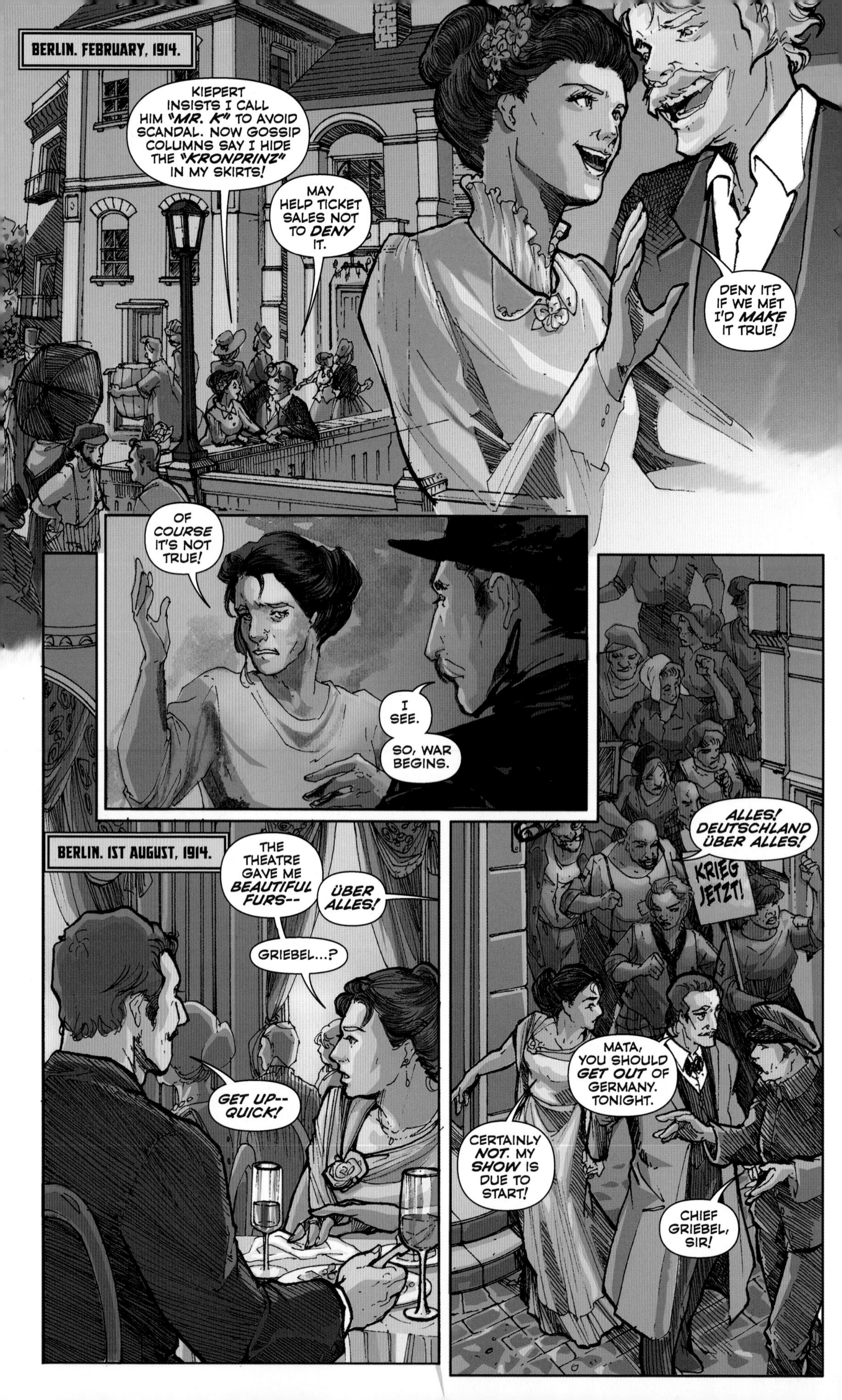
BERLIN. FEBRUARY, 1914.
KIEPERT INSISTS I CALL HIM "MR. K" TO AVOID SCANDAL. NOW GOSSIP COLUMNS SAY I HIDE THE "KRONPRINZ" IN MY SKIRTS!
MAY HELP TICKET SALES NOT TO DENY IT.
DENY IT? IF WE MET I'D MAKE IT TRUE!
OF COURSE IT'S NOT TRUE!
I SEE.
SO, WAR BEGINS.
BERLIN. 1ST AUGUST, 1914.
THE THEATRE GAVE ME BEAUTIFUL FURS--
ÜBER ALLES!
GRIEBEL...?
GET UP-- QUICK!
ALLES! DEUTSCHLAND ÜBER ALLES!
KRIEG JETZT!
MATA, YOU SHOULD GET OUT OF GERMANY. TONIGHT.
CERTAINLY NOT. MY SHOW IS DUE TO START!
CHIEF GRIEBEL, SIR!

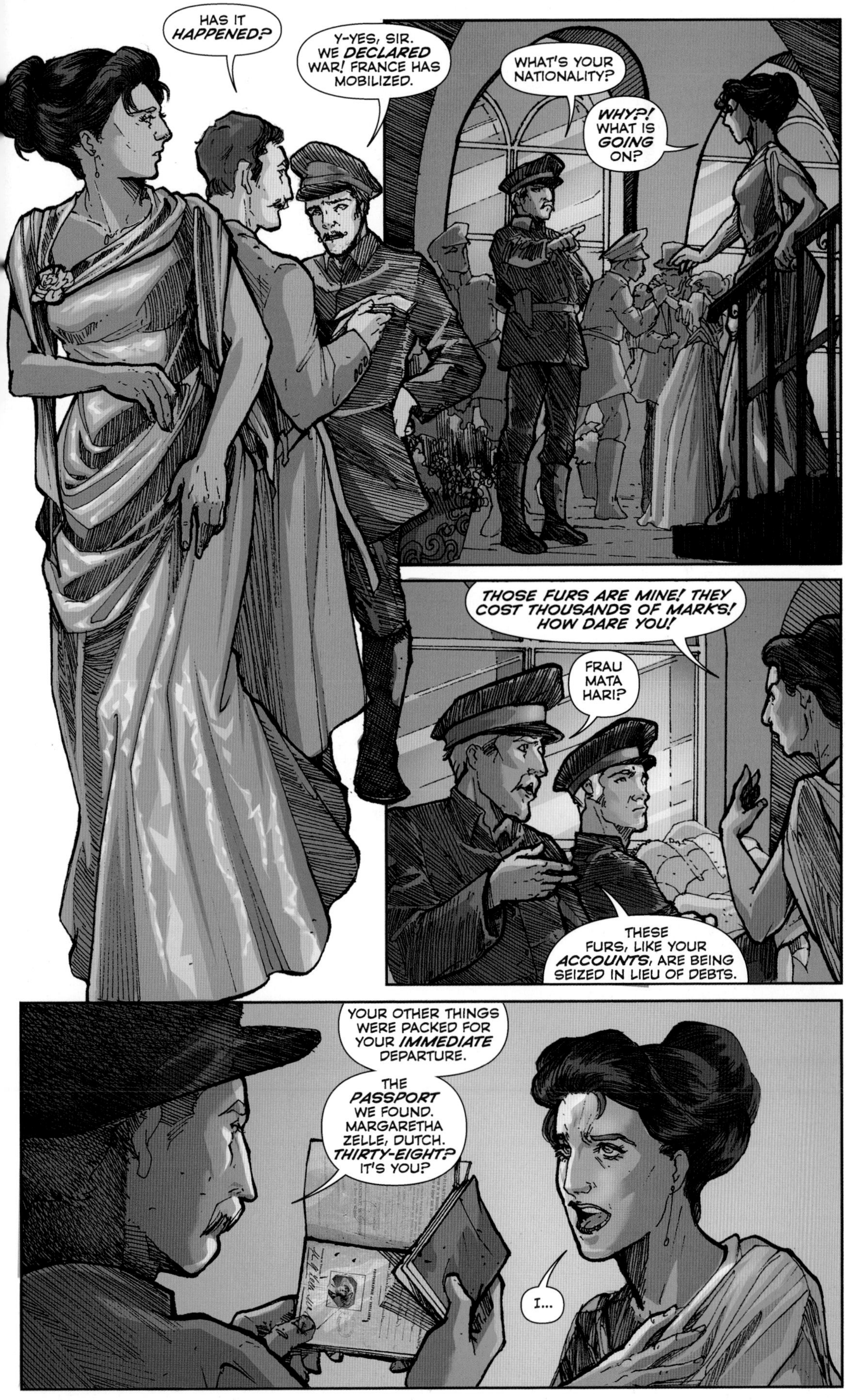

HAS IT *HAPPENED?*
Y-YES, SIR. WE *DECLARED* WAR! FRANCE HAS MOBILIZED.
WHAT'S YOUR NATIONALITY?
WHY?! WHAT IS *GOING* ON?
THOSE FURS ARE MINE! THEY COST THOUSANDS OF MARKS! HOW DARE YOU!
FRAU MATA HARI?
THESE FURS, LIKE YOUR *ACCOUNTS*, ARE BEING SEIZED IN LIEU OF DEBTS.
YOUR OTHER THINGS WERE PACKED FOR YOUR *IMMEDIATE* DEPARTURE.
THE *PASSPORT* WE FOUND. MARGARETHA ZELLE, DUTCH. *THIRTY-EIGHT?* IT'S YOU?
I...

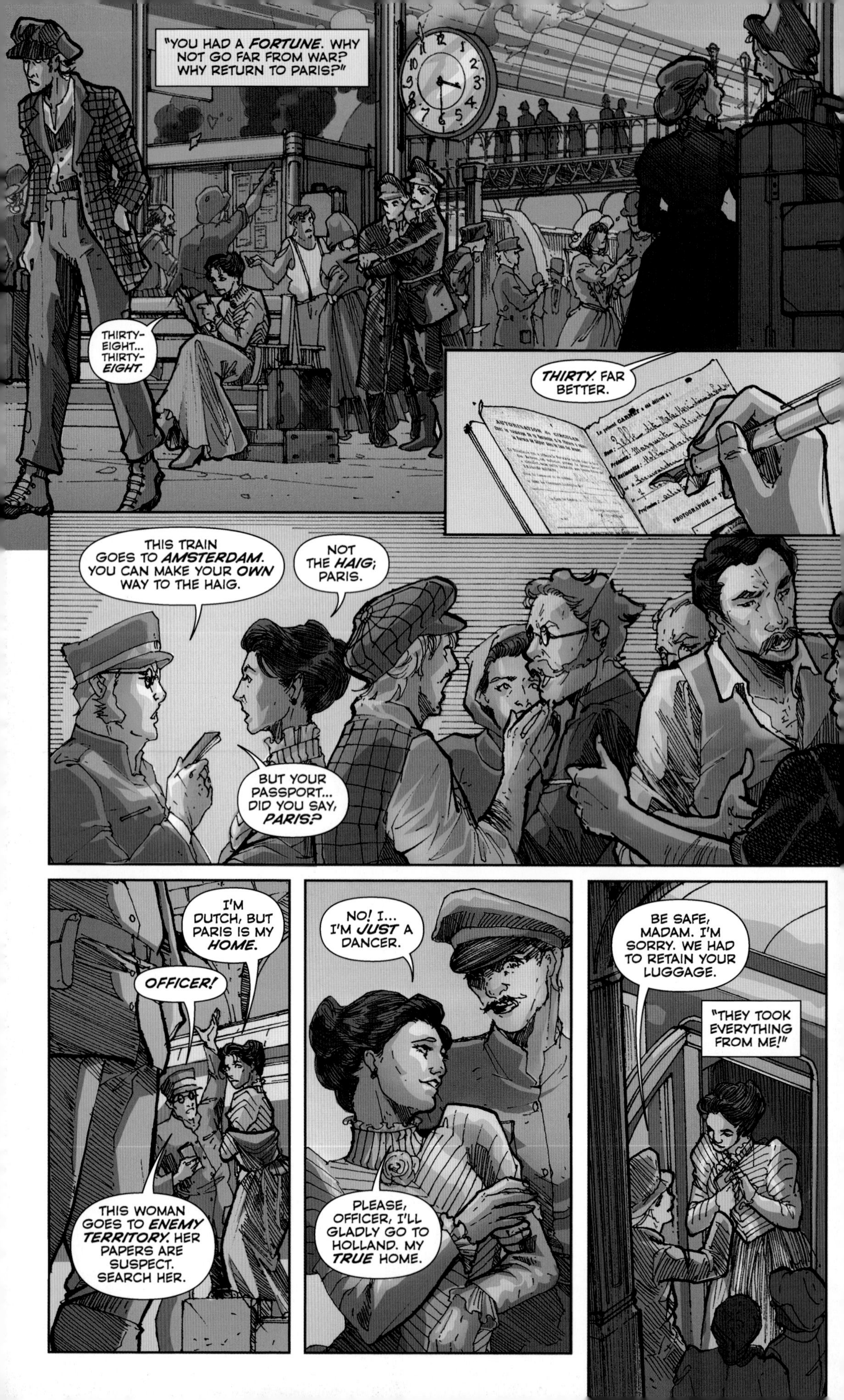
"YOU HAD A FORTUNE. WHY NOT GO FAR FROM WAR? WHY RETURN TO PARIS?"
THIRTY-EIGHT... THIRTY-EIGHT.
THIRTY. FAR BETTER.
THIS TRAIN GOES TO AMSTERDAM. YOU CAN MAKE YOUR OWN WAY TO THE HAIG.
NOT THE HAIG; PARIS.
BUT YOUR PASSPORT... DID YOU SAY, PARIS?
I'M DUTCH, BUT PARIS IS MY HOME.
OFFICER!
THIS WOMAN GOES TO ENEMY TERRITORY. HER PAPERS ARE SUSPECT. SEARCH HER.
NO! I... I'M JUST A DANCER.
PLEASE, OFFICER, I'LL GLADLY GO TO HOLLAND. MY TRUE HOME.
BE SAFE, MADAM. I'M SORRY. WE HAD TO RETAIN YOUR LUGGAGE.
"THEY TOOK EVERYTHING FROM ME!"

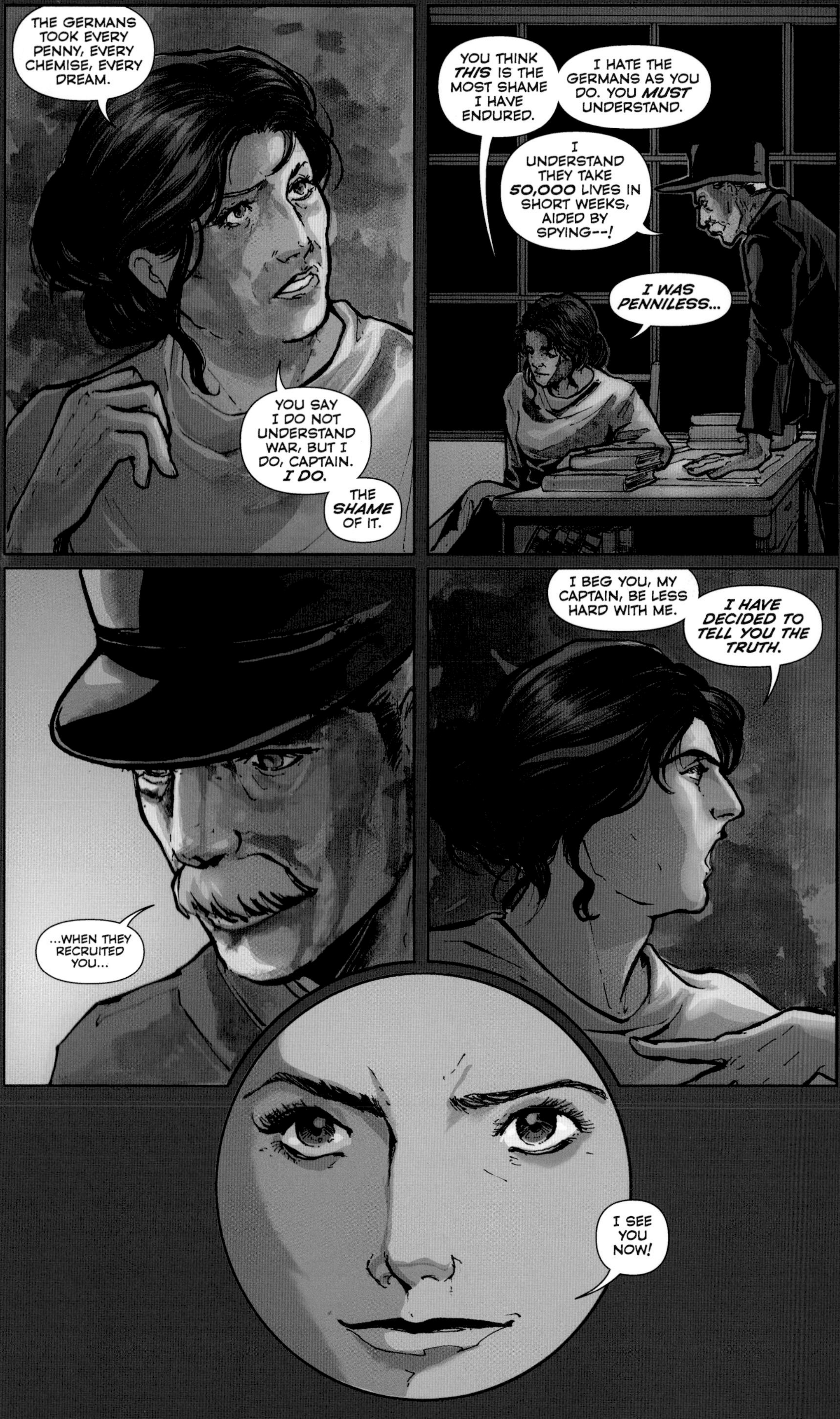
THE GERMANS TOOK EVERY PENNY, EVERY CHEMISE, EVERY DREAM.
YOU SAY I DO NOT UNDERSTAND WAR, BUT I DO, CAPTAIN. *I DO.*
THE *SHAME* OF IT.
YOU THINK *THIS* IS THE MOST SHAME I HAVE ENDURED.
I HATE THE GERMANS AS YOU DO. YOU *MUST* UNDERSTAND.
I UNDERSTAND THEY TAKE *50,000* LIVES IN SHORT WEEKS, AIDED BY SPYING--!
I WAS PENNILESS...
...WHEN THEY RECRUITED YOU...
I BEG YOU, MY CAPTAIN, BE LESS HARD WITH ME.
I HAVE DECIDED TO TELL YOU THE TRUTH.
I SEE YOU NOW!

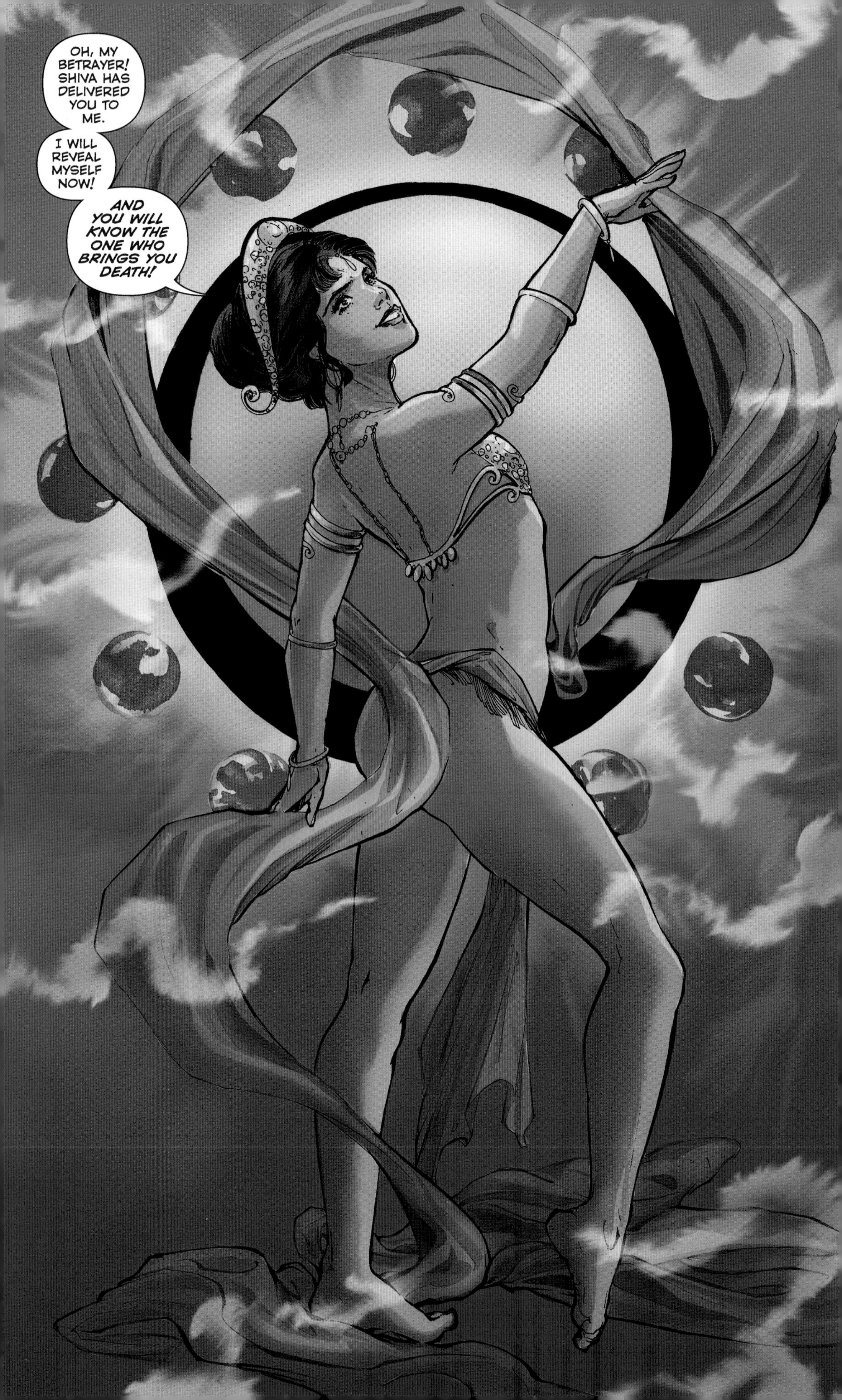
OH, MY BETRAYER! SHIVA HAS DELIVERED YOU TO ME.
I WILL REVEAL MYSELF NOW!
AND YOU WILL KNOW THE ONE WHO BRINGS YOU DEATH!

CHAPTER FIVE
BARE·ALL

"Ah! The wanton! The harlot!
Ah! The daughter of Babylon
with her golden eyes and her gilded eyelids!
Let the war captains pierce her with their swords,
let them crush her beneath their shields.
It is thus that I will wipe out all wickedness
from the earth, and that all women
shall learn not to imitate her abominations."

SALOMÉ:
A TRAGEDY IN ONE ACT
~ OSCAR WILDE ~

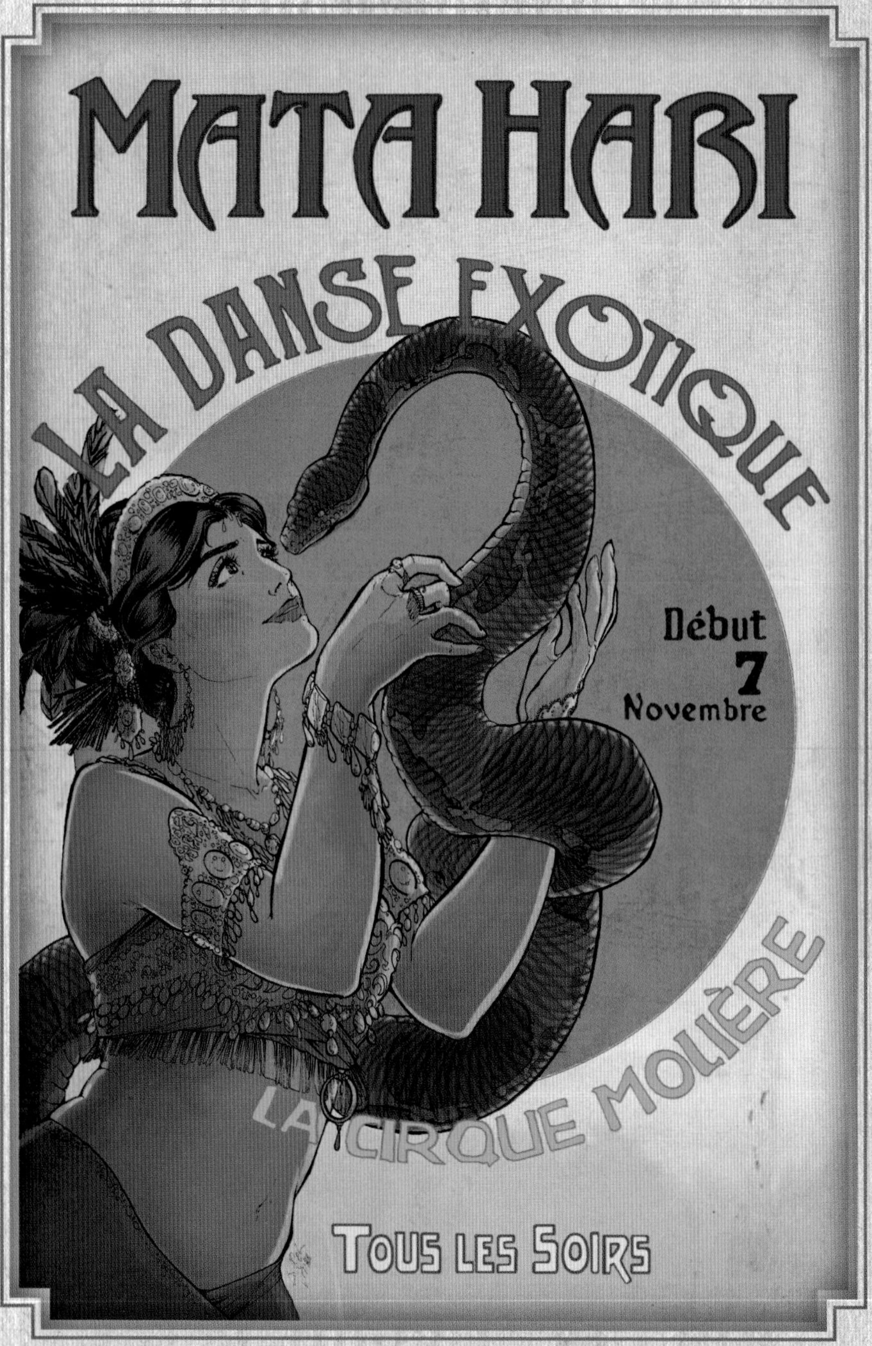
MATA HARI
LA DANSE EXOTIQUE
Début
7
Novembre
LA CIRQUE MOLIÈRE
TOUS LES SOIRS

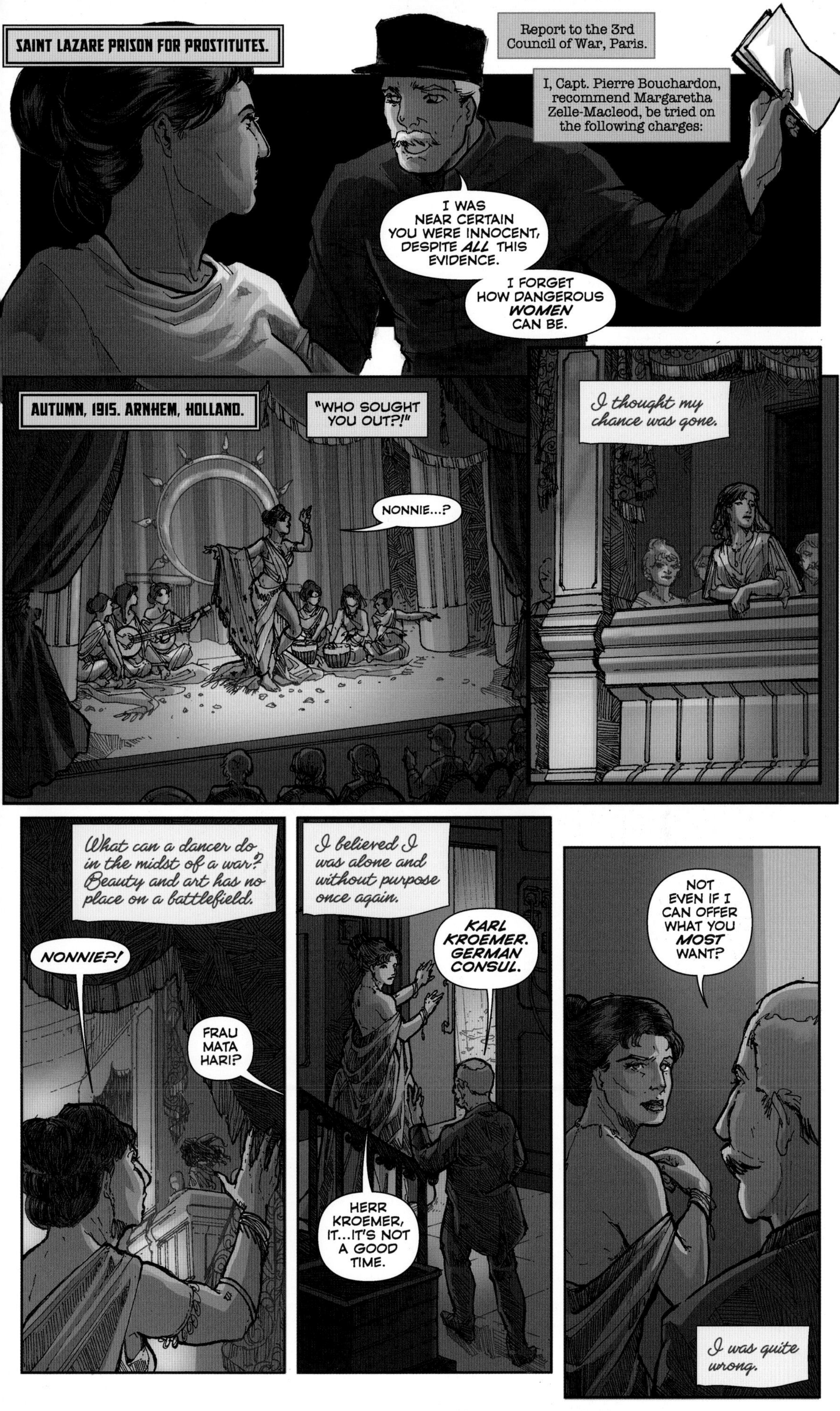

SAINT LAZARE PRISON FOR PROSTITUTES.
Report to the 3rd Council of War, Paris.
I, Capt. Pierre Bouchardon, recommend Margaretha Zelle-Macleod, be tried on the following charges:
I WAS NEAR CERTAIN YOU WERE INNOCENT, DESPITE ALL THIS EVIDENCE.
I FORGET HOW DANGEROUS WOMEN CAN BE.
AUTUMN, 1915. ARNHEM, HOLLAND.
"WHO SOUGHT YOU OUT?!"
NONNIE...?
I thought my chance was gone.
What can a dancer do in the midst of a war? Beauty and art has no place on a battlefield.
NONNIE?!
FRAU MATA HARI?
I believed I was alone and without purpose once again.
KARL KROEMER. GERMAN CONSUL.
HERR KROEMER, IT...IT'S NOT A GOOD TIME.
NOT EVEN IF I CAN OFFER WHAT YOU MOST WANT?
I was quite wrong.

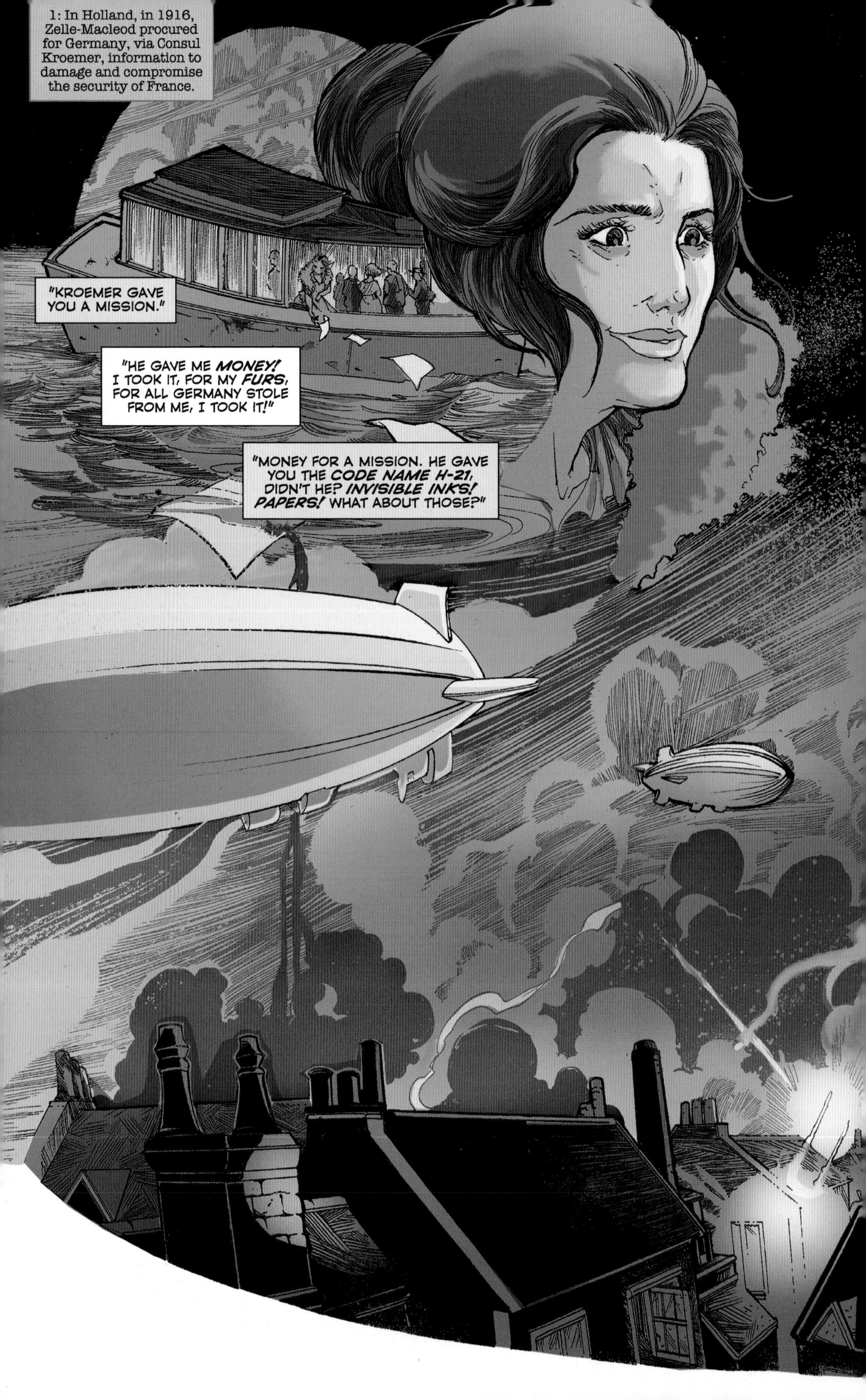
1: In Holland, in 1916, Zelle-Macleod procured for Germany, via Consul Kroemer, information to damage and compromise the security of France.
"KROEMER GAVE YOU A MISSION."
"HE GAVE ME MONEY! I TOOK IT, FOR MY FURS, FOR ALL GERMANY STOLE FROM ME, I TOOK IT!"
"MONEY FOR A MISSION. HE GAVE YOU THE CODE NAME H-21, DIDN'T HE? INVISIBLE INKS! PAPERS! WHAT ABOUT THOSE?"

PARIS, FRANCE. JANUARY, 1916.
"ALL I KNOW IS KROEMER GAVE ME ENOUGH TO RETURN TO MY *BELOVED PARIS*, WHERE ALL WOULD BE NORMAL AGAIN."
COME, MY LOVE, COME INSIDE.
I could do great things in this war. Such things that only a woman can achieve.
If only they had listened to me when I did.
"SHE'S A GERMAN SPY AND SHE'S HERE IN PARIS."

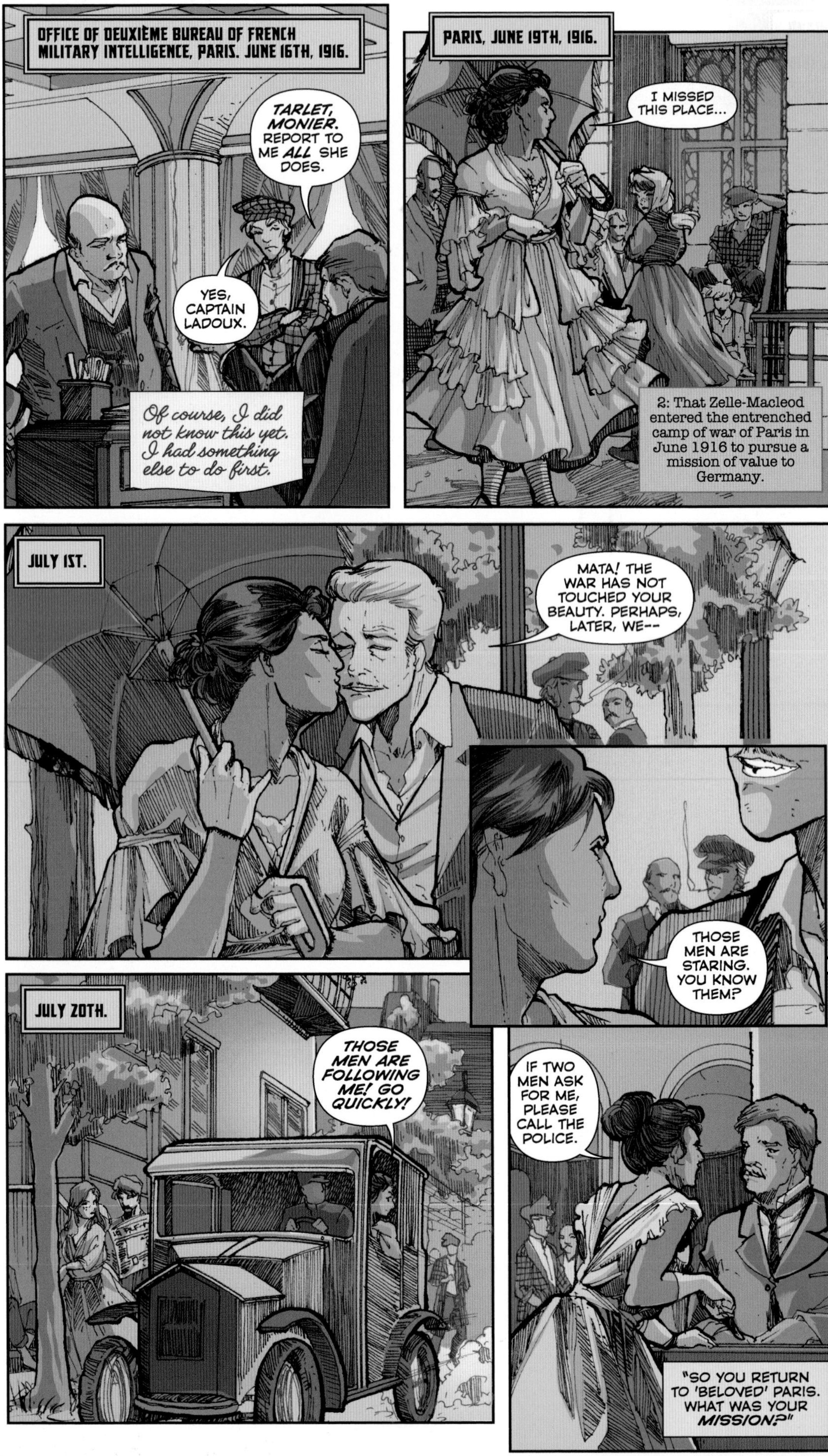
OFFICE OF DEUXIÈME BUREAU OF FRENCH MILITARY INTELLIGENCE, PARIS. JUNE 16TH, 1916.
TARLET, MONIER. REPORT TO ME ALL SHE DOES.
YES, CAPTAIN LADOUX.
Of course, I did not know this yet. I had something else to do first.
PARIS, JUNE 19TH, 1916.
I MISSED THIS PLACE...
2: That Zelle-Macleod entered the entrenched camp of war of Paris in June 1916 to pursue a mission of value to Germany.
JULY 1ST.
MATA! THE WAR HAS NOT TOUCHED YOUR BEAUTY. PERHAPS, LATER, WE--
THOSE MEN ARE STARING. YOU KNOW THEM?
JULY 20TH.
THOSE MEN ARE FOLLOWING ME! GO QUICKLY!
IF TWO MEN ASK FOR ME, PLEASE CALL THE POLICE.
"SO YOU RETURN TO 'BELOVED' PARIS. WHAT WAS YOUR MISSION?"

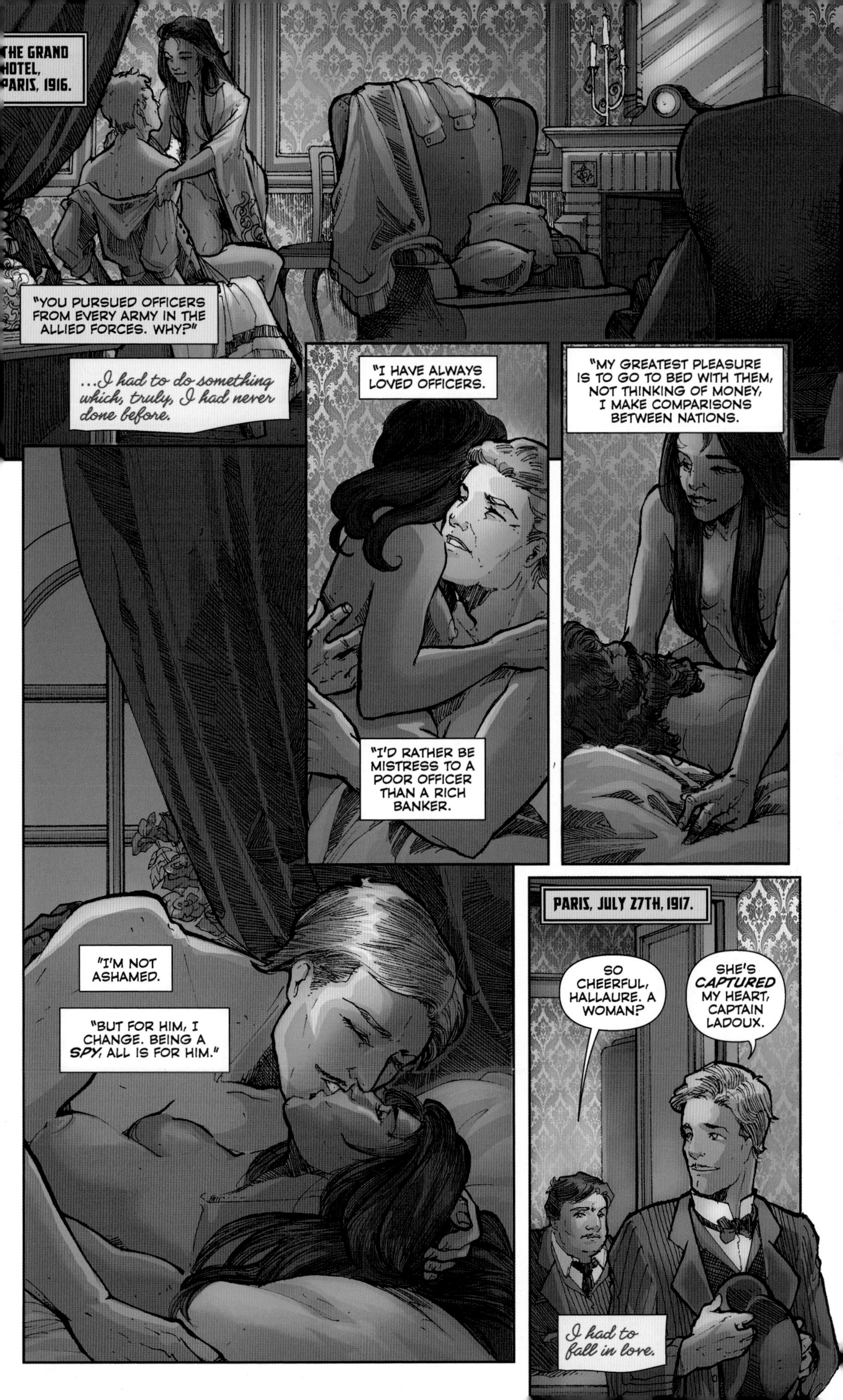
THE GRAND HOTEL, PARIS, 1916.
"YOU PURSUED OFFICERS FROM EVERY ARMY IN THE ALLIED FORCES. WHY?"
...I had to do something which, truly, I had never done before.
"I HAVE ALWAYS LOVED OFFICERS.
"I'D RATHER BE MISTRESS TO A POOR OFFICER THAN A RICH BANKER.
"MY GREATEST PLEASURE IS TO GO TO BED WITH THEM, NOT THINKING OF MONEY, I MAKE COMPARISONS BETWEEN NATIONS.
"I'M NOT ASHAMED.
"BUT FOR HIM, I CHANGE. BEING A SPY, ALL IS FOR HIM."
PARIS, JULY 27TH, 1917.
SO CHEERFUL, HALLAURE. A WOMAN?
SHE'S CAPTURED MY HEART, CAPTAIN LADOUX.
I had to fall in love.

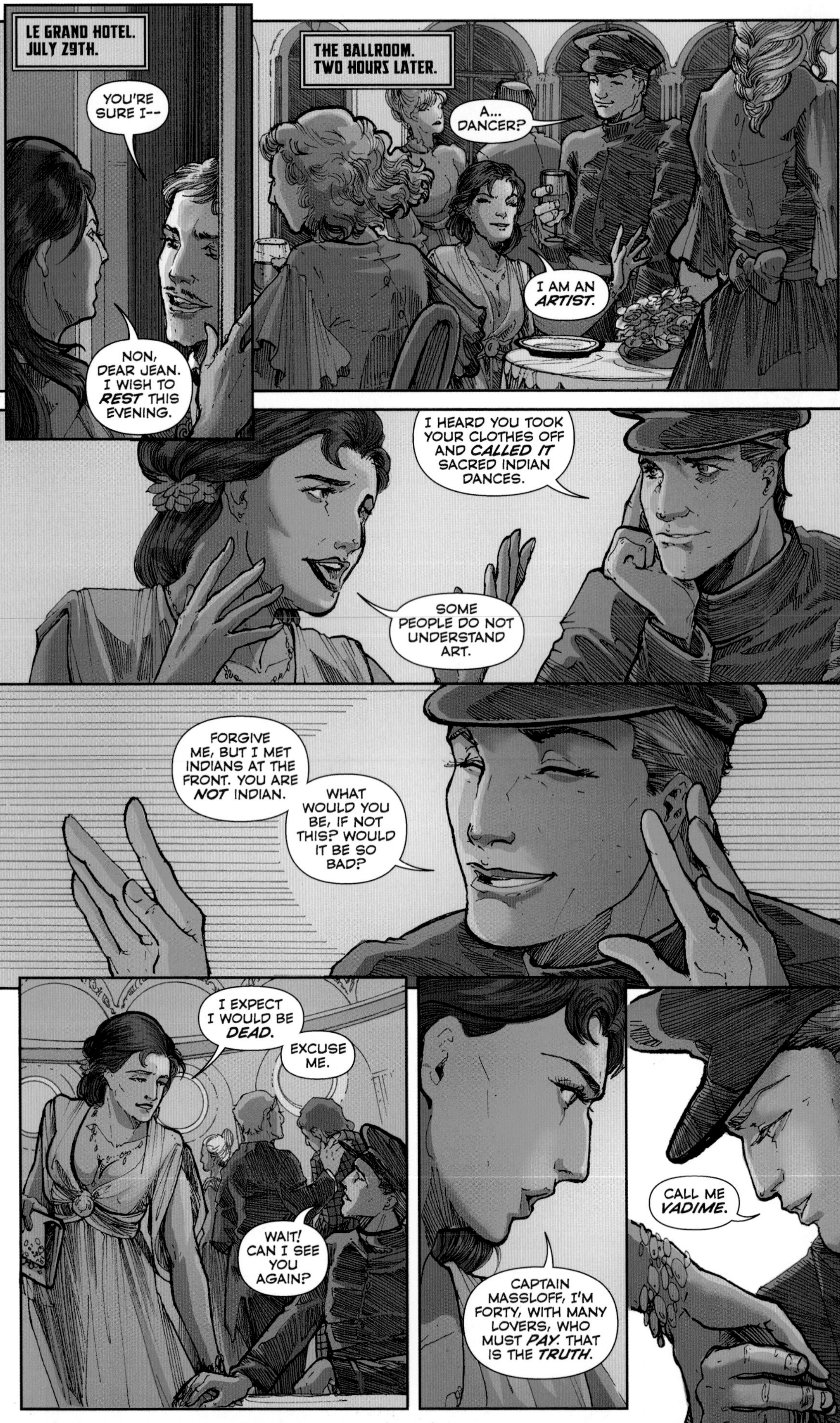

LE GRAND HOTEL. JULY 29TH.
YOU'RE SURE I--
NON, DEAR JEAN. I WISH TO *REST* THIS EVENING.
THE BALLROOM. TWO HOURS LATER.
A... DANCER?
I AM AN *ARTIST*.
I HEARD YOU TOOK YOUR CLOTHES OFF AND *CALLED IT* SACRED INDIAN DANCES.
SOME PEOPLE DO NOT UNDERSTAND ART.
FORGIVE ME, BUT I MET INDIANS AT THE FRONT. YOU ARE *NOT* INDIAN.
WHAT WOULD YOU BE, IF NOT THIS? WOULD IT BE SO BAD?
I EXPECT I WOULD BE *DEAD*.
EXCUSE ME.
WAIT! CAN I SEE YOU AGAIN?
CAPTAIN MASSLOFF, I'M FORTY, WITH MANY LOVERS, WHO MUST *PAY*. THAT IS THE *TRUTH*.
CALL ME *VADIME*.

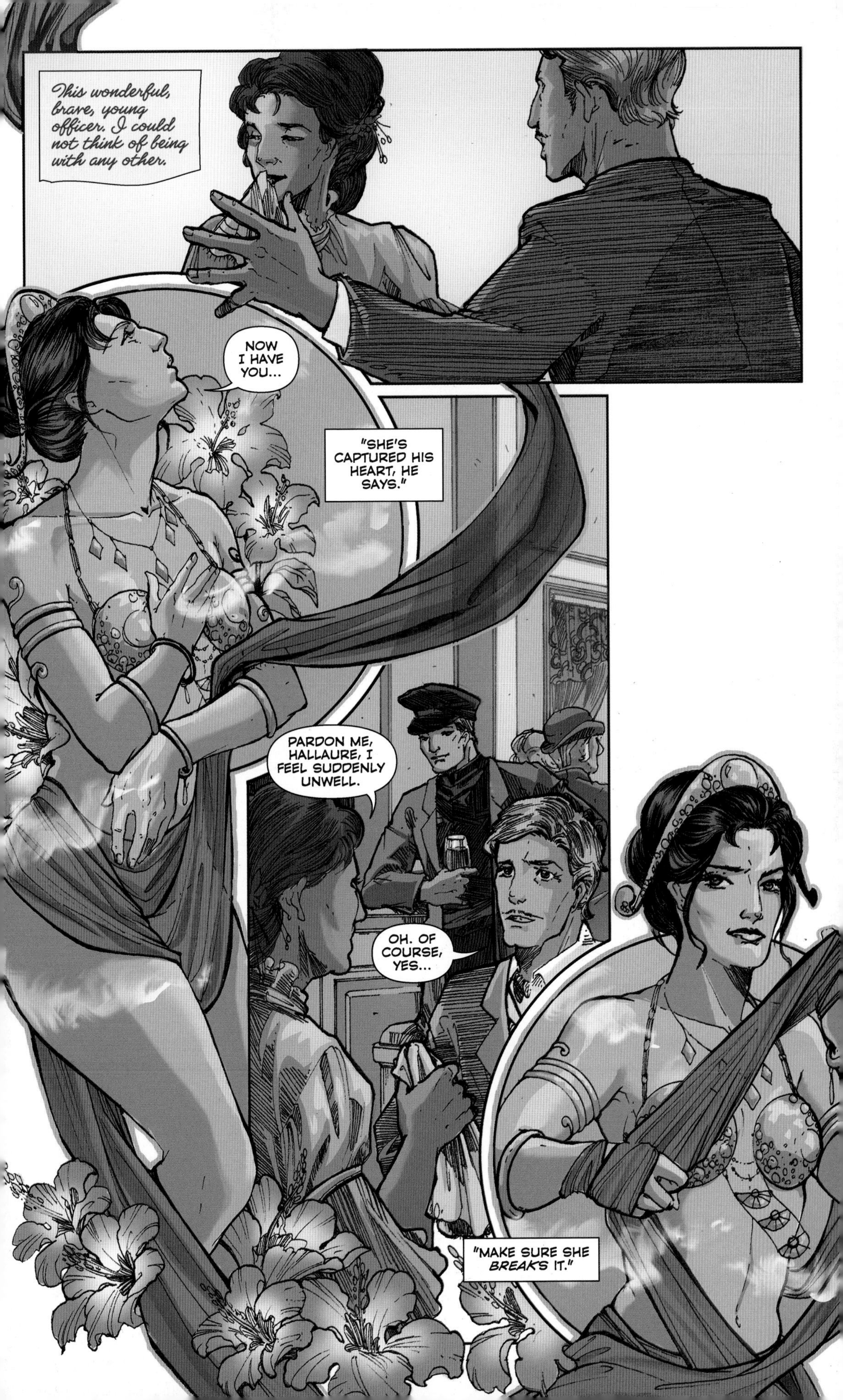
This wonderful, brave, young officer. I could not think of being with any other.
NOW I HAVE YOU...
"SHE'S CAPTURED HIS HEART, HE SAYS."
PARDON ME, HALLAURE, I FEEL SUDDENLY UNWELL.
OH. OF COURSE, YES...
"MAKE SURE SHE BREAKS IT."

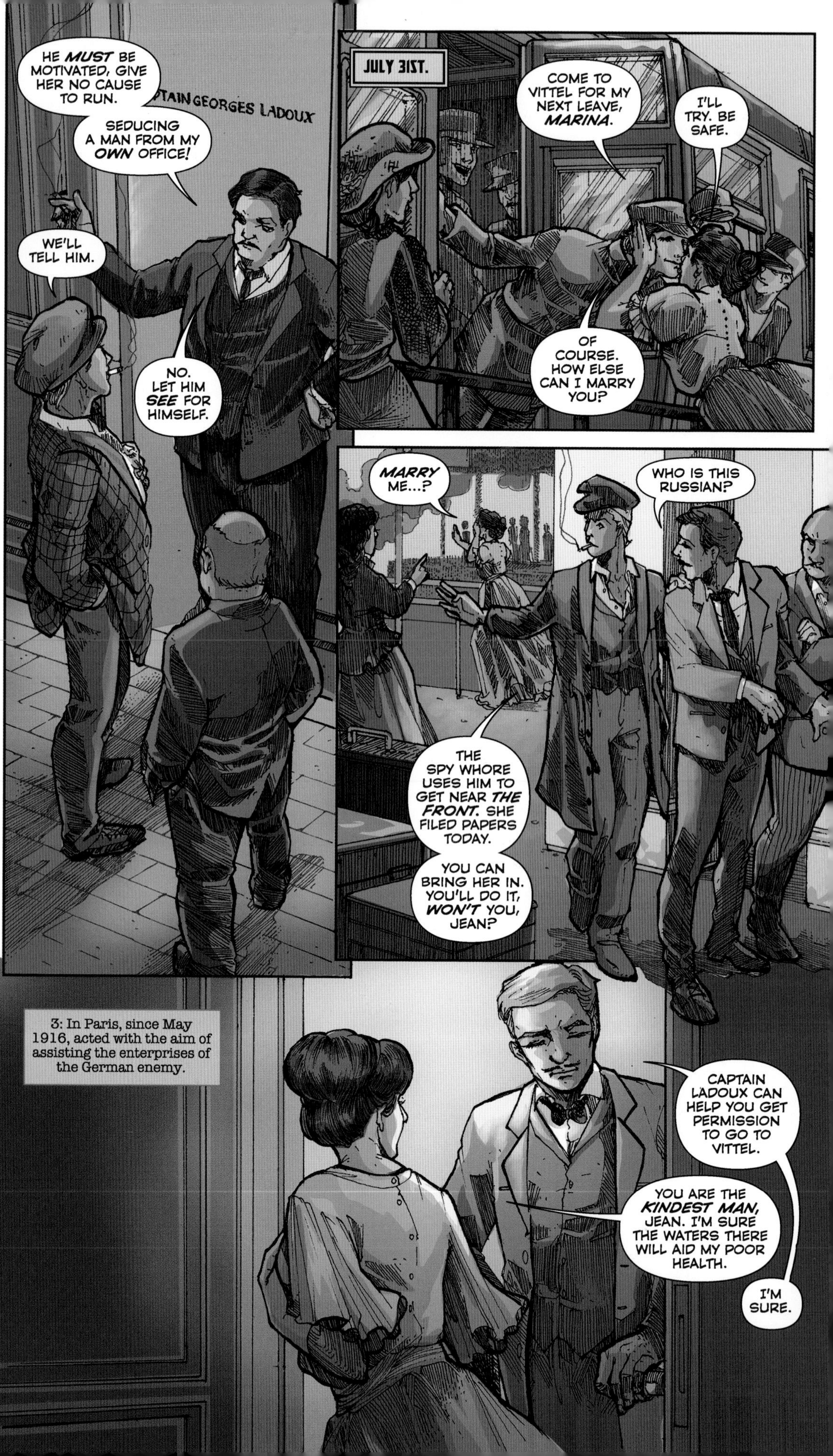

CAPTAIN GEORGES LADOUX
HE MUST BE MOTIVATED, GIVE HER NO CAUSE TO RUN.
SEDUCING A MAN FROM MY OWN OFFICE!
WE'LL TELL HIM.
NO. LET HIM SEE FOR HIMSELF.
JULY 31ST.
COME TO VITTEL FOR MY NEXT LEAVE, MARINA.
I'LL TRY. BE SAFE.
OF COURSE. HOW ELSE CAN I MARRY YOU?
MARRY ME...?
WHO IS THIS RUSSIAN?
THE SPY WHORE USES HIM TO GET NEAR THE FRONT. SHE FILED PAPERS TODAY.
YOU CAN BRING HER IN. YOU'LL DO IT, WON'T YOU, JEAN?
3: In Paris, since May 1916, acted with the aim of assisting the enterprises of the German enemy.
CAPTAIN LADOUX CAN HELP YOU GET PERMISSION TO GO TO VITTEL.
YOU ARE THE KINDEST MAN, JEAN. I'M SURE THE WATERS THERE WILL AID MY POOR HEALTH.
I'M SURE.

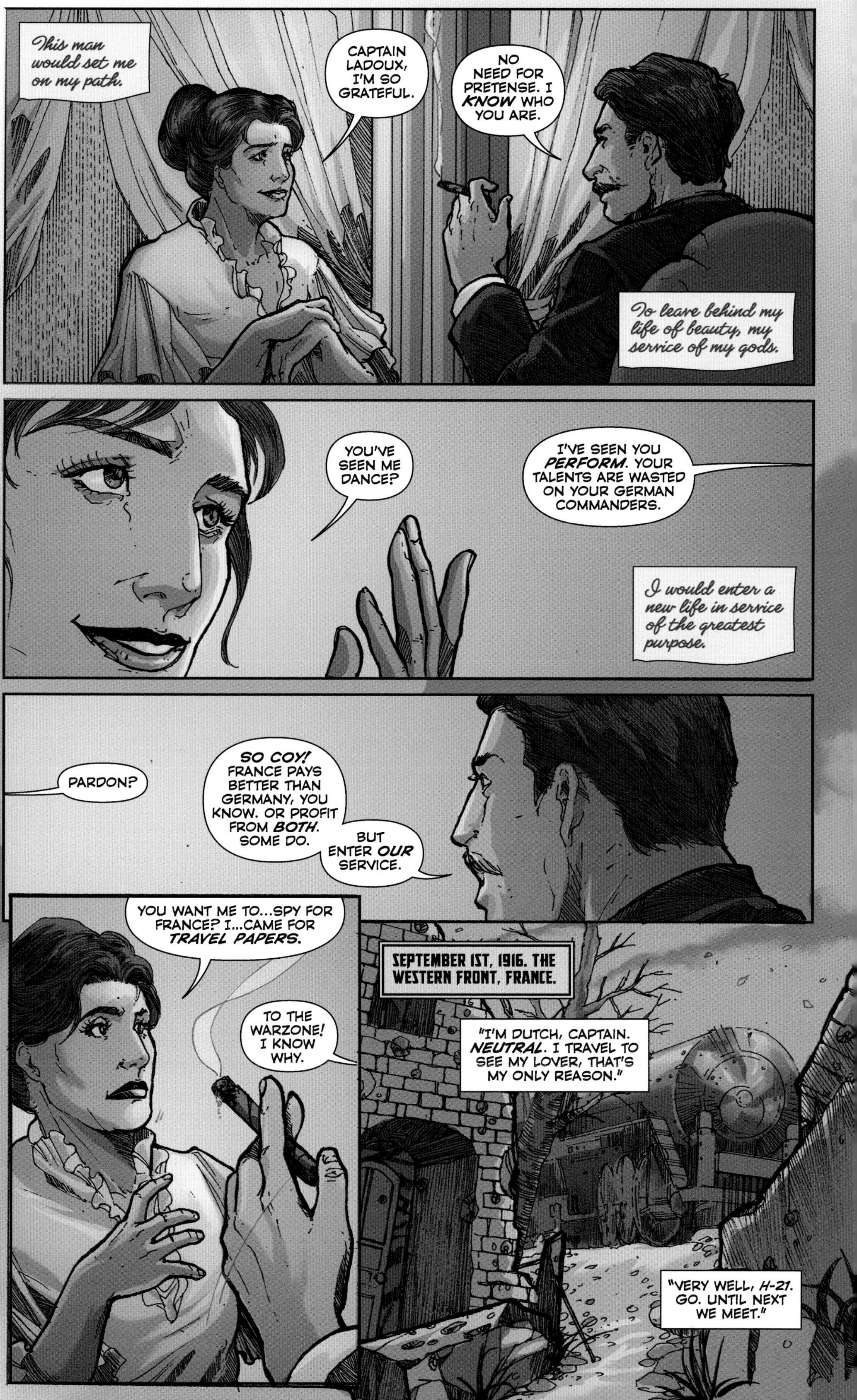
This man would set me on my path.
CAPTAIN LADOUX, I'M SO GRATEFUL.
NO NEED FOR PRETENSE. I KNOW WHO YOU ARE.
To leave behind my life of beauty, my service of my gods.
YOU'VE SEEN ME DANCE?
I'VE SEEN YOU PERFORM. YOUR TALENTS ARE WASTED ON YOUR GERMAN COMMANDERS.
I would enter a new life in service of the greatest purpose.
PARDON?
SO COY! FRANCE PAYS BETTER THAN GERMANY, YOU KNOW. OR PROFIT FROM BOTH. SOME DO.
BUT ENTER OUR SERVICE.
YOU WANT ME TO...SPY FOR FRANCE? I...CAME FOR TRAVEL PAPERS.
TO THE WARZONE! I KNOW WHY.
SEPTEMBER 1ST, 1916. THE WESTERN FRONT, FRANCE.
"I'M DUTCH, CAPTAIN. NEUTRAL. I TRAVEL TO SEE MY LOVER, THAT'S MY ONLY REASON."
"VERY WELL, H-21. GO. UNTIL NEXT WE MEET."

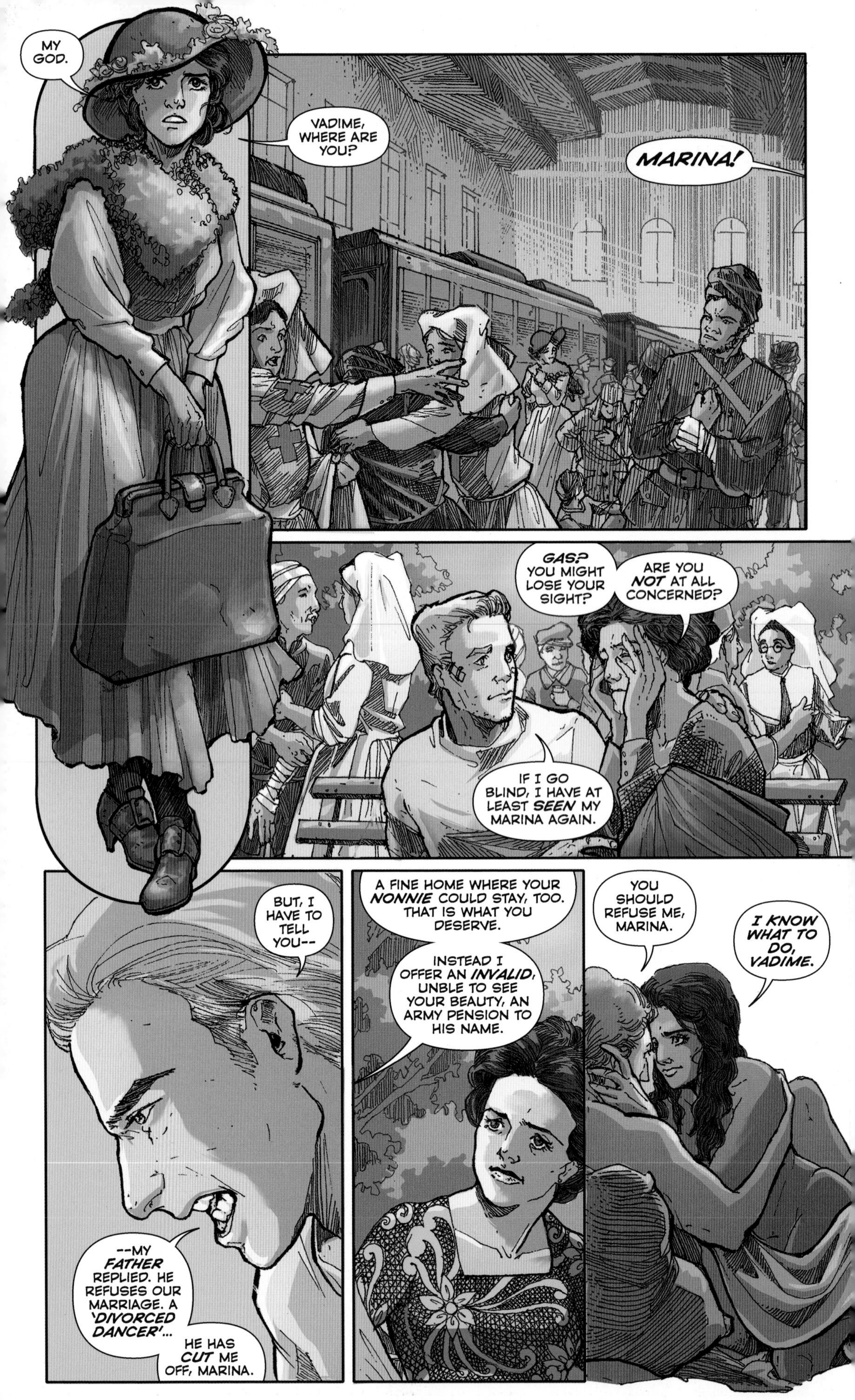

MY GOD.
VADIME, WHERE ARE YOU?
MARINA!
GAS? YOU MIGHT LOSE YOUR SIGHT?
ARE YOU NOT AT ALL CONCERNED?
IF I GO BLIND, I HAVE AT LEAST SEEN MY MARINA AGAIN.
BUT, I HAVE TO TELL YOU--
--MY FATHER REPLIED. HE REFUSES OUR MARRIAGE. A 'DIVORCED DANCER'...
HE HAS CUT ME OFF, MARINA.
A FINE HOME WHERE YOUR NONNIE COULD STAY, TOO. THAT IS WHAT YOU DESERVE.
INSTEAD I OFFER AN INVALID, UNBLE TO SEE YOUR BEAUTY, AN ARMY PENSION TO HIS NAME.
YOU SHOULD REFUSE ME, MARINA.
I KNOW WHAT TO DO, VADIME.

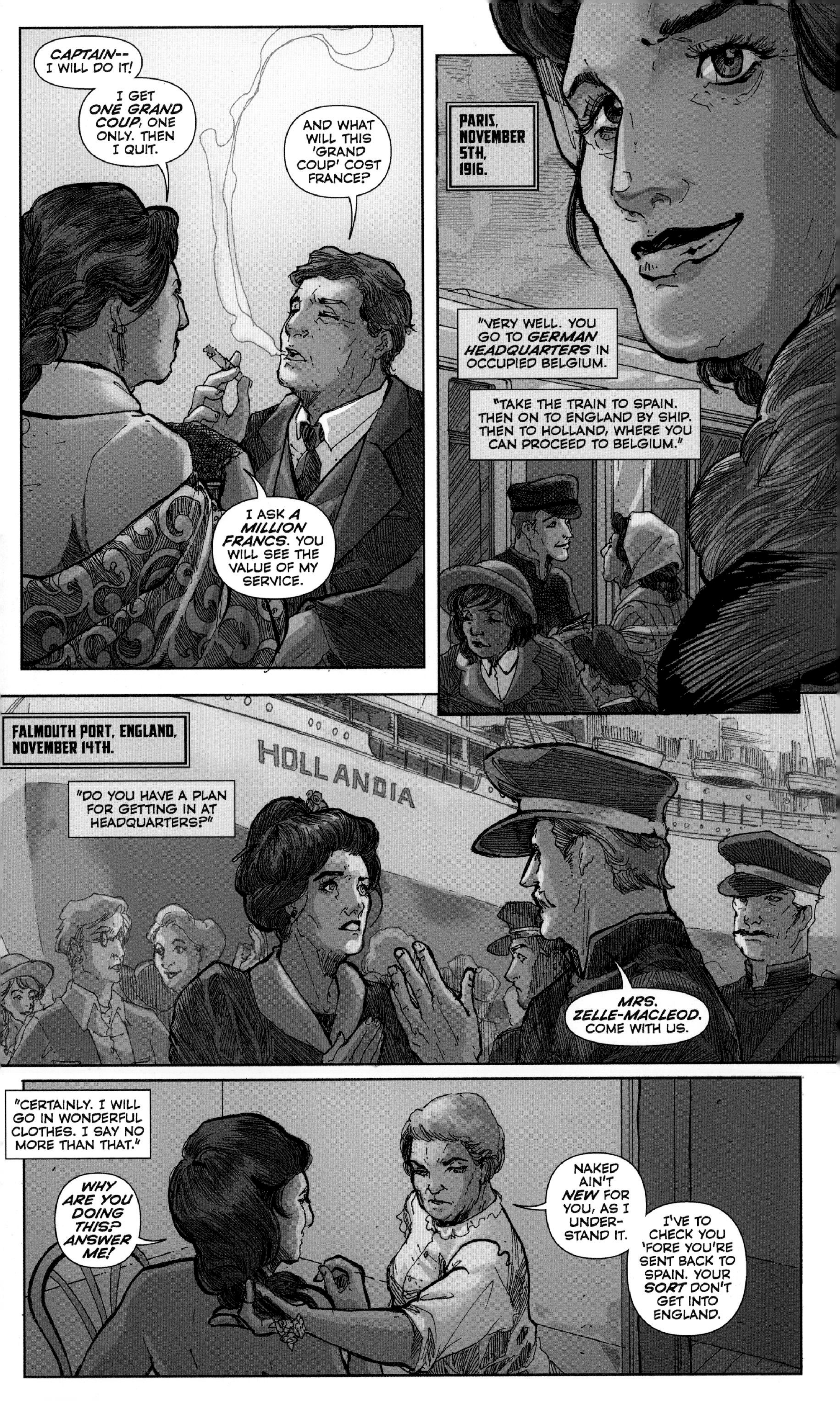
CAPTAIN-- I WILL DO IT!
I GET ONE GRAND COUP, ONE ONLY. THEN I QUIT.
AND WHAT WILL THIS 'GRAND COUP' COST FRANCE?
I ASK A MILLION FRANCS. YOU WILL SEE THE VALUE OF MY SERVICE.
PARIS, NOVEMBER 5TH, 1916.
"VERY WELL. YOU GO TO GERMAN HEADQUARTERS IN OCCUPIED BELGIUM.
"TAKE THE TRAIN TO SPAIN. THEN ON TO ENGLAND BY SHIP. THEN TO HOLLAND, WHERE YOU CAN PROCEED TO BELGIUM."
FALMOUTH PORT, ENGLAND, NOVEMBER 14TH.
HOLLANDIA
"DO YOU HAVE A PLAN FOR GETTING IN AT HEADQUARTERS?"
MRS. ZELLE-MACLEOD. COME WITH US.
"CERTAINLY. I WILL GO IN WONDERFUL CLOTHES. I SAY NO MORE THAN THAT."
WHY ARE YOU DOING THIS? ANSWER ME!
NAKED AIN'T NEW FOR YOU, AS I UNDER-STAND IT.
I'VE TO CHECK YOU 'FORE YOU'RE SENT BACK TO SPAIN. YOUR SORT DON'T GET INTO ENGLAND.

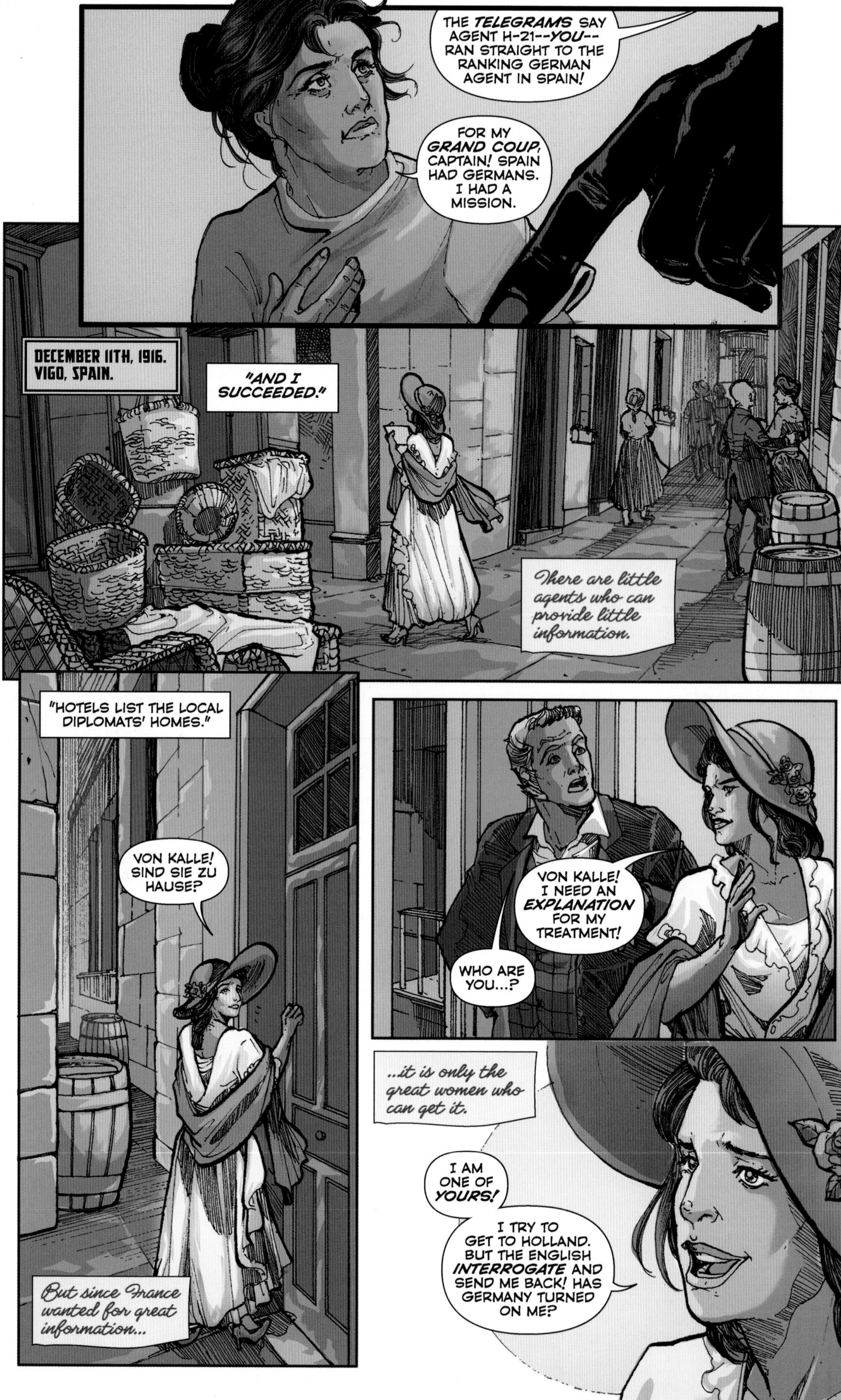
THE TELEGRAMS SAY AGENT H-21--YOU--RAN STRAIGHT TO THE RANKING GERMAN AGENT IN SPAIN!
FOR MY GRAND COUP, CAPTAIN! SPAIN HAD GERMANS. I HAD A MISSION.
DECEMBER 11TH, 1916. VIGO, SPAIN.
"AND I SUCCEEDED."
There are little agents who can provide little information.
"HOTELS LIST THE LOCAL DIPLOMATS' HOMES."
VON KALLE! SIND SIE ZU HAUSE?
But since France wanted for great information...
VON KALLE! I NEED AN EXPLANATION FOR MY TREATMENT!
WHO ARE YOU...?
...it is only the great women who can get it.
I AM ONE OF YOURS!
I TRY TO GET TO HOLLAND. BUT THE ENGLISH INTERROGATE AND SEND ME BACK! HAS GERMANY TURNED ON ME?

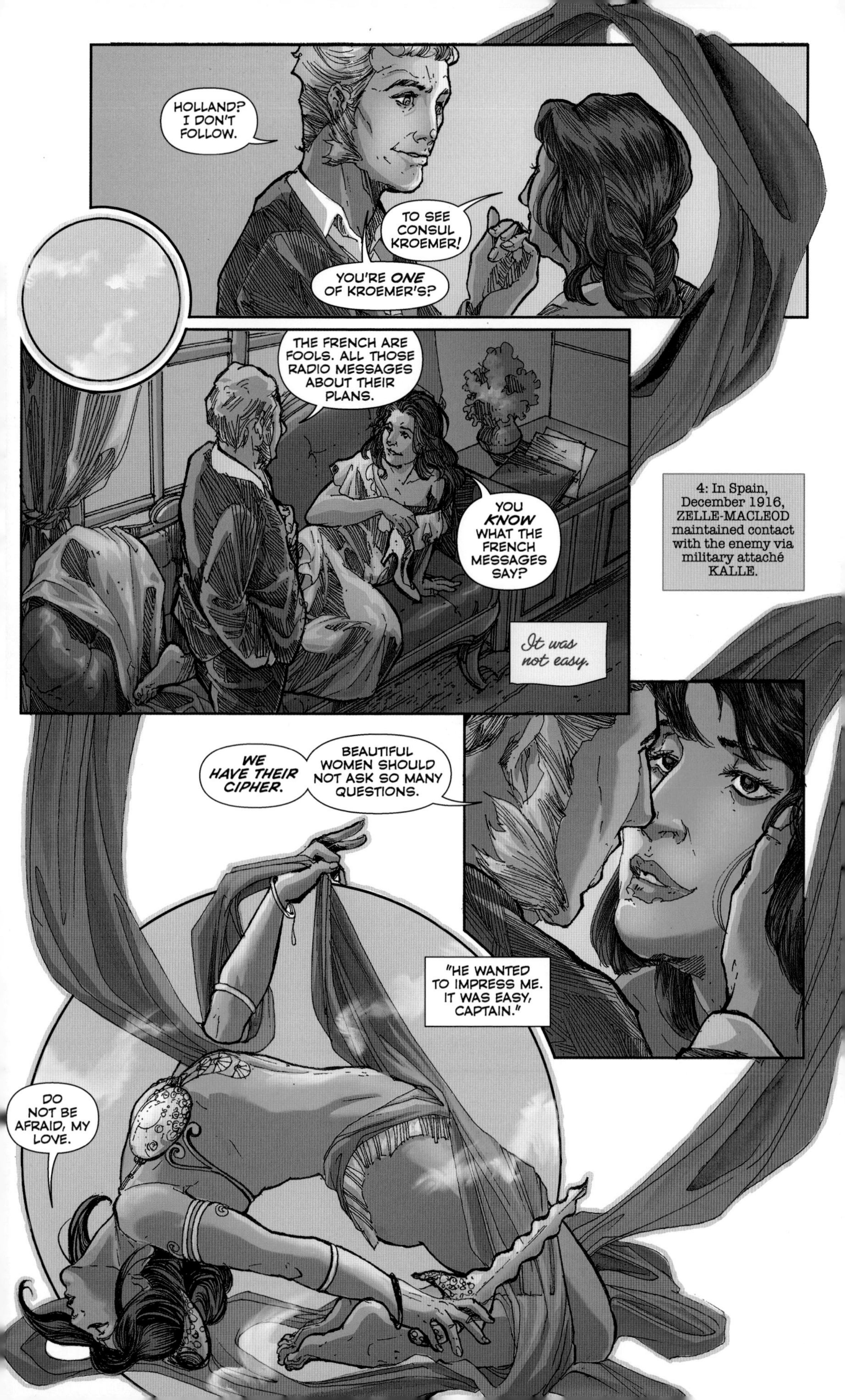
HOLLAND? I DON'T FOLLOW.
TO SEE CONSUL KROEMER!
YOU'RE ONE OF KROEMER'S?
THE FRENCH ARE FOOLS. ALL THOSE RADIO MESSAGES ABOUT THEIR PLANS.
YOU KNOW WHAT THE FRENCH MESSAGES SAY?
It was not easy.
4: In Spain, December 1916, ZELLE-MACLEOD maintained contact with the enemy via military attaché KALLE.
WE HAVE THEIR CIPHER.
BEAUTIFUL WOMEN SHOULD NOT ASK SO MANY QUESTIONS.
"HE WANTED TO IMPRESS ME. IT WAS EASY, CAPTAIN."
DO NOT BE AFRAID, MY LOVE.

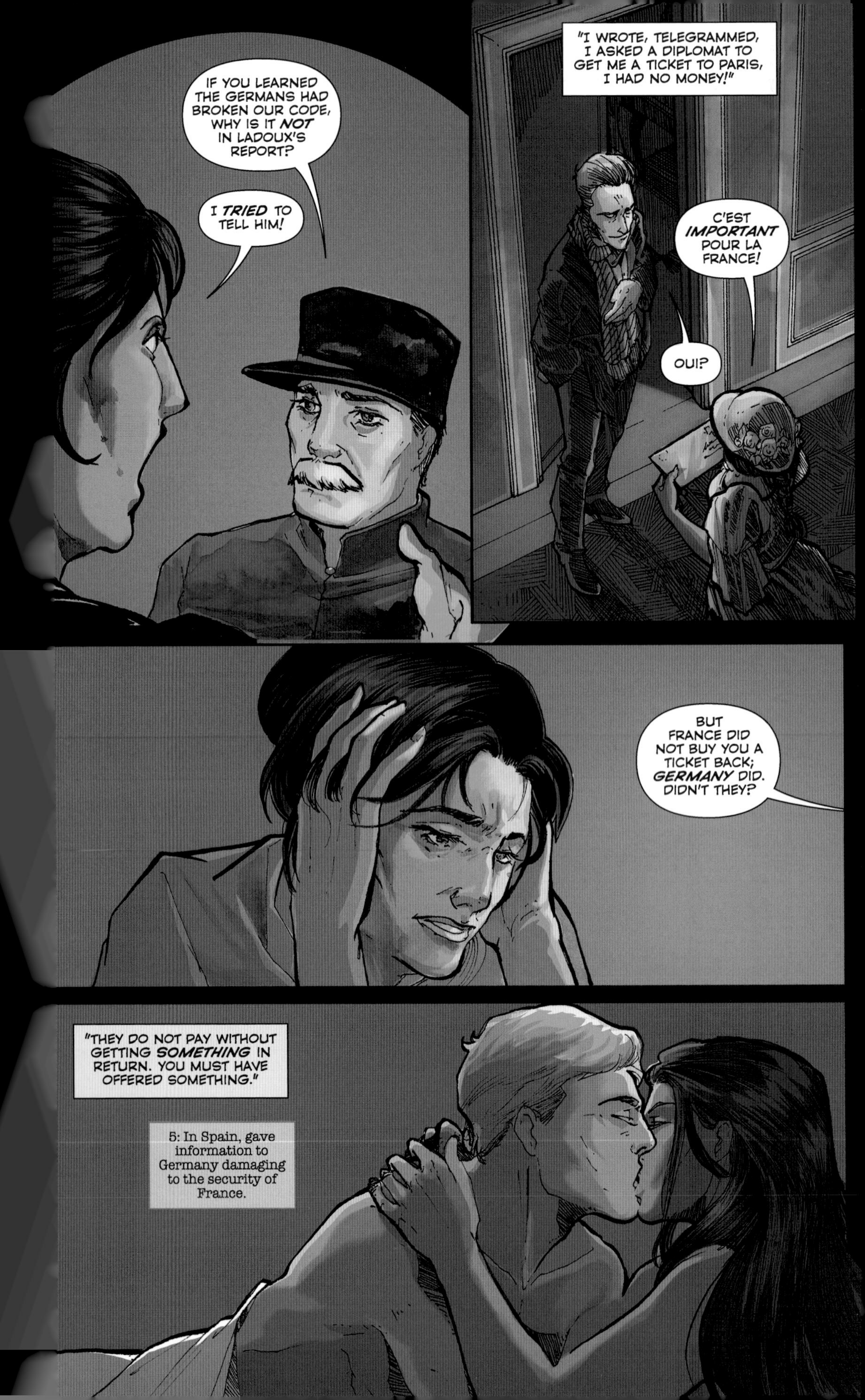
IF YOU LEARNED THE GERMANS HAD BROKEN OUR CODE, WHY IS IT NOT IN LADOUX'S REPORT?
I TRIED TO TELL HIM!
"I WROTE, TELEGRAMMED, I ASKED A DIPLOMAT TO GET ME A TICKET TO PARIS, I HAD NO MONEY!"
C'EST IMPORTANT POUR LA FRANCE!
OUI?
BUT FRANCE DID NOT BUY YOU A TICKET BACK; GERMANY DID. DIDN'T THEY?
"THEY DO NOT PAY WITHOUT GETTING SOMETHING IN RETURN. YOU MUST HAVE OFFERED SOMETHING."
5: In Spain, gave information to Germany damaging to the security of France.

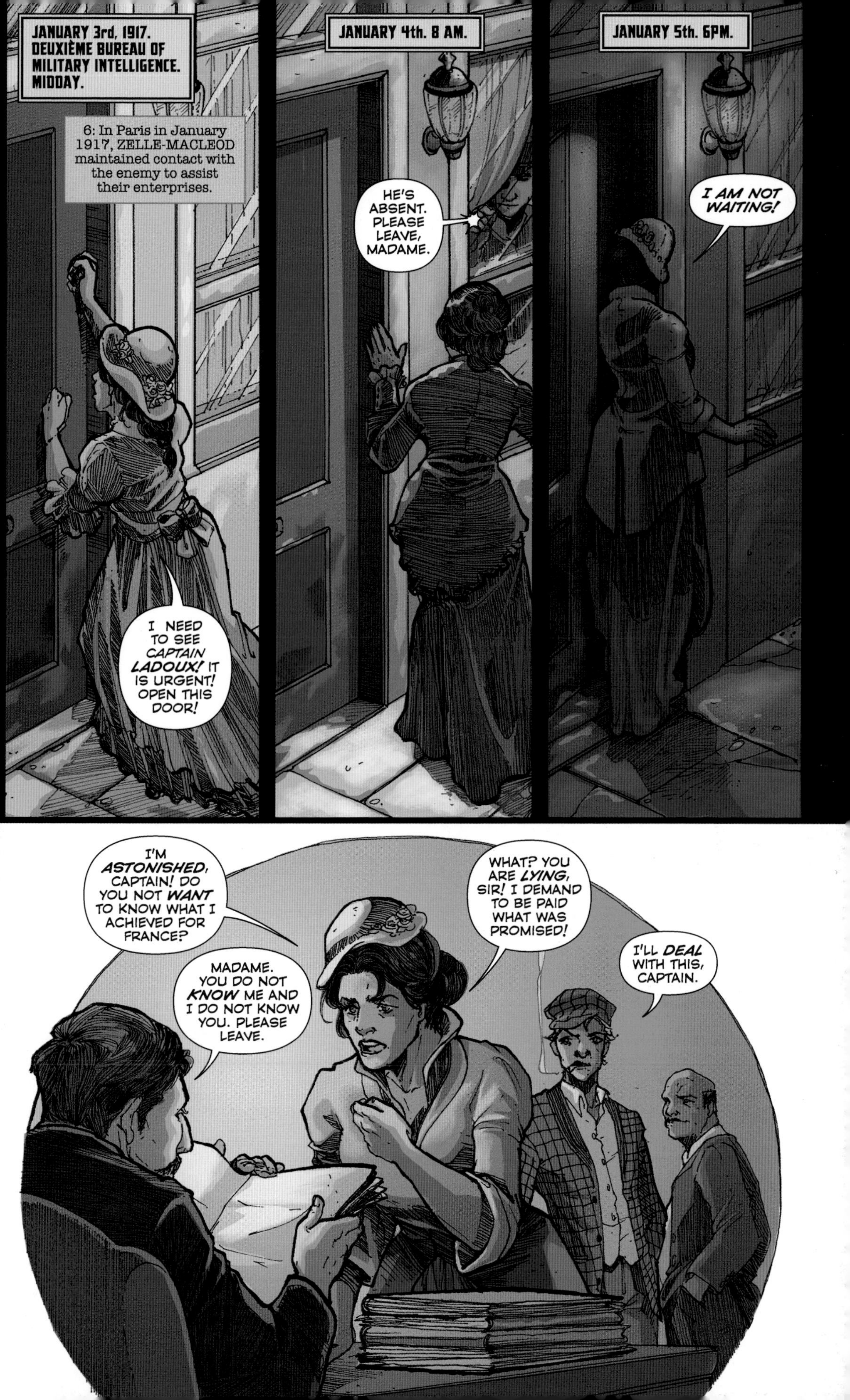
JANUARY 3rd, 1917. DEUXIÈME BUREAU OF MILITARY INTELLIGENCE. MIDDAY.
6: In Paris in January 1917, ZELLE-MACLEOD maintained contact with the enemy to assist their enterprises.
I NEED TO SEE CAPTAIN LADOUX! IT IS URGENT! OPEN THIS DOOR!
JANUARY 4th. 8 AM.
HE'S ABSENT. PLEASE LEAVE, MADAME.
JANUARY 5th. 6PM.
I AM NOT WAITING!
I'M ASTONISHED, CAPTAIN! DO YOU NOT WANT TO KNOW WHAT I ACHIEVED FOR FRANCE?
MADAME. YOU DO NOT KNOW ME AND I DO NOT KNOW YOU. PLEASE LEAVE.
WHAT? YOU ARE LYING, SIR! I DEMAND TO BE PAID WHAT WAS PROMISED!
I'LL DEAL WITH THIS, CAPTAIN.

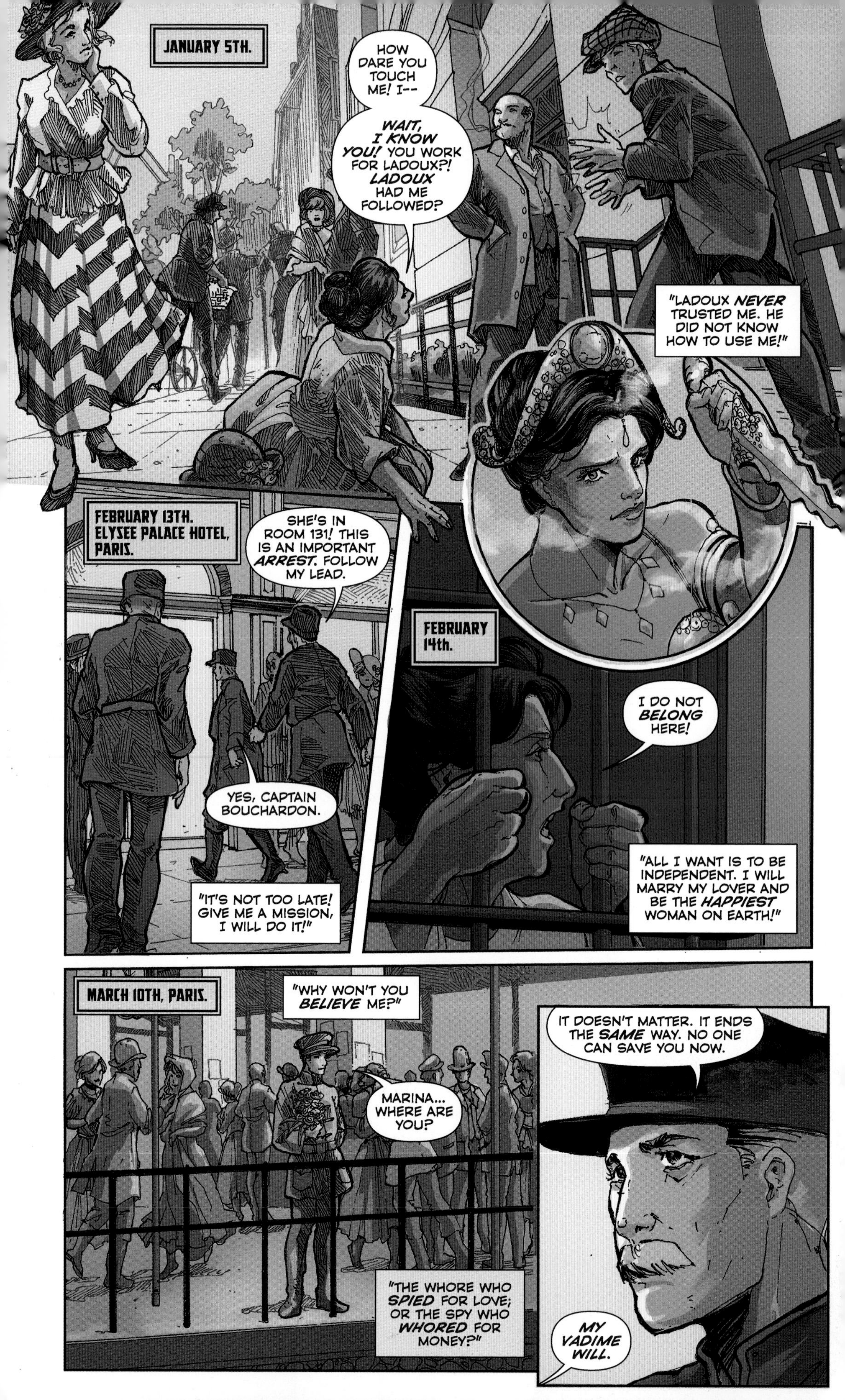
JANUARY 5TH.
HOW DARE YOU TOUCH ME! I--
WAIT, I KNOW YOU! YOU WORK FOR LADOUX?! LADOUX HAD ME FOLLOWED?
"LADOUX NEVER TRUSTED ME. HE DID NOT KNOW HOW TO USE ME!"
FEBRUARY 13TH. ELYSEE PALACE HOTEL, PARIS.
SHE'S IN ROOM 131! THIS IS AN IMPORTANT ARREST. FOLLOW MY LEAD.
YES, CAPTAIN BOUCHARDON.
"IT'S NOT TOO LATE! GIVE ME A MISSION, I WILL DO IT!"
FEBRUARY 14th.
I DO NOT BELONG HERE!
"ALL I WANT IS TO BE INDEPENDENT. I WILL MARRY MY LOVER AND BE THE HAPPIEST WOMAN ON EARTH!"
MARCH 10TH, PARIS.
"WHY WON'T YOU BELIEVE ME?"
MARINA... WHERE ARE YOU?
"THE WHORE WHO SPIED FOR LOVE; OR THE SPY WHO WHORED FOR MONEY?"
IT DOESN'T MATTER. IT ENDS THE SAME WAY. NO ONE CAN SAVE YOU NOW.
MY VADIME WILL.

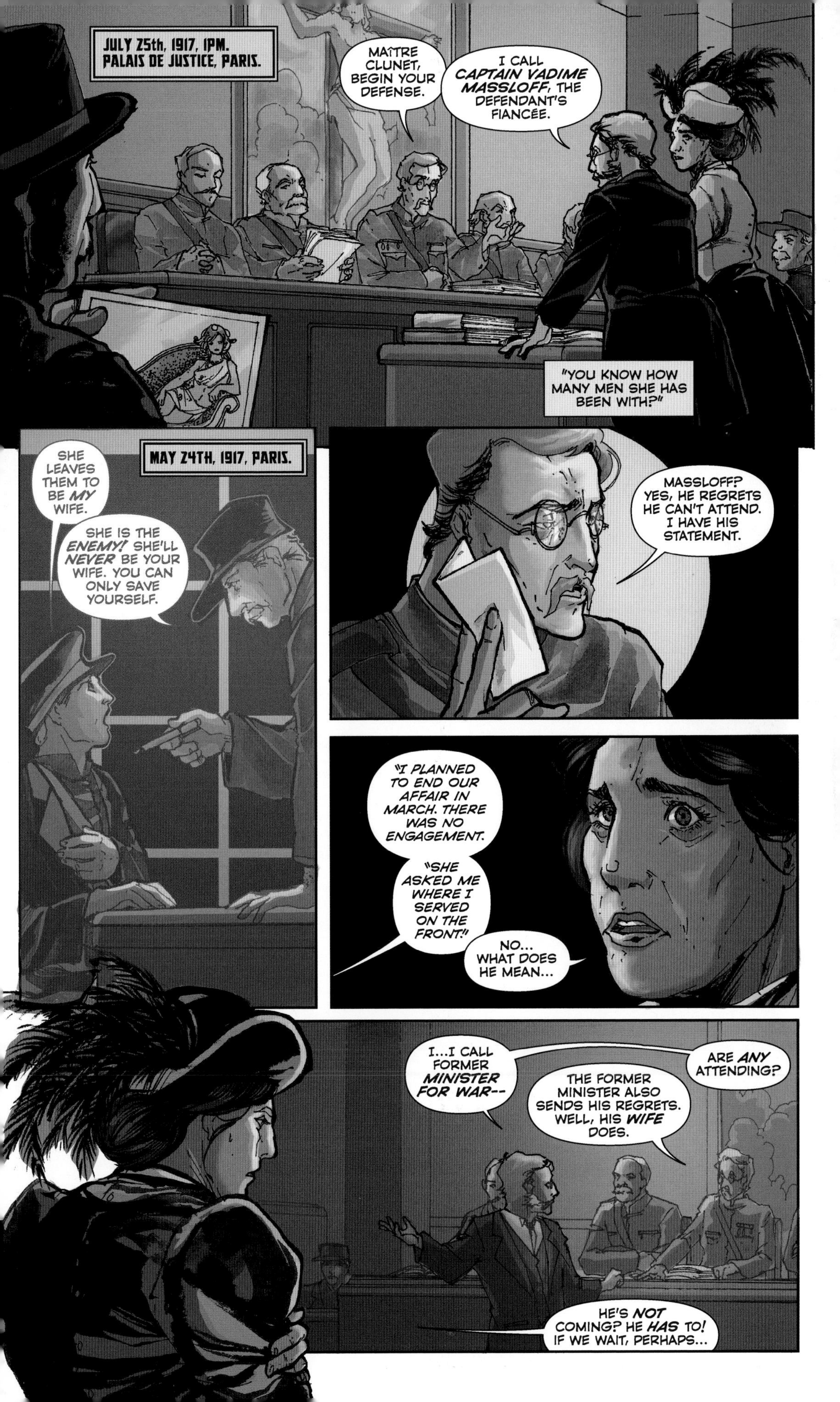

JULY 25th, 1917, 1PM. PALAIS DE JUSTICE, PARIS.
MAÎTRE CLUNET, BEGIN YOUR DEFENSE.
I CALL CAPTAIN VADIME MASSLOFF, THE DEFENDANT'S FIANCÉE.
"YOU KNOW HOW MANY MEN SHE HAS BEEN WITH?"
MAY 24TH, 1917, PARIS.
SHE LEAVES THEM TO BE MY WIFE.
SHE IS THE ENEMY! SHE'LL NEVER BE YOUR WIFE. YOU CAN ONLY SAVE YOURSELF.
MASSLOFF? YES, HE REGRETS HE CAN'T ATTEND. I HAVE HIS STATEMENT.
"I PLANNED TO END OUR AFFAIR IN MARCH. THERE WAS NO ENGAGEMENT.
"SHE ASKED ME WHERE I SERVED ON THE FRONT."
NO... WHAT DOES HE MEAN...
I...I CALL FORMER MINISTER FOR WAR--
ARE ANY ATTENDING?
THE FORMER MINISTER ALSO SENDS HIS REGRETS. WELL, HIS WIFE DOES.
HE'S NOT COMING? HE HAS TO! IF WE WAIT, PERHAPS...

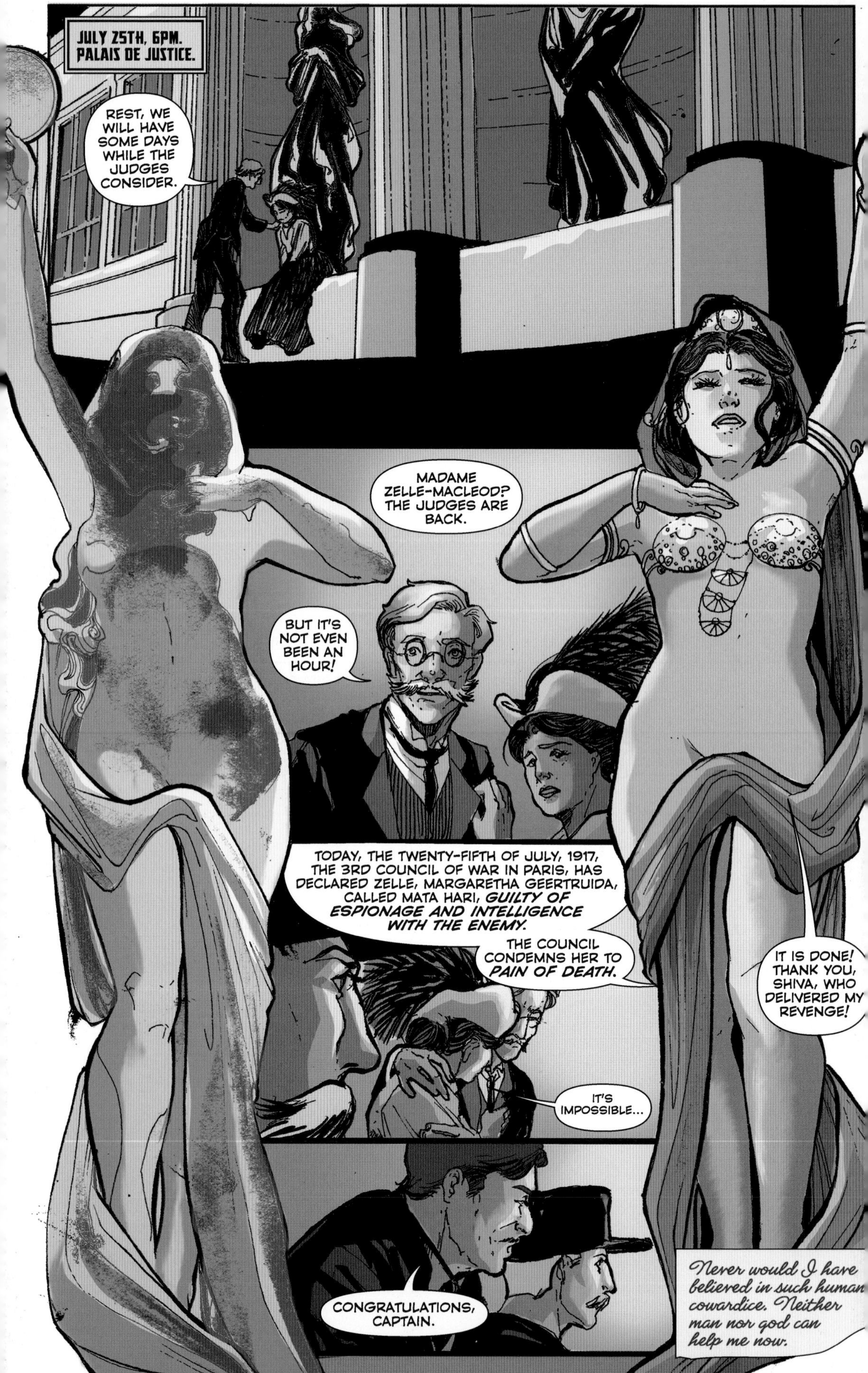

JULY 25TH, 6PM. PALAIS DE JUSTICE.
REST, WE WILL HAVE SOME DAYS WHILE THE JUDGES CONSIDER.
MADAME ZELLE-MACLEOD? THE JUDGES ARE BACK.
BUT IT'S NOT EVEN BEEN AN HOUR!
TODAY, THE TWENTY-FIFTH OF JULY, 1917, THE 3RD COUNCIL OF WAR IN PARIS, HAS DECLARED ZELLE, MARGARETHA GEERTRUIDA, CALLED MATA HARI, GUILTY OF ESPIONAGE AND INTELLIGENCE WITH THE ENEMY.
THE COUNCIL CONDEMNS HER TO PAIN OF DEATH.
IT IS DONE! THANK YOU, SHIVA, WHO DELIVERED MY REVENGE!
IT'S IMPOSSIBLE...
CONGRATULATIONS, CAPTAIN.
Never would I have believed in such human cowardice. Neither man nor god can help me now.

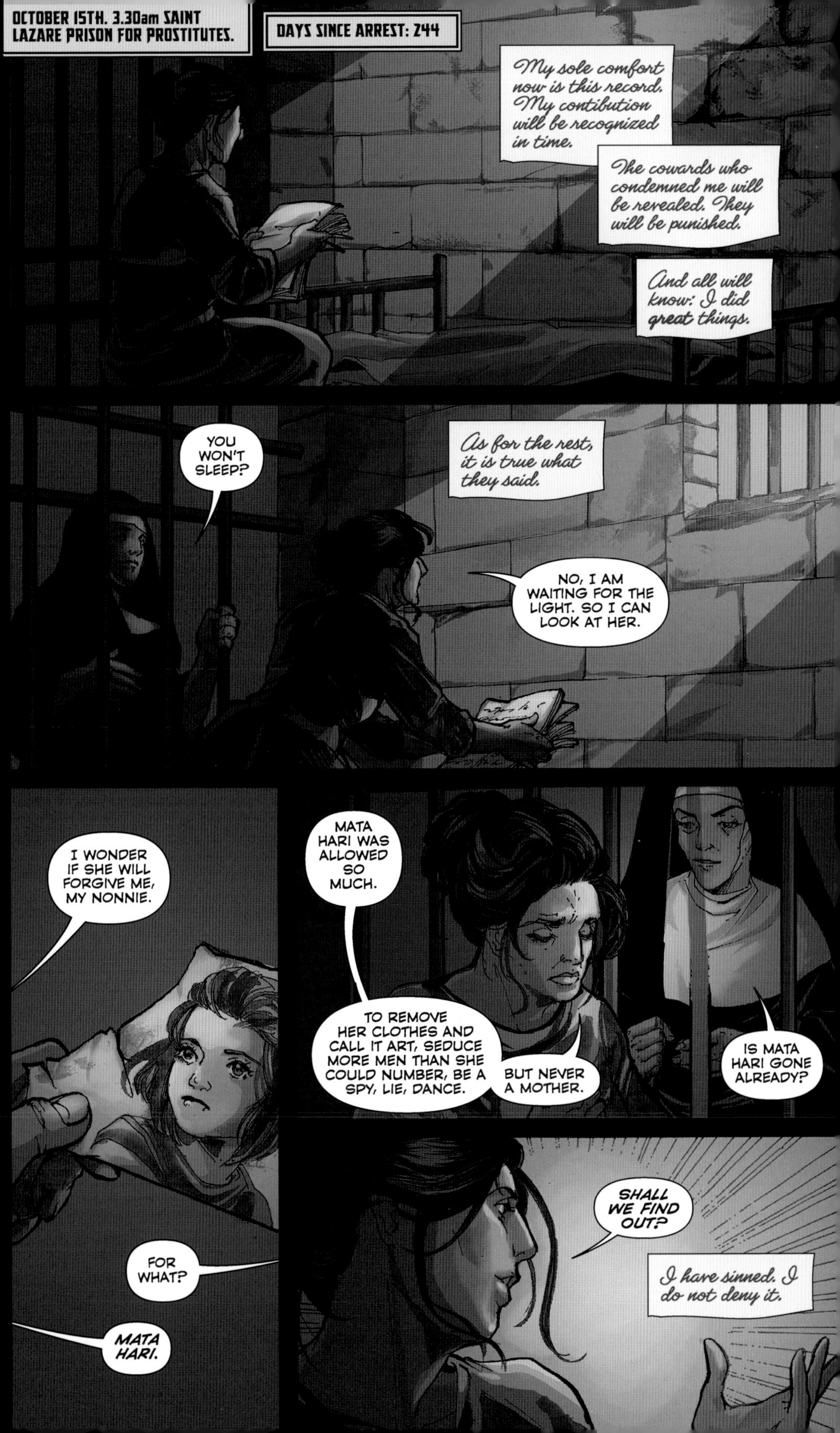
OCTOBER 15TH. 3.30am SAINT LAZARE PRISON FOR PROSTITUTES.
DAYS SINCE ARREST: 244
My sole comfort now is this record. My contibution will be recognized in time.
The cowards who condemned me will be revealed. They will be punished.
And all will know: I did great things.
YOU WON'T SLEEP?
As for the rest, it is true what they said.
NO, I AM WAITING FOR THE LIGHT. SO I CAN LOOK AT HER.
I WONDER IF SHE WILL FORGIVE ME, MY NONNIE.
FOR WHAT?
MATA HARI.
MATA HARI WAS ALLOWED SO MUCH.
TO REMOVE HER CLOTHES AND CALL IT ART, SEDUCE MORE MEN THAN SHE COULD NUMBER, BE A SPY, LIE, DANCE.
BUT NEVER A MOTHER.
IS MATA HARI GONE ALREADY?
SHALL WE FIND OUT?
I have sinned. I do not deny it.

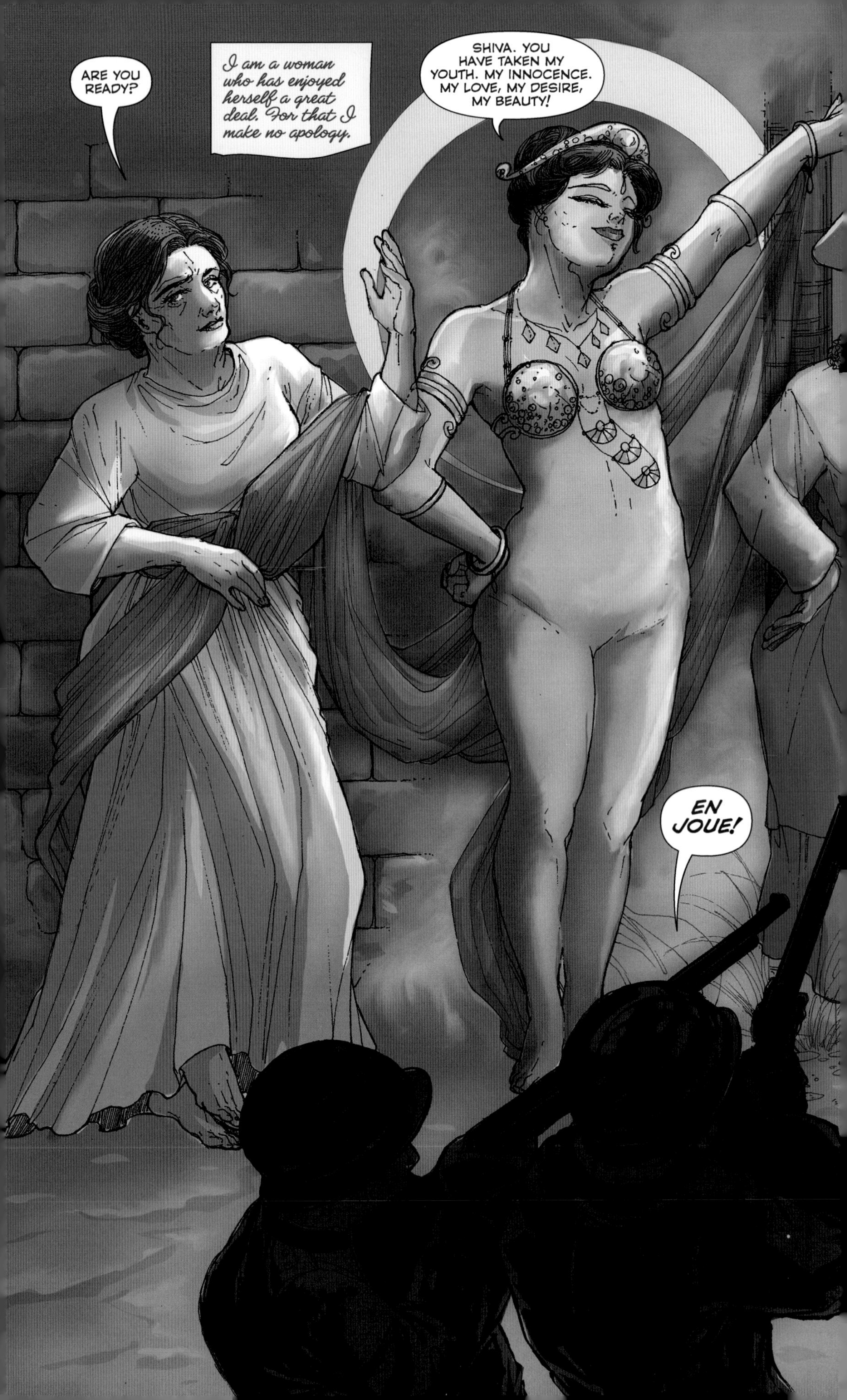
ARE YOU READY?
I am a woman who has enjoyed herself a great deal. For that I make no apology.
SHIVA. YOU HAVE TAKEN MY YOUTH. MY INNOCENCE. MY LOVE, MY DESIRE, MY BEAUTY!
EN JOUE!

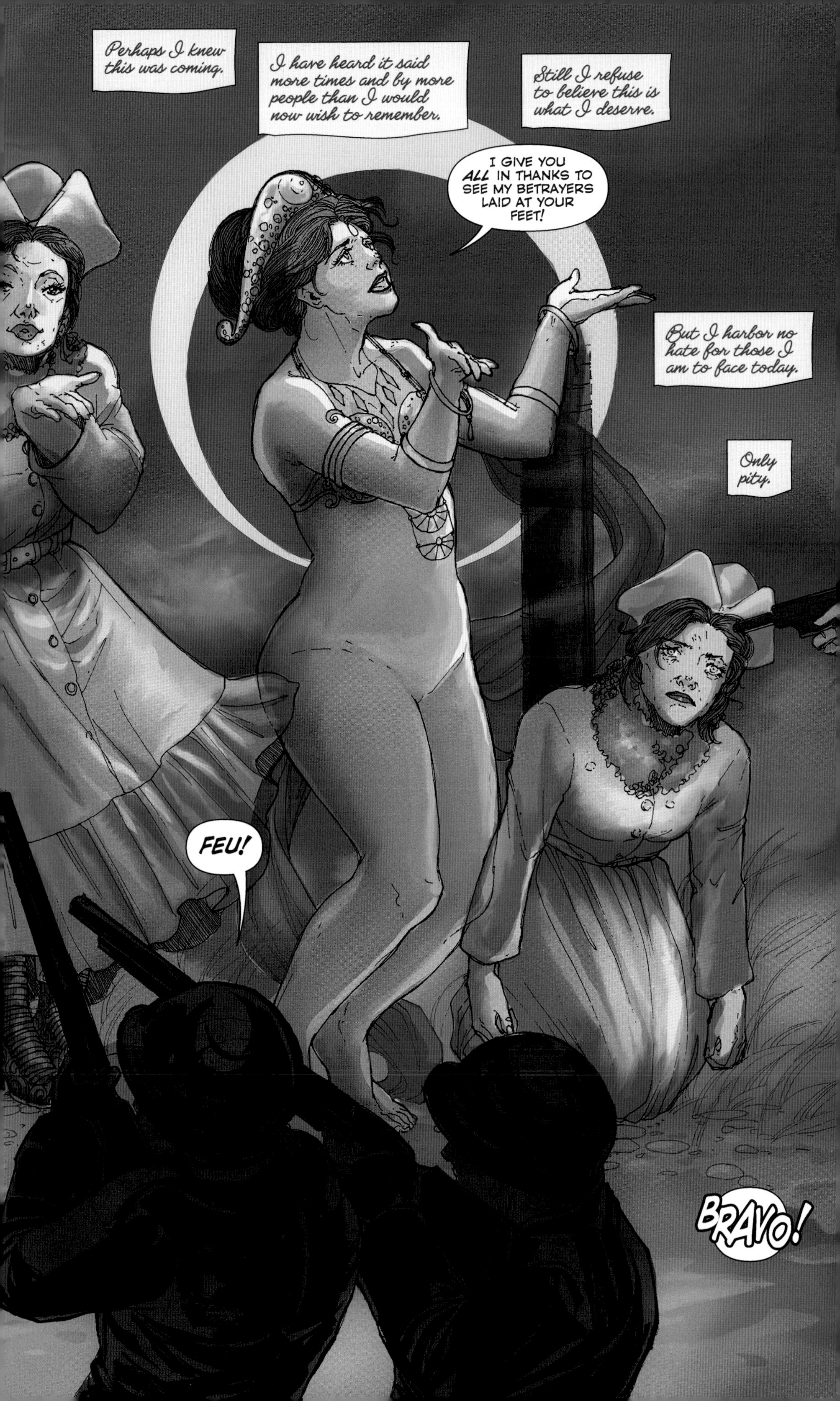
Perhaps I knew this was coming.
I have heard it said more times and by more people than I would now wish to remember.
Still I refuse to believe this is what I deserve.
I GIVE YOU ALL IN THANKS TO SEE MY BETRAYERS LAID AT YOUR FEET!
But I harbor no hate for those I am to face today.
Only pity.
FEU!
BRAVO!

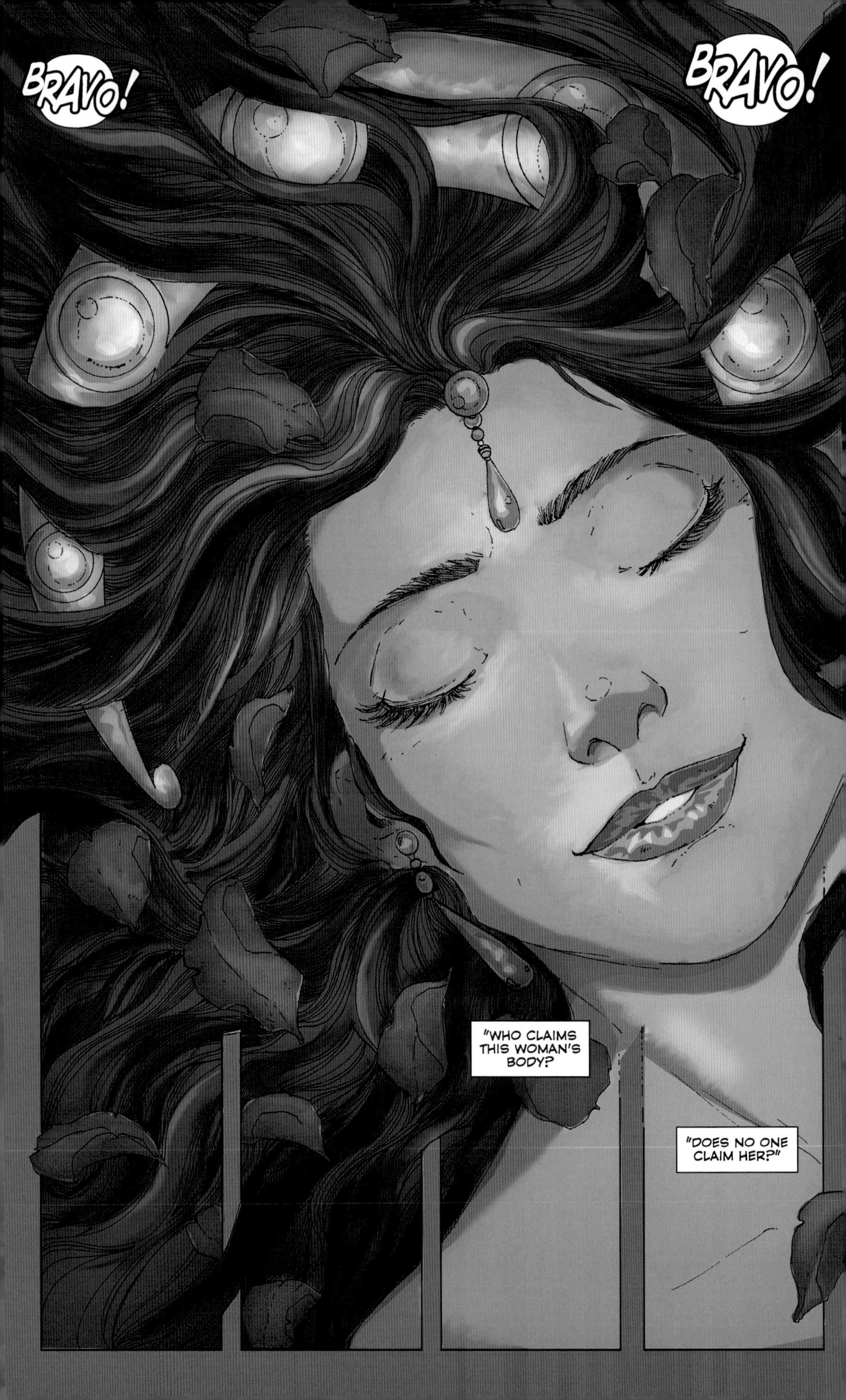
BRAVO!
BRAVO!
"WHO CLAIMS THIS WOMAN'S BODY?
"DOES NO ONE CLAIM HER?"

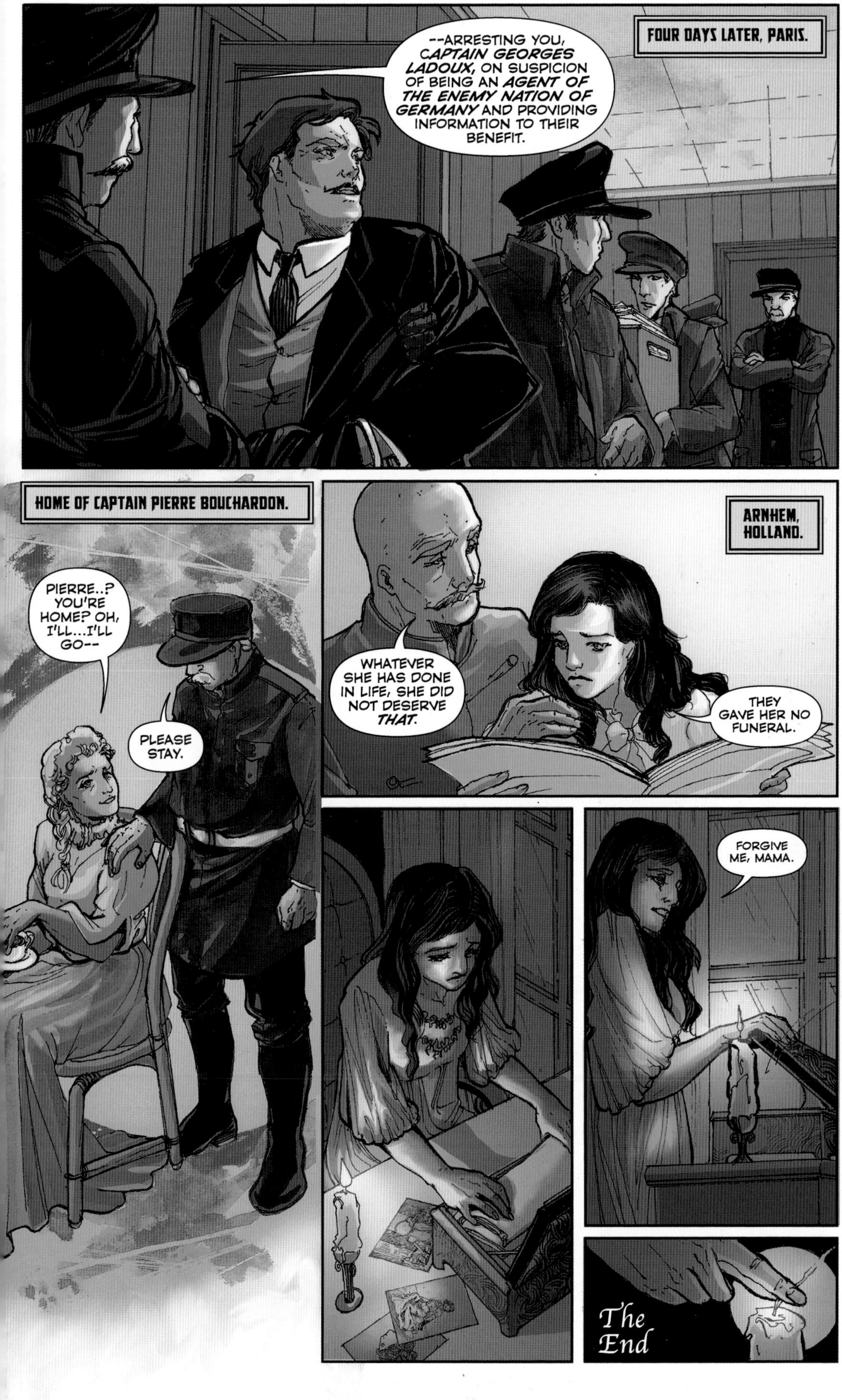
FOUR DAYS LATER, PARIS.
--ARRESTING YOU, CAPTAIN GEORGES LADOUX, ON SUSPICION OF BEING AN AGENT OF THE ENEMY NATION OF GERMANY AND PROVIDING INFORMATION TO THEIR BENEFIT.
HOME OF CAPTAIN PIERRE BOUCHARDON.
PIERRE..? YOU'RE HOME? OH, I'LL...I'LL GO--
PLEASE STAY.
ARNHEM, HOLLAND.
WHATEVER SHE HAS DONE IN LIFE, SHE DID NOT DESERVE THAT.
THEY GAVE HER NO FUNERAL.
FORGIVE ME, MAMA.
The End

Mata Hari's conviction

made Captain Pierre Bouchardon a public hero, profiled and praised in French newspapers for his techniques in breaking spies.

After his arrest, Captain Georges Ladoux spent almost two years in prison before he was acquitted and released on May 8, 1919. He claimed that the evidence against him was manufactured, and retired four years later.

Louise 'Nonnie' MacLeod died on August 10, 1919 of a brain hemorrhage, less than two years after her mother, at the age of 21. Her death was likely due to complications from congenital syphilis. She was due to return to the Dutch East Indies that week to take up a position as a schoolteacher.

Mata Hari left no will. The profit from the sale of her many fine possessions was claimed by the French government to cover the cost of the trial; other possessions simply disappeared. In 1924, jewels and other items resurfaced at an auction held by the clerk of the French Council of War.

Mata Hari's remains were taken to the Museum of Anatomy in Paris. Her head was preserved and put on display as an example of 'the criminal type,' until it went missing sometime after 1954.

It has never been recovered.

• On the Day of her Arrest •
February 13, 1917

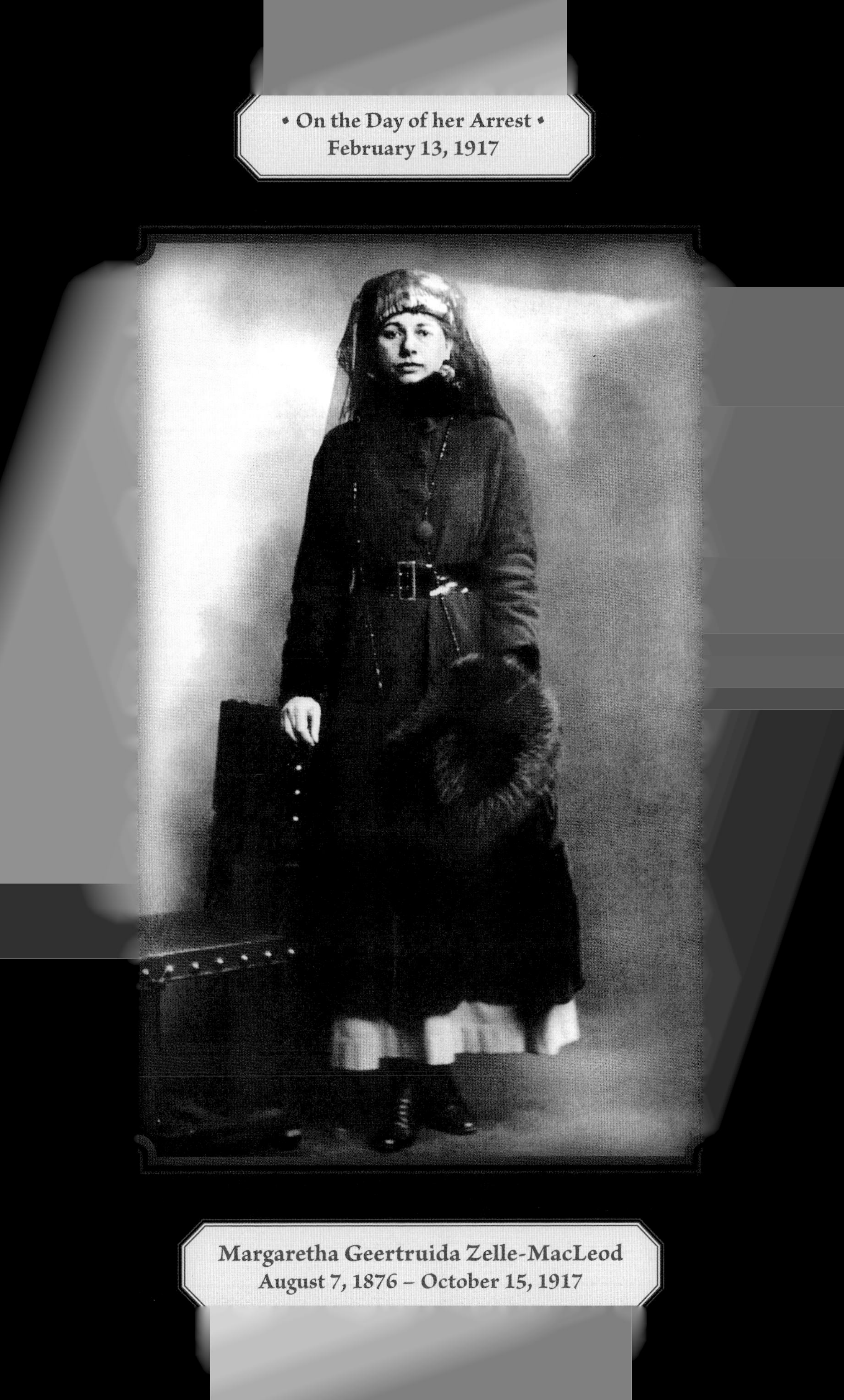

Margaretha Geertruida Zelle-MacLeod
August 7, 1876 – October 15, 1917

WAS MATA HARI A MARTYR?

Not long after the run of the MATA HARI series finished, a reader asked me this question, which I didn't know how to answer at the time.

I'd never considered it. My first instinct was a "no."

Margaretha Zelle-MacLeod is famous for taking her clothes off, for lying, for spying and perhaps most of all, for sex. Lots of sex, with lots of men. I've tried to give a fuller picture of who she was in this, to give that reputation context rather than judgement, compassion rather than titillation. To me her story is a survival story. That is how I saw her. She ran toward money, luxury, sensuality — all the things so often stripped from her life without warning. It made sense as a survival story, even if the heroine doesn't get to survive. But a martyr? That's a different story. Martyrs have principles, beliefs they are willing to die for.

What did Mata Hari believe in?

I've seen her called a feminist martyr. Despite the time she lived in, with women across Europe on the verge of getting the vote, she was no suffragette; she seemed to dislike them. She made no pleas in prison or court on the rights of women, only that she wasn't like the other women and shouldn't be treated the same way. She enjoyed and greatly profited from her sexual objectification, an objectification that was a fetishistic portrayal of the women of a culture she didn't belong to. Even for her time, it's not great.

If she could have thought of a story, true or otherwise, to get her out of prison she'd probably have told it. Her moral position was that she should be allowed to do whatever she wanted. She would sleep with who she wanted, go by whatever name she wanted, take money from whoever offered it and promise nothing in return, to be a mother and not have to be a wife. I think what started out of the necessity of survival and not wanting to need anyone turned into an often genuine joy in putting herself and the things she enjoyed first — to be selfish and hedonistic.

She sought and flaunted personal, financial, and sexual freedoms. Mata Hari existed at the far end of what it can mean for women to have those freedoms. We still have trouble with it.

Having those freedoms means having the right to be selfish, to not do the most moral, expected thing, and use our bodies as we like. That's an ongoing battle, not just in law, but within ourselves. Women still die because of the absence of those freedoms (and still get the blame).

So yes, I would say Mata Hari is a martyr, if not a traditional one. A patron saint of bad behaviour, perhaps.

I wish it had been possible to fit more in to this series. I'd have loved to show Mata being approached by the Russians to spy for them as well (though she never did); or how at her wedding, she paid a taxi to drive her father all around town to make sure he missed it; or how when the formidable mother of one of her lovers came to the house he'd bought her to end the affair, she was so charmed by Mata she stayed for months. The biographies by Prof. Pat Shipman or Julie Wheelwright or Mary W. Craig are all excellent choices for reading more.

This telling owes all to the talents of Ariela, who brought life to the history of several countries and decades, their wars, boulevards and jungles, doing so much research and turning my strange ideas about interweaving narratives and dancing between the panels into something I couldn't have imagined being so beautiful. It's all perfectly complemented by Pat's gorgeous, rich colours, even more impressive given the absence of colour photography as source material. I think we relied on lettering for storytelling more than most comics, and Sal is a master. I'm so grateful to Karen for bringing us all together and being a patient guide when there never seemed to be enough pages.

Thank you for reading.

—Emma